On Mockingbird Hill

Caitlin Press Inc.
8100 Alderwood Road
Halfmoon Bay, BC V0N 1Y1
www.caitlin-press.com

Text and cover design by Vici Johnstone
Copy edited by Meg Yamamoto
Cover image courtesy Daniel Stark
Printed in Canada

Caitlin Press Inc. acknowledges financial support from the Government of Canada and the Canada Council for the Arts, and the Province of British Columbia through the British Columbia Arts Council and the Book Pub-lisher's Tax Credit.

Library and Archives Canada Cataloguing in Publication

Kelly, Mary Theresa, author
          On Mockingbird Hill : memories of dharma bums, madcaps, and fire lookouts / Mary Theresa Kelly.

ISBN 978-1-987915-51-8 (softcover)

          1. Kelly, Mary Theresa. 2. Fire lookouts—Alberta—Biography. I. Title.

SD421.375.K45 2017   363.37'9092   C2017-904599-7

On Mockingbird Hill

Memories of dharma bums, madcaps,
and fire lookouts

MARY THERESA KELLY

CAITLIN PRESS

With gratitude for friendships, those that endure and those in the past.

Contents

Prologue

They memorized the texture and contour of every ridge, valley, and slope that fell within a forty-kilometre radius, carrying their binoculars the way other men carried a gun. At night they stood outside to photograph sheet lightning, tasting the metal on their tongues, or watching the dazzling play of northern lights. They ran low on food some months, boiling withered root vegetables or dry spaghetti, waiting like refugees for the helicopter pilot to drop groceries and water. They logged thousands of hours looking for smoke, eyes sore and fatigued, scanning the forest for telltale wisps of an ember. Some seasons they endured the isolation the way an inmate yearns for early parole, counting the weeks, the days, or the hours. In winter, after the fire season was done, the stories flowed from their lips like rain, *Roger this* and *Copy that*, stories about radio mishaps, hidden smokes, the number of visitors they'd had, and, in good years, stories about hikers who transformed into lovers.

During the late 1980s and early 1990s, I lived in Calgary and belonged to a group of friends who worked on fire lookouts in the mountains of southwestern Alberta. Among them were five couples; four of the men and one of the women were employed by Alberta Forestry to watch for fire in the spring, summer, and early fall. Although only one member from each couple had the lookout job, we had all cultivated the "lookout lifestyle." The core of this lifestyle involved practising or teaching Maharishi's Transcendental Meditation; reading and, at parties, referencing Jack Kerouac's *The Dharma Bums*; making art; and being a vegetarian. We were young, in our thirties, and although the lookout season meant romantic partners were left behind, we idealized sitting on top of a mountain in a twelve-by-twelve-foot cabin as the perfect way to earn a living. I, myself, worked at a large natural foods store, selling vitamins, and telling customers how to grow alfalfa sprouts or cook tofu. At work, I answered questions all day from men wanting to buy herbal aphrodisiacs and women wanting to lose weight.

Each spring my partner, Daniel, and I waited for his official phone call from Forestry. Usually toward the end of April, when the poplar trees started to leaf, Daniel would announce, "They're putting me up next week," and our small house became a place of reckoning for what he would bring and what he would leave behind for five months.

The first year he became a lookout man, Daniel was sent to northern Alberta, and the rangers took bets on how many weeks he would last before the solitude or mosquitoes broke him. The head rangers were convinced men like Daniel, who wore jewellery, rings, or wooden beads, weren't tough enough to endure what they perceived as the lonely life of a lookout. By the time we met, Daniel's seniority meant he could request one of the locations in the south with road or hiking access: Moose Mountain, Mockingbird, Carbondale, Blue Hill, or Kananaskis Lookout. This suited us both. In the south, he would still be flown in for the season by helicopter, but I would be able to travel there on weekends. Visiting the lookout became a refuge from the monotony of my own job.

If I left Calgary right after work, I could drive our old blue Chevy up the Forestry Trunk Road west of Cochrane and arrive at Mockingbird by dusk. When Daniel was posted on Moose Mountain, I would drive to the trailhead outside Bragg Creek and then hike for three hours to reach the lookout at the 2,400-metre summit. Even though I passed between these two worlds, Daniel and I exchanged letters throughout the season, and because I was an "insider," friends on other lookouts wrote me letters as well. I would mail my letters to the district ranger's office. The ranger would pass the mail to the helicopter pilot, who might deliver it on a routine fire detection tour or when he serviced the lookout with groceries and water. Outgoing mail was the same in reverse, but Daniel more often entrusted hikers with his mail.

The letters stayed with me after friendships disintegrated into the four directions, as though blown apart by a chinook wind. They came with me when I packed up my belongings and crossed over the Rockies, moving to Vancouver. Then, one rainy evening in the week after Christmas, I purged my files in honour of the new year. Assembling the letters in one heap, I unfolded the pages, pressing them flat, sorting and remembering. I had saved a couple of dozen letters from Daniel and two male friends, written during

their time on lookouts. I had not kept copies of the letters I wrote to them.
The letters were smoky, unfiltered narratives of our younger lives, gendered
reflections that inspired me to recapture our fire lookout years.

In 1956, Maharishi Mahesh Yogi broke the deep silence of his meditation
retreat in a cave-like room at Uttarkashi, north of Rishikesh in the Hima-
layas, inspired by the conviction that his destiny was to teach meditation
in the West.

That same year, Jack Kerouac watched the clouds float over the Cascade Mountains from a fire lookout on Desolation Peak, writing passages
that would later show up in *The Dharma Bums* and *Desolation Angels*, trying
to not think, to let consciousness flow onto the page.

In 1956, Jack Carter manned Moose Mountain, looking for smoke
in the foothills of the Rockies near Bragg Creek, and imagined a plan to
do more with his life. Maybe he would become an assistant ranger, at least.

It was a matter of scale and depth of consciousness, but solitude in
the high mountains could awaken the inner purpose of an individual's life,
a faint voice, softer than the swoosh of a raven's wing, heard only in the
absolute quiet.

While the two Jacks and the Maharishi Yogi contemplated existence
amid the serenity of mountain peaks, in 1956, Tomas, a young child, fled
with his family from the violent uprisings in Budapest, Hungary, escap-
ing from behind the Soviet Iron Curtain, and, journeying from Europe to
Canada, at last settled outside Calgary, in Cochrane, Alberta, where the
Rocky Mountains were ever present on the horizon.

Daniel, a toddler, drove with his raven-haired mother, an award-win-
ning markswoman, to the indoor shooting range on Kensington Drive in
Calgary, captivated by the moment when she squeezed the trigger, her
cheek against the rifle's cold steel, body taut in concentration on the target,
until the aroma of gun smoke exploded into the room, saturating his senses
and memory.

In Vancouver, McNeal, four years old, sprawled in the corner of the
ballet studio where his mother played the piano, accompanying dancers at
the barre. Indoors he tracked dancers' outstretched limbs, and outdoors he
tracked the North Shore Mountains towering over the city.

In the small town of Napanee, Ontario, John slid down the banister
in his grandparents' funeral home, anticipating the feeling of the void at

the bottom of the stairs in the basement morgue, curious about the trolleys on each side of the stairwell, where shrouded dead bodies were laid out for embalming.

Thousands of kilometres from the Rockies, in the Toronto suburbs, I practised walking across the kitchen linoleum, stepping clumsily in heavy, brown oxfords, as my mother coached me to resist a pigeon-toed gait, promising patent-leather shoes when I reformed the abnormal curvature of my big toes.

In 1956, how and when our lives might one day intersect was still emergent, open to the great play of Spirit and infinite possibilities.

The Dragon

I first met Daniel not long after my common-law husband and I split up. It was November 22, 1986, and I had recently graduated from the University of Calgary with a degree in psychology, although the truth is I had taken so many dance courses my transcript had an extra page of jazz and modern dance classes that didn't count toward the degree. I worked in a health food store, at the same job that had driven me back to school, and I was poised for change, except that I had no plan.

In my twenties I had dropped out, surviving like a gypsy or nomad, grabbing temporary jobs, which were plentiful, when absolutely broke. I feared losing myself in the grind of consumer society. I mean this in an existential way because I was well aware most citizens of the world struggled merely to survive. Then intellectual studies sparked my enthusiasm, and I began to feel maybe I could participate in society without succumbing to the machine. In other words, worn down by retail and clerical jobs, I wanted to drop back in, but I wasn't sure how.

I trusted the feeling that something bigger than myself would come along to guide my life.

Despite my emergent optimism about developing a career, joblessness had spiked in the 1980s, reaching the highest levels since the 1930s.

That night in November, Daniel and I danced side by side at a house party in Calgary, a gathering where everyone had some connection to the natural foods industry and herbal medicine, or had at least survived a liver cleanse, or ten days of fasting on maple syrup, cayenne pepper, and lemon juice.

Hummus, salsa, and guacamole splattered the kitchen table, pot smoke wafted through the living room, and half-empty wineglasses teetered on the edges of second-hand furniture. People held idealistic conversations about permaculture, organics certification, and straw-bale houses. It was as though the 1970s had never ended and we'd all grown up in northern California. Political leadership had swerved right, but we persisted in the utopian dream, as though the progressive swing toward environmentalism, gender equality, and social justice begun in the 1960s would, by necessity, fulfill itself.

The Talking Heads' *Burning Down the House* was playing when Daniel and I bumped into each other. Daniel revelled, flailing his arms and legs in rhythm, without a hint of self-consciousness. He sang along with David Byrne, his throat wide open in ecstasy, improvising a gospel-style harmony. At 4:00 a.m. we were the last guests to leave, and he drove me home in his red Volkswagen van, narrating the story of his recent divorce as we rolled through the dark, empty streets of Calgary, his two shih tzu dogs, Zip and Joe, at my feet. He talked about his ex-wife, Eileen, his exit from an American spiritual community in Seattle, and his seasonal job on Carbondale Fire Lookout.

The next evening Daniel took me to Laurie Anderson's new movie, *Home of the Brave*, at the Plaza Theatre in Sunnyside. His friends, two married couples, John and Dinah and Christos and Alice, went to the same showing and gathered afterwards, peeping at me across the lobby, curious about Daniel's latest date.

It was Dinah's thirty-second birthday.

"Come on, I'll introduce you to everyone!" Daniel crossed the lobby and I tagged along, apprehensive about meeting his friends on our first date.

To show off my anti-consumer identity, I wore a faux fur coat I had purchased in a second-hand clothing shop on Tenth Street NW. Dinah and Alice admired the coat and their approval put me at ease. They dressed in hippie-chic, exotic, layered clothing woven from Indonesian ikat and Guatemalan cotton, but to me, Daniel exuded more flair than both women. He wore a knee-length denim coat, unbuttoned and open, so that it trailed behind him, cape-like, and around his neck he'd wrapped a hand-painted scarf, all sea blues and teals that matched the turquoise knit beanie covering his wavy, black hair.

Chameleon-like, Daniel could pass for many ethnicities and identities, and, depending on the day, might evoke an Italian director, an Egyptian musician, or a Mexican potter. A decade before the term came into use, he had cultivated a metrosexual look. Artistically, he was a potter who specialized in high-fired clay. Musically, he played the sarod, a fretless stringed instrument native to India and Pakistan, similar to the sitar, but he had trouble growing his fingernails long and strong enough to manipulate the twenty-five strings, which caused him considerable distress.

It was hard to tell who adored Laurie Anderson more, Daniel or John, Dinah's husband.

"Isn't that tape-bow violin cool?" John drawled, widening each vowel in his soft, breathy voice. John wore a beard, and tied his curly brown hair into a ponytail. He had no inclination to compete with Daniel's fashion sensibility, settling for blue jeans and a down vest with hiking boots.

Daniel nodded in excitement. "Did you get what was happening? Every time she touched a violin string, it played back an electronic loop."

"Yeaaah." John smiled as though ready for the Rapture, dragging his vowels into infinity. His agreement with Daniel sparked a round of accord.

In "Smoke Rings," Anderson sang only for them:

Standby, you're on the air…
> Smoke makes a staircase for you
> To descend. So rare.
> Ah desire! So random so rare
> And every time I see those smoke rings
> I think you're there.
> *Que es mas macho,* staircase or smoke rings?

What is more macho? Everyone delighted in the lyrics, I expect because there was no macho in this crowd. Lookout men were peaceful, artistic nature lovers who appreciated women. We were all high on Laurie Anderson, androgynous in her white suit and tie, her avant-garde performance playing with gender and mocking male voices of authority.

"I bet you enjoyed those backup singers," Dinah teased Daniel. Sensuous and flowing, the femininity of the two black performers contrasted with Anderson's lanky body and spastic movements.

Daniel swooned. "Ah, geez. I find them so beautiful, you know. Wow, that's all I can say, wow."

Dinah was petite, dark-haired and feminine, like the backup singers. Standing next to the diminutive statures of her and Alice, I felt more like Laurie Anderson. Despite my dance and fitness regime, next to these soft-spoken, small women, I felt large and awkward.

I would have self-described as feminist, but I had no inclination to become androgynous.

The theatre was closing and John needed a cigarette, so we moved outside, huddling in a clump under the neon light of the marquee. The November temperature had dipped well below zero, and our exhalations hung like smoke in the cold Alberta air. The only smoker among us, John stood apart, inhaling his hand-rolled Drum. He tilted his head back and exhaled perfect smoke rings as the group relived the movie.

John's buddy, Christos, towered over us all like a friendly giant, his big 'n tall frame nodding in agreement.

Daniel leaned into me as he gestured, imitating Laurie Anderson on keyboards and Laurie Anderson on electric violin, provoking screams of delight from Dinah and Alice.

Forgetting the Alberta cold for a moment, I joined in the laughter. But I felt like an outlier and kept asking myself: were these lookout folks my new tribe?

In early December Daniel cooked dinner for me at his apartment. Crossing the doorway threshold, I was met by the aroma of sweet, heavy Padmini incense, imported from India, Daniel said. He had prepared a vegetarian Thai recipe: tofu, veggies, and noodles in a peanut and miso sauce, a special effort since he could go all day forgetting to eat, and by late afternoon often staggered around in a state of low blood sugar. He was so used to running out of food on the lookout he could last for days in the city with little more than a bag of brown rice in the cupboard before driving to a grocery store. Whereas I danced and counted calories to stay slim, and often complained about feeling hungry, for Daniel food was mere biological duty. But on that first dinner date, he blended flavours like a sommelier of vegetarian cuisine, crushed garlic, salty soybean miso, buckwheat honey, and crunchy peanut butter.

"What do fire lookouts *do*?" I asked, impressed by how he sliced carrots into tiny matchsticks, julienne-style. I knew he had worked for eight seasons with Alberta Forestry, but I couldn't picture the day-to-day job.

"I'm basically a white-collar office worker, except my office is on top of a mountain."

"Oh, come on. Really, what's it like? You must go hiking sometimes?" I imagined fire lookout observers tromping through the woods in their spare time, and hiking up and down the sides of mountains.

"Not really. Most lookouts are above the treeline, for the sightlines, right, and it's so rocky and steep you can't walk anywhere too easily."

"Really, you're in these beautiful wilderness places and you don't go hiking?"

"We're looking for smokes all the time—inside, looking out the window, that's basically what we do. We're looking for smoke and fire. Fire lookouts are the Eyes of the Forest."

The Eyes of the Forest sounded far more appealing than my retail sales job at Community Natural Foods. I was in charge of the vitamins and nutritional supplements, which were shelved behind a long, high counter that looked like a pharmacy, and every time a customer wanted an item, even a bottle of vitamin C, they had to consult with me. The pharmacy display invited customers to ask questions about supplements and health, and all day I advised customers on products for everything from constipated colons to advanced cancer.

I sold a lot of psyllium powder and herbal laxatives to the colon customers, pau d'arco and red clover tea to the cancer customers, and B vitamins and ginseng to the fatigued customers. And in those pre-Viagra years, I also had requests from men struggling to maintain an affair and a marriage. "Damiana and ginseng might help," I would say, handing the cheater a bottle of capsulated herbs known in folklore for their aphrodisiac effects.

Many customers fasted to overcome health obstacles, and after forty days on the maple syrup cleansing program they wanted to share the intricacies of their fasting experience with me, a total stranger. I entertained stories about all kinds of purification rites; many health seekers leaned against the counter and pondered how to correct their ballooned and spastic colons, describing the green bile and black debris that had passed from their colonic or high enema. One of the grocery cashiers attempted to keep working while she fasted on the maple syrup diet, until day twenty-one, when we sent her ninety pounds of rejuvenated flesh home to recover from dizzy spells.

And there were the eccentric shoppers, many of whom turned completely orange from drinking too much raw carrot juice. One of my customers was convinced he was the reincarnation of Mozart and needed special supplements to compose music. I sold him a harmless homeopathic remedy, suspecting he suffered from a delusional personality disorder.

Some days I felt that every wacky health seeker in Calgary burdened me with his or her problems.

Desiring my own freedom from the stress of vitamin sales, I could understand why Daniel chose to work on top of a mountain.

As he cooked, I surveyed his apartment, trying to get a sense of this unusual man. He had chosen a suite with linoleum floors throughout so he could set up a pottery studio at home. He said he planned to make clay pots all winter, and by the time the lookout season came around in the spring, he'd be ready for a break from ceramics. I quickly got the picture that it wasn't only pots he made. He was afflicted with the impulse to fashion or refashion everything in his environment. He confessed that he usually spent more time perfecting the studio set-up than he did making pots.

"Show me your studio then," I said, poking my head into the other room.

He had made a pottery wheel with a hand stick that spun the clay, rather than purchase an electric one. Next he planned to build wooden counters for a workspace, and drying racks for the raw clay pots waiting their turn to be fired. And then there was kiln type and kiln construction, an unending source of study for a clay artisan. Should he keep firing pots in the gas kiln at the community centre or rebuild a wood kiln out in the country near Bragg Creek?

"I did make pots this fall, in case you're wondering. I had a table at the Waldorf School Christmas sale a few weeks ago. You met Dinah; she works there and her kids go to school there. The Waldorfians love my pottery." Daniel laughed at his own remark.

I picked up a tea bowl from a cluster of pots on the linoleum floor. "I like your pottery too. It's beautiful."

Daniel shuffled around the maze of equipment and clay. "Thanks. It's tenmoku, that one. The best pieces already sold though. I saved a couple things for my friends, Athena and Tomas, but mostly it's just these few tea bowls left."

"So, do you ever want to quit lookouts and do pottery full-time?" I asked.

"All I really want is to move to a beautiful place in the country and make pots. I plan to quit fire lookouts, eventually. I just haven't figured out a way to make the money work, you know."

I certainly did. With two failed communes and two parcels of land in my own past, the move-to-the-country plan alarmed me. My romance with smoky wood stoves, muddy back roads, and cold winters in the bush was over. Maybe Daniel with his clay and binoculars was not the man for me? I could back out gracefully before we got too involved, but I felt uplifted and energized when we were together—the world intensified in colour, brighter and more vivid.

"Move to the country? I already did the back-to-the-land thing. I want to live in the city, build a career, and get out of debt."

"But you have a cool job. Best natural foods store in town. Nice people, good products, it's not so bad, is it?"

"I am so fed up with that job. I didn't go to university to work in a retail store."

Daniel appeared uncomfortable with my declaration; I softened my statement.

"Well, I don't mean I'd *never* move to the country. I guess under the right circumstances I might. But I don't know what I'd do for work." And then, for good measure, I bragged about my wilderness resumé. "I've lived off the grid, split wood, hauled water, chased off bears, all of it."

"Then you'd be fine on a fire lookout," he said. "You don't need to make a big salary if you live in the country. Grow your own food, build things instead of buying everything."

I was suited to voluntary simplicity, but I was skeptical. Years of traipsing around the bush in northern Alberta and British Columbia were the reason I had ended up in the health food store. The organic folks were my people, true, but I didn't want to stand on the retail floor with them for the next few decades. Besides, there was no dance performance in the country—or art of any kind. There were probably a lot of potluck dinners with barefoot couples and cranky babies. It didn't seem to me that the leading edge of culture was ever located in the country.

"I've been thinking about studying dance therapy or counselling psychology, maybe. I'd have to do more training."

"More education?" Daniel frowned. "Don't you think you've been in school long enough?"

I was thrown off guard by his lack of support. "Well, didn't you go to art school?"

"No way. I study artists I admire, read books, and learn by doing. I have no interest in the history of European art, which is a big part of art school. Yucko."

We bantered like this all evening, the subtext of our conversation the negotiating terms for a romantic contract. I would have to agree to live in the country. He, in turn, would have to quit the fire lookout. He would build a studio and make pots, while I figured out what I wanted.

And just like a woman, I put the relationship first.

After the spicy Thai dinner, Daniel and I formed a stable, fair-weather system, floating between our two apartments, sometimes sleeping at his place, sometimes mine. When I stayed overnight at his apartment, he drove me to work in the morning. Getting up to take me to the natural foods store was a morning ritual that helped him prepare to dip his hands into wet clay.

"Did you make any pots?" I'd ask in the evening, and Daniel would grimace. I quickly learned that he was plugged into divine inspiration and channelled ideas at such a ferocious rate it was difficult to focus on making pots. On a good day, his mind pelted out creative ideas like hail falling from the sky, and all he could do was run for his notebook. He kept a sketchbook handy to illustrate the flashes of invention: kiln plans, functional clay objects, and large-scale designs like fully fired clay houses. Some days he roamed around the city, buying magazines on art and architecture, observing fashion trends, and nurturing his insatiable appetite for beautiful objects. Even on a bad day, the Muse hummed loudly enough that his own inner voice became like radio static, a place between two channels, unintelligible, garbled, and strangely comforting.

We were fast friends and I fell in love with his creative spirit, gentle nature, and gregarious mind. I latched onto his creativity as if it were partly my own, confusing his steady stream of inspiration with my own course of action.

One afternoon on my day off, Daniel said, "Let's go to the perfume counter," and we drove downtown to the Bay on Stephen Avenue Mall. He dabbed his favourite scent on the inside of my wrist and pulled my hand to his face. "Oh good," he said, taking a deep whiff, "your skin mixes with this perfume," as though the chemical reaction was proof of our compatibility. Then we went to the Laughing Rooster bookstore and hovered in the aisles, scanning for books important to our lives. *Zen and the Art of Motorcycle Maintenance*? Yup, read it. *The Crack in the Cosmic Egg*? Years ago. He showed me the books he would buy, visual books with photographs and drawings, Asian art books, each one with more images than language.

"The less words the better," he said, smiling at the provocation.

One evening in mid-December, Daniel invited his friends, Tomas and Athena, to his apartment to look at the pots he had left from the firing at the Mount Pleasant community centre. He needed to sell these during the Christmas season or he'd be left with pots in January, and this would squelch the motivation to make more. Athena had expressed interest in buying some pottery, but I knew he wanted me to meet more fire lookout friends.

In celebration of the Christmas season, Daniel had bought a small Shinto shrine at a Japanese import store and turned it into an irreverent nativity scene, substituting a green Gumby figure for the usual religious figures, and trimming the shrine with tiny coloured lights. Gumby, with his green slanted head and block legs and feet, faced the street, mocking passersby from inside the apartment window.

Tomas remarked dryly on the display, "You're creating your own mythology, I see, Mr. Stark."

Daniel ignored the comment, rushing about to take coats and make introductions. Athena, a five-foot-ten-inch, elegant brunette, made a dramatic impression next to Tomas, lean, wiry, and barely her height. They had brought along their three-year-old daughter, Willow, and the three of them sprawled across a big upholstered armchair as though it were the family bed, Athena on the seat cushion, Tomas on the wide arm, and their blond little girl clasped between them.

Daniel brewed herb tea and served it in his own pottery, ceramic bowls without handles. None of his tea bowls had handles, a choice reflecting his Japanese esthetic. Coffee mugs with handles were on the banned list in his kitchen.

Athena selected pots, setting aside a few pieces to consider. She had a natural gracefulness and modesty in her style that complemented Tomas's focussed intensity.

"What's the glaze on these bowls, Daniel?" Athena ran her fingers around the surface.

"That milky white is a Shino glaze, an old Japanese recipe." He had let the Shino flow freely, brushing it thinly in places so that the coral-brown clay contrasted under the translucent white.

"I like this bowl—and the teapot you have there, too. We could use a new teapot, Tomas, and we don't have a really large salad bowl."

"That teapot doesn't drip, either; I think I got the spout just right." Daniel lingered, as though not ready to let it go. "The handle is bamboo. I soaked it in the bathtub for days."

"They're beautiful. Who knows when we'll have another chance to buy some of your pottery." Athena examined the fit of the teapot's lid.

"Yeah, and who knows when I'll throw large bowls again. I'm not exactly prolific—the whole lookout thing makes it hard. You know me, I spend all winter getting the studio ready and then it's time to go back to the lookout."

"What do you call this style of pottery, Daniel?"

"I love a Japanese tradition called wabi-sabi. It's about seeing perfection in the imperfect. I don't try to make perfectly formed bowls." Daniel held up a tea bowl, happy to point out its uneven features. "I like thicker walls on my pots, so I use a lot of clay. I'm not so fond of more feminine pottery. A pot should have some weight to it."

"Very nice work, Daniel, very nice." Tomas was sincere. "All right, let's get them both then." He pulled out a chequebook.

Daniel dug out some bubble wrap, packaged the pots for Athena, and after a few more swigs of tea, the young family departed into the December night.

"They seem nice," I said, after the door clicked shut. I had been quiet, feeling shy around Daniel's lookout friends.

"They are nice," answered Daniel, "and so different. Tomas is a total minimalist. I swear he could be happy living in a bare motel room without any possessions. He and Athena have done Mockingbird Lookout together for years now. In fact, he named Athena!"

"What do you mean, he named her?"

"Exactly that. She was Beverly when she met Tomas and he named her Athena. The name stuck."

I read classical mythology and knew Athena was famous for her ability to go head to head with men, comfortable dealing with power and strategy.

I didn't want to be too judgmental, having just met them, but it seemed paternalistic, as though she had given up her own identity, reshaped by her husband.

"I don't get it," exclaimed Daniel, "all this name swapping. Dinah used to be Nancy! But I'm not sure how that happened. And John changed his own name too, a long time ago. His birth name is David."

"Wow, David and Nancy transformed into John and Dinah. That's interesting, because Dinah is close to Diana, the Greek goddess Artemis. Artemis represents women's independence and creative expression. Ha, I wonder if John is aware of *that* myth?"

"Who knows? He reads Carl Jung, Carlos Castaneda. He's really into shamanism—which I'm not in the least."

"And what's Tomas into?" I was enjoying the backstory on fire lookout people.

"Tomas, he's into transcendence, yogic transcendence of the material world, especially the writings of Krishnamurti. He rode the Greyhound bus all the way to Ojai, California, a few years ago to hear Krishnamurti give a talk."

"And what about the wabi-sabi you were talking about tonight? What's that about?"

"Oh geez, how can I explain it? It has more to do with a Zen Buddhist view. It's a specific esthetic and way of seeing life. It's about accepting things as they are and living in a rustic, simple way. Wabi-sabi is part of the Japanese tea ceremony. Ceramics are high art in Japan. Pottery in Asia is the equivalent to fine painting in the West."

"I don't know anything about the Japanese tea ceremony or pottery," I said. I truly didn't.

"Well, for example, your teeth are wabi-sabi."

"What—my teeth! Why are they wabi-sabi?" I had crooked front teeth, and I was self-conscious about them. My left front tooth protruded forward a little, and the right one tilted back, making my bite uneven. My front teeth had grown in crooked when I was a child, and my parents couldn't afford dental braces. Whenever I smiled, I was conscious of my toothiness.

Unlike me, Daniel had perfect, bright white, evenly spaced teeth.

"Your teeth are wabi-sabi because they aren't perfect; their crookedness is a natural aspect of who you are. Perfection is artificial in nature. I like your crooked teeth, they're uniquely you."

I flashed him a toothy smile.

Daniel was so peculiar, in a perfect kind of way.

During the Christmas holiday season that winter, John and Dinah threw a potluck dinner party. This was my first evening with the whole lookout gang, and my first social outing with Daniel as a couple. As was my tendency, I plied Daniel with questions about his friends, how they met, their values, their work, everything. I wasn't a Greek goddess—I was more like Lois Lane, smart investigative reporter, always extracting more details of the story. I had always been this way, and years before had entered the journalism program at Ryerson in Toronto, but changed my mind and withdrew when I discovered Chaucer and medieval English literature were required reading. Many people found my insatiable questions annoying; Daniel accommodated, sharing the backstory on his friends.

John and Dinah rented a small farmhouse on Bearspaw Road in the country, northwest of Calgary, not far off the 1A highway. The acreage was near the Bearspaw Dam, which controlled winter ice packs and spring runoff on the Bow River upstream from Calgary. Christos and Alice rented a small house next door on the same property.

"They spend a lot of time together in the winter," said Daniel. "I think they have dinner together every night, just like an extended family."

John had provided Christos with a lookout reference, and for several seasons now, Christos and Alice worked on a fire tower in northern Alberta, sharing the salary. Dinah worked as part-time administrator at the Calgary Waldorf School, a private elementary school she had helped establish with a small group of dedicated educators.

"John's always going out to the Dragon to make a fire," said Daniel. "It's not really my thing. He and Tomas love to walk out there, smoke, and talk about philosophy and stuff."

"The Dragon? Catch me up before we get there."

"It's hidden in the hills, behind their farmhouse in a secluded gully, protected from the winds."

Daniel described how John had built the dragon sculpture with field rocks, in part influenced by his reading of Jung, and in part inspired by his own creative imagination. He had chosen a flat, secluded area in a stand of aspen trees, out of sight from the road and neighbours, a short walk from his house. He recruited Christos, and for weeks and months during the fall they collected round rocks, piling and arranging them into the shape of a huge reptile with a long tail. The men hauled hundreds of smooth rocks from the surrounding fields and gullies, piling them into a monument with a head over five feet tall and a long, tapered serpent body. When the hills were picked clean, John persuaded friends to bring rocks from Calgary, and supporters of John's project would show up with backpacks full of rocks. In time, the Dragon grew a body about six metres long, the creature's tail disappearing into a spiral of stones among the aspen trees.

The Dragon became a kind of mecca for John, Christos, Tomas, and other friends and acquaintances who journeyed from Calgary to Bearspaw Road, sitting around an outdoor fire, while John consulted the *I Ching* and advised them on life challenges. The Dragon inspired awe; it also provided solid, nature-based proof of John's shamanic identity.

"I was never into the whole Dragon thing," said Daniel. "It's art that John and I have in common."

By "the whole Dragon thing," Daniel meant both the rock sculpture and the philosophy of Jung. I, on the other hand, devoured writings about Jungian psychology and psychological growth. Jung believed the true work of the individual involved bringing material from the unconscious into awareness, becoming intimate with its nature, and assimilating it back into the conscious self. He depicted this task as an inner battle between the conscious and unconscious self, or the hero and the dragon, a decidedly masculine metaphor. To develop one's full creative potential, the hero had to seek out and slay the fire-breathing dragon, or risk letting the dragon sabotage one's life by unleashing destructive, pent-up energy.

By the time we arrived at Dinah and John's, I had a snapshot of each person's disposition. In the living room, we lolled about on Persian carpets and propped ourselves up on decorative cushions. Daniel sprawled horizontally across the floor, pleased there was no couch. He had worn a fishnet T-shirt, turquoise, and the black hairs on his chest poked through all the fishnet openings. I studied him from across the room; being of slender build, he could pull it off. The fishnet shirt was a bit glitzy; it certainly wasn't a regular button-up man's shirt.

Tomas caught my eye. "Mr. Stark is such an androgynous creature, don't you think? And such a hook for women."

I was unsure how to answer or what he meant by "a hook." The others laughed affectionately.

Tomas persisted, determined to engage me in debate. "What kind of psychology did you study?" he asked. "I hope you're not an Aristotelian or one of those white-coat behavioural scientists."

I flushed, unfamiliar with Tomas's wry humour. Daniel had told me that Tomas was the only one in the lookout gang with a university degree. Clearly, he wanted to spar.

"Don't worry, I did an arts degree, I'm not a behaviourist."

"Well, I'm glad you're not into running rats in a lab somewhere."

I tilted my beer, annoyed by Tomas's screening. Usually I loved to discuss ideas, but I felt intimidated; his words were like electric prods.

Athena breezed by with a bowl of homemade dip and tortilla chips, long skirt swishing. I was grateful for the diversion. I could feel Tomas's eyes follow me as I plunged a chip into the layers of sour cream and black beans with one hand, and gripped the can of Olympia beer with the other.

His eyes narrowed, lips pursed. "So Dionysian all of this, isn't it?"

"Oh come on, Tomas!" Daniel rolled his eyes, listening from across the room. He had been talking to Dinah about design, admiring a rosewood end table. "Not the Dionysian thing again."

"Watch out or soon we'll be dancing too, wineglasses to the sky," I said. A flicker of a smile creased Tomas's face.

Like the three Graces, Dinah, Alice, and Athena laid out the food on the dining room table, banquet-style, encouraging everyone to serve themselves. Dinah had made the main course, bouillabaisse, or fish stew, a French recipe that had taken her the better part of the day to coax along, starting with fresh ingredients, garlic, saffron, leeks, and several kinds of fish to make the base. We ate the soup in wide bowls with crusty bread, salads, and plenty of wine despite Tomas's Dionysian concerns, the eight of us crowded around the table, elbow to elbow.

If I became partner to a fire lookout man, I would share the seasonal cycle: spring would always be a time of separation, winter a time of coming together.

I had squeezed into a place at the table opposite Daniel. I could feel John check out my energy without addressing me directly.

"So, any thoughts about going back to Carbondale next year?" John was a soft speaker. He cast a look toward Daniel.

"Oh gee, I don't know. I'd kinda like to get a lookout closer to Calgary. How about you? Going back to Cline?"

"Oh yeah. Cline is the most beautiful lookout I've ever done, really. I wish Dinah could visit more easily, but I'm going back for sure."

"He loves it there," said Dinah, shaking her head. "I'll visit once a season, maybe, but that's it."

"Where's Cline?" I asked, unfamiliar with all the lookout names and places. A cascade of laughter followed.

"It's extremely remote," said Dinah dryly. "Basically John couldn't have picked a more difficult place for me to get to."

"That's not true, Dinah. And it's worth the hassle, it's a sacred, beautiful place."

"Cline is northwest, toward Jasper," explained Christos. "It's a four-hour drive and then a helicopter ride. Basically he didn't have any visitors for five months—aside from Dinah, once."

"I wish he'd get a lookout down south again like you and Tomas." Dinah glanced approvingly at Daniel.

"Yeah, well, I'm staying out of it." Daniel laughed, hands up, fending off a debate.

"Let's talk about something besides lookouts," interrupted Athena. "I'm enrolling in classes at the University of Calgary next semester."

Tomas sighed. "We're discussing it. I think Willow is too young to be away from her mother so much."

Daniel twirled his fork in disbelief. I stared across at him and raised my eyebrows as if to say, what decade is this?

"What do you want to study?" I asked.

"Maybe women's studies, I'm not sure yet."

"Ah, the dark comedy of the masculine and the feminine. The alchemy of the sun and the moon." Tomas spoke to anyone at the table who might listen.

"Not the Jungian thing." Daniel laughed. "Not tonight, Tomas."

"Well, I'm going to work full-time," Dinah said, as though in defence of Athena. "We need the money and the Waldorf School is considering a full-time administrator."

"Dinah, that's wonderful," Athena exclaimed. "You'd be perfect."

"I might as well be at work," she added. "John's usually getting up about the time we get home from school."

Christos laughed. "That's a bit of an exaggeration, Dinah. I've come by in the early afternoon and found him brewing the espresso."

Dinah rolled her eyes. "He stays up all night, every night."

"I like to paint late at night," said John quietly. "And I love the feeling of being in alpha and not really falling asleep. It's like lucid dreaming."

"Hypnagogic," quipped Daniel. "It's called hypnagogic, the edge of sleep."

"I don't know how he gets up to do 7:00 a.m. weather at the lookout." Dinah shrugged. "I'm the only one getting up at 7:00 a.m. in this house."

"We've decided to spend more time down south in Central America." Everyone turned to Alice.

"Yes, one more lookout season and then we're leaving the Alberta deep-freeze." Christos was Greek-Canadian, his name given at birth; but he did resemble images of Christ with his long dark hair, beard, and Mediterranean features.

"I have zilch interest in travelling," Daniel moaned. "That's why I got the dogs, so I'd stay in one place. All I want to do is to move to the country and build a hill-climbing kiln."

I chimed in my approval, conscious everyone's gaze was now on me. I harboured my resistance silently, mulling over the possibility in my mind. Would I move to the country with this man?

John, animated by the good company, food, and alcohol, marked the moment: "You guys can all be in my movie."

On one level, I assumed he simply wanted to buy a camera and make a movie about his life. But in a cosmic sense, John was referring to the Hindu teaching that we are all characters in each other's dream of life, or movie, in the same way that every character in a dream represents an aspect of ourselves.

The night of the fish stew, we birthed the Lookout Supper Club, celebratory suppers that would continue for years and that we would remember for the rest of our lives—long after the Dragon breathed fire out its nostrils, forever altering the ending to the movie.

Later that winter, Tomas and Athena announced that they were giving up Mockingbird and applying for Blue Hill Lookout. Blue Hill was farther from Calgary, but the cabin provided more space for a family, and after four years on Mockingbird, they were ready for a change.

"This is so lucky," exclaimed Daniel. "I didn't want you to have to drive all the way down to Carbondale; it's a good three hours. If I get Mockingbird, it will be way easier for you to visit. You'll like Mockingbird, it's close to Calgary and it's pretty up there."

In the months leading up to the next fire season, Daniel made lists of all the potential supplies he might need on the lookout, ensuring he had every conceivable tool for any project he might undertake. This meant his days were occupied with a lot of shopping, bargain hunting for the best deals before he left town.

In mid-February I became unwell with flu-like symptoms, nausea, and fatigue. I would come home from work and lie on the couch, too exhausted to go to dance class. Then it occurred to me that maybe I did not have the flu. I hurried to the drugstore and bought a home pregnancy test. Within five minutes, a blue line materialized on the test strip. I watched in horror as the blue colour emerged from nothingness, first appearing like a faint possibility, and then darkening and eliminating any question of the result. The test was positive; I was pregnant.

I called Daniel and broke the news. Our news.

"Well, hon, I'm okay with whatever you want to do. It's your decision."

I was shocked because I'd expected him to freak out and tell me he was ill-equipped to be an artist and a father.

"People do have children and work on lookouts," he said. "It's possible, right?"

"You mean like Athena and Tomas? I'm making an appointment at the birth control clinic tomorrow, for an abortion."

"Like I said, whatever you decide, I'll support the decision. We can always do this later." He meant have children together.

Did I want to have a child now? The image of chasing a toddler around the fire lookout or raising a child alone terrified me. I had known Daniel for only three months and I wanted the chance to develop a relationship based on mutuality, not the responsibility of parenthood. If we had a child now, I would never enjoy the freedom of an adult relationship without children. For some reason, I held no romantic notions about babies and children. Rather, I worried about becoming a mother and getting stuck in a mundane job. And I didn't want to be the reason Daniel stopped pursuing pottery; he might end up resenting me, trapped into becoming a provider. I belonged to the first generation of women who were expected to balance marriage, career, and children, and in my estimation, the prospect lacked appeal. Where was the liberation in raising young children and dragging myself to work sleep-deprived?

I was four weeks pregnant and had to wait eight more weeks for a safe abortion. A nurse informed me that before the College of Physicians and Surgeons approved the procedure, I must agree to go on the pill or have an IUD inserted several weeks after the abortion. She sat next to me in a small, windowless room, gripping her clipboard, ready to record my pledge.

"Condoms don't count as effective birth control," she reprimanded.

I promised to get an IUD, a choice I subsequently regretted but felt coerced into carrying out. The procedure was scheduled for April 15 at Foothills Hospital.

One day after work I lay down on my bed, placed my hands on my belly, and inwardly sensed the unborn soul. It was a boy; I was absolutely sure. I explained my reasons for the decision and made peace with the being on the inner planes.

While I waited for my date with the surgeon, Daniel was officially assigned Mockingbird Lookout. Now he was in standby mode too, monitoring the warming temperatures and mountain snowpack, anticipating a start date. As soon as Forestry approved all the hires, and weather conditions reached a specified level of dryness and daily highs, the fire season would commence. Sometime around the beginning of April, he received word.

"They're putting me up on April 24," he said, happier than I expected.

Then my day finally arrived. At the hospital, there was a lineup of women in the waiting room. A nurse called us one by one into the operating room. I had had a general anesthetic once before, as a child, for dental surgery. It was exactly the same: the anesthetist's voice, the mask, counting one, two, and then total blackness. When I regained consciousness, my first impressions were the fuzzy yellow of fluorescent lights on the ceiling and the faint chatter of nurses nearby. I could barely sense the contours of the room—it was blurry and out of focus. Then, I lurched awake, conscious of dull aching pain and sharp contractions in my abdomen. A nurse draped a hot, heavy compress across my pelvis and wheeled the hospital bed into a recovery room. I fell into a deep, dreamless sleep.

When I woke up the second time, a nurse was gently shaking my arm. "Come on, dear, time to go home." I could see the other beds in the room were empty. "You're the last one, come on, wake up."

I desperately longed to sleep but commanded myself to sit up on the edge of the bed. The nurse handed me a glass of juice. "Your blood is Rh-negative," she said. "If you get pregnant again, it's possible your body would produce antibodies that attack the fetus. But don't worry, we've given you an injection so that won't happen."

She handed me my bag of clothes. "Everyone else is gone, so you can get dressed right here if you want."

I could not imagine how the other women had recovered so quickly; I felt drugged and weak.

Back at Daniel's apartment, I collapsed in the corduroy armchair for the rest of the day and ate green grapes.

"We can split the wages you lost today," he offered.

"Thanks," I muttered from inside the hangover of anesthesia. It was kind and thoughtful, but I had nothing else right then, nothing.

"Are you going to be all right, hon?"

"I'll be fine," I said. "I just need a long sleep."

The next day I woke up, relieved to know I was no longer pregnant. Daniel drove me to work as usual.

A week later, he packed the van tight, all the way to the ceiling. He had saved apple boxes, and bought Rubbermaid containers with fitted lids, so he could cram as much as possible in the vehicle. He boxed up bedding and towels, fabric for curtains and hangings, tea bowls and clay pots, his favourite artwork to decorate walls, photograph albums and negatives, boxes of clay and clay tools, the sarod, books and magazines, stationery, postage stamps, sketchbooks, the remaining dry and fresh food from his kitchen, and a stash of chocolate bars. He moved his large furniture, the couch, armchair, and pottery wheel into storage in his grandmother's garage. Then he scrubbed the empty apartment, leaving it cleaner than when he had moved in.

I expected we would spend the last evening together, but Daniel was compelled to dart about the city and visit friends, capitalizing on his last chance to socialize.

"Come on, hon, I'm gonna see you in just a couple weeks. I'm not going away forever."

I relented with a pout and a fresh memory of the stern nurse admonishing me: "Don't even think about sex for four weeks. Off limits. I mean it, your body needs time to heal."

The next morning, April 24, 1987, Daniel drove off to Mockingbird Fire Lookout and I walked to my job at the natural foods store.

That night after work I went home to an empty apartment, popped an Olympia beer, and sipped from the metal can, the taste strangely comforting. I could smell exhaust from the rush-hour traffic on Memorial Drive. It would be only ten days or so until I could drive all the way up to the lookout, but I could feel how Daniel had vanished into another world.

It was still April and already I contemplated the end of the fire season.

Mockingbird Lookout

On a Saturday evening in early May, I cashed out the last customers and raced around the store balancing till receipts, tossing the bank deposit into the safe, and setting the alarm. After stopping by the house to throw some clothes into a pack, I headed out of town in the blue Chevy. The giant cottonwood poplars lining Memorial Drive shimmered pale green, buds coaxed open by the warming days, their sticky scales glazing the banks of the Bow River.

I was a nervous driver and planned my travel routes to avoid left turns. Luckily, I could drive all the way to the lookout without having to turn left even once. I veered right off Sixteenth Avenue to shop in Bowness on the west side of the city. Daniel had phoned with a short grocery list the night before: chocolate, coffee cream, lettuce, and fruit, the things fire lookouts long for and often do without. I bought some Cinzano liqueur for him and a six-pack of Olympia beer for myself. Daniel hated the aluminum beer cans, but I was not going to give up my modest beer drinking for esthetic reasons, or pour a good American beer into one of his clay tea bowls.

After coasting down the big hill into Cochrane, I continued west on the 1A highway, looking for the Forestry Trunk Road, a right-hand turn that led north, first through open ranch and grazing country, then deeper into the forest reserve and the foothills. The tiny community of Waiparous Village appeared, just as Daniel had described, then the Ghost district ranger station. After driving for fifteen minutes on the trunk road, the pavement ended, turning to gravel.

Dust billowed out in a plume behind me. A semi-trailer hauling cut trees barrelled toward me on the trunk road, lurching and swaying from side to side, forcing me to slow down and hug the gravel shoulder. The Alberta government had designated the forest a "multi-use area," which meant logging operations, oil and gas development, and recreational activities, such as camping, hiking, and hunting, coexisted. Every square kilometre of the

Alberta foothills had been bulldozed by seismic cuts in the search for oil and gas, leaving a scarred meshwork of straight lines throughout the forest. Seismic cuts in Alberta forests were so plentiful and systematic that authors in the *Journal of Environmental Management* estimated the total length of cuts would stretch between the earth and the moon—four times over.

I crossed the one-lane bridge over the Waiparous Creek. On my left, the forest opened up into a cleared strip of land along the roadside. A group of young men tore back and forth on motorized all-terrain vehicles, ripping up the earth for the weekend. I must have been in the right place, because Daniel had complained about the squealing noise of ATVs. When I saw the sign for the Mockingbird Girl Guide Camp, I knew I was close and slowed down, afraid of missing the unmarked fire road. The dirt road swerved right. Around the first bend I saw the yellow-and-brown forestry sign, Dangerous Road Closed to All Vehicles. Beyond the sign and out of view from the main road, the green metal forestry gate blocked public road access.

I pulled over, turned off the engine, and walked to the gate; it was locked with a heavy chain. Reaching inside the hollow metal bar, I searched for the spare key with my fingertips—found it. After driving through, I locked the gate behind me. The gate kept out the ATVs, but the whine of their engines reverberated through the valley on weekends.

The dirt road traversed back and forth through the lodgepole pines in long switchback turns. I gained elevation quickly and small openings in the forest offered glimpses of the Rocky Mountains to the west. Putting my trust in the old blue Chevy, I discovered the right speed to creep uphill and take the turns without stalling on the steep slope. Daniel would hear the engine as I got closer. I had left a phone message with the radio operator asking her to relay my 8:30 p.m. arrival time. The whole forest would have heard the message: rangers, guardians, and other lookouts, many wishing for their own intimate visitor.

The road levelled out at the top and I found myself in a large clearing surrounded by a pine-tree forest that sloped off in all directions. I pulled up next to the lookout building, transfixed by the vista, a blood-orange western sky touching the grey jagged edges of the Rocky Mountains.

It truly was a job on top of the world. At 1,900 metres, I could see the Waiparous River valley, the foothills, and a stretch of mountain ranges to the west and north. Devil's Head jutted out, a black protruding thumb surrounded by the Front Ranges and layers of peaks in the distance. To the east, a grid-like pattern of fields, farms, and ranchlands rolled toward a distant horizon. I could almost scope out the glint of office towers in downtown Calgary, head offices for Big Oil, angular lines rising out of the flatness of the prairie. This was Mockingbird Lookout—juxtaposed between the wide expanse of parkland, rolling foothills, and the vertical rock face of mountain peaks.

I stood outside for a moment, collected myself, and gazed at the sheer breadth of place. The sky supported and held the mountains and prairie in its vastness. My frustrations with the workweek disappeared, soothed away by the immensity of the space here.

The steel door to the lookout building was wide open; Daniel's voice and the crackling of the two-way radio filtered outside. A Forestry staffer was talking about a loud drunken party in the Waiparous campground and asking Daniel to radio a message to the ranger at the Ghost station. I carried the groceries inside, sat down at the table on the main floor, and popped an Olympia beer, listening to the radio mayhem, the call signs and insider language of "copy" this and "copy" that. The radio reception was chopping off words, but Daniel seemed unperturbed, at home with the static.

Finally, he put down the microphone, wrapped his arms around me, and squeezed my ribs.

"Hey, you made it!"

"I sure did. I missed you." I stepped back to examine him. He wore a denim Japanese happi coat and a bright yellow ball cap with a big brim. His long dark ponytail dangled through the hole at the back of the cap, a hybrid fashion of schoolgirl and sportsman.

"Nice outfit," I kidded, amused by his style.

"This is Mockingbird, no one sees me on the radio. Glad you're here, hon! Easy drive, isn't it?"

"Yeah, super easy. The hardest part is getting out of Calgary. I had to bust through an invisible magnetic field to get here."

"I know what you mean. And as soon as you hit the gravel it's like being set free, right?"

"Yeah, driving on gravel suits me. Except for the damn logging trucks."

"I have a few things on the go, so hold that thought. Give me a sec."

Daniel cranked up the volume on the radio speaker in the kitchen. "There's a bunch of stuff going on in the campground. I just need to listen in case the ranger calls me."

"What kind of stuff?"

"I have to relay information between the rangers and guardians. There's a problem at the campground down below. A drunk camper has shot a deer or something crazy like that. Sometimes the rangers end up behind a hill and they lose radio reception. I'm not only the Eyes of the Forest, tonight I'm the Ears too."

Ignoring the radio, I launched into my own report on what had happened in the organic work world that week. Two punks, a woman and her boyfriend, had become regular shoppers at the store. They were real punks with all the trappings: mohawk head spikes, shaved skulls, nose rings, and black army boots. They could clear a crowded aisle of yoga moms in seconds. I rather enjoyed how their black fashion death message complemented the vitality-longevity motif of the health food industry.

Every now and then Daniel stopped my monologue and leaped for the microphone, forcing me to wait my turn.

"XMD58 here."

"Dan, we have a situation at the Waiparous campground. I need you to relay a message to the office. I'm about to lose reception behind this hill to your southwest."

"Go ahead, Owen."

"Yeah, Dan, tell them this: there's a guy in the campground with a chainsaw and he cut the head off a dead elk. I'm on my way there now and I need backup. Tell them to send a couple guardians over."

"Copied, Owen."

"Thanks, Dan. I've called the RCMP."

"D58 clear."

Daniel clicked the microphone closed. "This is a first. It's not usually this insane. I can't believe I have to repeat this message straight up." He inhaled, collecting himself for a moment and then opened the microphone and relayed the message as though stating the relative humidity in the morning weather report.

For much of the evening he was lost to me, absorbed in radio shorthand, call signs, and utterances I was unable to decipher.

While Daniel juggled radio messages about drunken campers and deer beheadings down in the valley, I poked around the lookout. The main living space had a galley-style kitchen, lots of cupboard and counter space, a kitchen table with two chairs, and a fridge and stove powered by propane. Off the kitchen, there was a small bedroom, and he had hung colourful cotton fabric across the bedroom doorway for privacy. The fabric brightened and domesticated the space. The bedroom contained a double bed, nightstand, dresser, and clothes closet. On the dresser there was a stack of photographs in a small woven basket. Next to it, a solitary photograph lay on its own, as though the viewer had put it there for later reflection. Innocently, I picked up the photograph and met the radiant image of Daniel's ex-wife, Eileen.

It would be an understatement to say Eileen was beautiful. She was the Elizabeth Taylor of fire lookouts, a gorgeous brunette, so stunning she could have been her own Calgary Stampede event, Most Beautiful Woman in Alberta. The photo, obviously taken by Daniel, had been staged with a western narrative and showed off her best features. She leaned against the front end of a 1951 Willys Jeep, decked out in a cowboy hat and boots, tight blue jeans accentuating wide hips and cinched waist, long brown hair flowing past her shoulders. Her large brown eyes were almond shaped, her mouth and lips full, her smile magnetic. Eileen had a model's facial structure, high cheekbones with eyes and mouth in accord with some mysterious mathematical ratio that translated into universal beauty.

I froze, photograph in hand. Why was Daniel looking at a photo of Eileen at the lookout? More to the point, why had he even brought the photo in the first place? I felt betrayed—by a photograph. Did I need to make an issue of it on my first night at the lookout? Maybe I should wait and just see how things went.

Back in the kitchen Daniel was cooking a pasta dinner, one ear toward the mic, the other reserved for me. I flopped into a chair and popped the metal on another Olympia.

"It's starting to quiet down. I'll show you the cupola tomorrow in the daylight. That's where I usually work. The windows down here aren't big enough to look for smoke."

"Sure." I faked a half smile.

"Basically this place is an ATCO trailer, you know, Alberta Trailer Company."

"What?"

"This building, its industrial, grey aluminum siding, like a trailer, right?"

I nodded in agreement from inside my self-pity. He told me how he longed for the rustic lookout buildings of the past, the original one-room wooden cabins, twelve feet by twelve feet.

Mockingbird Lookout had been built here in 1952, and the original cabin sheltered fire lookouts for over twenty years before Alberta Forestry replaced it in the 1970s with the modern industrial design.

"And did you know the lookout is named after the song?"

"No, tell me about it." If I didn't ask him about the photo, how could I sit here and hold a grudge? It was unfair, but I was afraid of coming across as jealous and insecure by bringing up Eileen.

"Well, when the work crew surveyed the site back in the fifties, one of the guys pulled out a transistor radio to test the reception up here and Wilf Carter's song "Mocking Bird Hill" was playing. So the guys said, 'Let's call it Mockingbird Hill,' and the name stuck. There aren't any mockingbirds here by the way, but Forestry kept the name anyway. There're crows, magpies, and whisky jacks though. *Tra la la, tweedle dee dee dee, it gives me a thrill, to wake up in the morning on Mockingbird Hill!* Come on, hon, what's wrong? Are you okay?" Daniel studied my face.

When I was really upset, my upper lip twitched involuntarily.

"I'm fine," I lied. I didn't want to ruin the night with an argument; I wanted to try out the new IUD, since I had the damn copper wire inserted inside my body now.

"Are you sure?" he said. "What's up?"

"Nothing, I'm fine, just scattered energy leaving the city." I would wait for a better time to confront the ghost of Eileen.

Finally by 10:00 or 10:30 p.m. the radio went silent and it was safe to get in bed without a forest interloper. We were shy with each other after weeks apart, the abortion, and the radio commotion.

"We fit together perfectly," I said, admiring the length of our long, slim bodies. "But you have the blackest, thickest leg hair I've ever seen on a man."

"I know! They shed all over the sheets too, just like at home."

"Oh, God help me. A knitter could make socks with all that leg hair."

We slid easily into the curves and folds of each other's bodies, savouring the taste of sweat, skin, and tangled hair. Daniel was a generous, eyes-open lover, keeping me in his presence, ready to please. My body was familiar terrain, every ridge, valley, and hill, his to explore.

The next morning the radio woke me at seven thirty. I rolled over in the empty bed; he must have been up in the cupola.

"Good afternoon, all stations, XMC26 for the morning weather. Go ahead." The voice of a female radio operator streamed into the lookout.

One by one, the half-dozen fire lookouts in the north Bow-Crow district read their weather findings. I recognized Tomas's voice beaming in from Blue Hill Lookout. Then Daniel was on the air.

"Good morning, everyone, Mockingbird weather. Present temperature is eight degrees Celsius, minimum five, max twelve, relative humidity thirty-seven percent, dew point six percent, precip zero, wind speed is ten kilometres from the west, visibility clear with a few cumulus clouds, snow patches remaining. Forest greening up. Over to you, Barrier."

The radio intrusion ended and I fell back into a deep sleep. When I got up mid-morning, Daniel was still in the cupola. He heard me moving around, bounded down the outdoor stairwell, and burst through the main door.

"Good morning! I turned the radio down so you could sleep in. Grab your coffee and come upstairs with me."

We climbed up a metal ladder through a trap door in the ceiling, a shortcut to the upstairs room. The cupola, or lookout man's workspace, had huge windows on all four sides for maximum visibility. An iron catwalk wrapped around the perimeter of this upper level, so the lookout person could stand outside, or pace back and forth, observing the countryside and weather conditions. In the middle of the cupola, an Osborne fire finder was bolted to the floor, a bulky apparatus that looked like a telescope and giant compass mounted on a stand. Key to the job, the fire finder oriented to true north and the lookout man relied on it for calculating the bearings and direction of a smoke sighting. It was remarkable how much farther one could see from the cupola. Daniel was paid to look for smoke within an eighty-kilometre-wide circle and, ideally, spot a smoke before it ignited into a fire. Using test flares, forest managers had determined forty kilometres was the farthest distance a lookout observer could be expected to detect smoke in this terrain. Based on this formula, Alberta Forestry had positioned and spaced fire lookouts along the entire east slope of the Rocky Mountains. Tomas, on Blue Hill, was located forty kilometres to the northwest.

After a few sweeps of the western ranges, Daniel focussed the binoculars on one spot.

"Do you see that black peak over there? It's Black Rock Mountain."

He handed me the binoculars. "Look," he commanded. "You can see a black bump at the very top. That's the remains of the abandoned lookout cabin."

At more than 2,400 metres altitude, Black Rock stood alone, protruding slightly east of the Rocky Mountain Front Range. The sights from the top would be panoramic—an unimpeded view of the Rockies, Banff National Park, and the prairies spreading east beyond Calgary.

I tried to focus the binoculars on the dark speck, unable to hold the landscape steady. I could not imagine staring through binoculars for hours every day.

"Occupational strain. These are heavy to hold up," I said.

"Heavy?" Daniel took the binoculars from me. "Pentax binocs are lightweight. I bought them to replace the ones Forestry issues—they're heavy." He pressed the binoculars to his eyes, pinpointing the summit again.

"Forestry built that cabin up there in 1929. They hauled all the building supplies up the mountainside on horseback."

He was intrigued by everything about Black Rock, and I was about to get a history lesson.

"The forest service ran a telephone line all the way up the side of the mountain—from the ranger station to the cabin at the top. The lookout man had to telephone the ranger to pass weather or report a smoke until 1938, when two-way radio systems were installed," Daniel explained.

He said it got so cold up there during rainy spells, the lookout man spent days huddled in his sleeping bag. And during electric storms, he cowered under the windows, ready to dodge explosive lightning strikes. The blustering winds were so powerful the outhouse had been built of stones to make sure it didn't blow off the side of the mountain. It took the ranger three days each month to pack in supplies on horseback, and the horses, unable to make the final ascent, were tethered below the lookout cabin for a day. Other than a monthly visit from the ranger, the lookout man's only visitors were ravens and mountain goats.

"I want a forestry pilot to fly me up there sometime," said Daniel, as though planning a vacation with frequent flyer points.

"So, why'd they close it if the sightlines are so good?" I could tell, despite the austerity, if Black Rock Lookout had been in operation, Daniel would have applied for the job; for some reason he wanted to go higher and higher.

He said by the 1950s, Alberta Forestry was forced to admit that the mountain was too darn high to be useful. The observer was sealed off by clouds so often the forest service deemed Black Rock unfit for fire detection or weather reporting. They abandoned the cabin, letting it deteriorate in the elements, and then built Mockingbird Lookout to replace the gap in the fire detection network.

"You wouldn't be able to drag as much stuff up there by helicopter." I looked around at all the things he had brought from his apartment. There was the sarod, boxes of clay, the eighty-pound pottery wheel, sewing supplies, photography equipment, magazines, books—and a lot of photographs.

The picture of Eileen still lay on the dresser in the bedroom where I'd found it yesterday.

"I'm going for a walk," I said. Why didn't I march back into the bedroom, pick up the photo, and ask him why it was on display? Because I was a coward, afraid to let him know that it bothered me.

"There's not really anywhere to walk," said Daniel. "I mean, there's the road. But there aren't any trails or ridges to explore. It's straight down and straight up. Not really a walkabout kind of place."

"Well, I'm going to check it out," I insisted. I struck off into the pines on the east side of the hill and immediately had to grind the edges of my shoes into the soft pine needle loam to break the descent. He was right; I thrashed around in the forest for a while and then climbed back to the top, defeated. Daniel hovered outside in front of a little white miniature weather station.

"I'm doing the afternoon weather now." He smiled, jotting things into a notebook.

"What do you have to record?"

"Well, a bunch of stuff." Daniel opened the screen on the station.

He checked thermometers for minimum and maximum daily temperatures; a psychrometer, which had wet and dry bulbs to compute the relative humidity; and a glass funnel to measure the precipitation. Nearby on the ground, a rain gauge captured moisture. To record wind direction a weather vane was mounted to the building; an anemometer measured the wind speed.

"That's it," he said. "Now I record all these numbers on another government form and when Karen calls, I'm ready to pass the weather."

"It's so technical," I said, lost at the part about the psychrometer and wet and dry bulbs.

"Not really," he said. "Once you've done it for a while, it takes minutes. In fact, once you know the weather patterns in your district, you barely have to check the instruments; you just know the numbers you're gonna get." He looked up at the sky. "High cumulus. Good, I want dry weather so I feel like I have a purpose here. The fire hazard's not very high yet."

We wandered inside and then I stammered, unable to quash my insecurity any longer, "Uh, that picture, in the bedroom. Why do you have a picture of Eileen here?"

Daniel faced me. "Oh gee, does that bother you?"

"Well, it seems kind of strange that you brought photos of your ex-wife here."

"Hon, I brought all kinds of photos to consider. It's a beautiful photograph, that's all."

"Obviously it's a beautiful photo. I get that."

"No, I mean compositionally. I like that photo, not because it's Eileen, but because it's beautiful from an esthetic perspective. I have tons of photos of Eileen. It's the photo itself, not her I'm considering."

I didn't know what to say. How could he separate his marriage to Eileen from the photograph of Eileen?

"Are you afraid she and I might get back together?"

"I wasn't until I saw that photo."

"I'm sorry, I'll put it away if it bothers you." He pulled me toward him in an embrace.

"XMC26 here for your afternoon weather." Karen's voice intruded over the radio waves.

"Sorry, just give me a minute—the weather calls. I'll be right back." He dashed up the ladder, pushed open the trap door, and reached for the microphone.

"And over to you on Mockingbird, Daniel." Perfect timing. It was odd to hear Tomas over the radio. His studious tone could make a high cirrus cloud sound like a Jungian metaphor.

"Good afternoon, everyone, Mockingbird weather." The numbers flowed from Daniel's lips like a song. His radio persona was friendly and upbeat, as though he had not a care in the world.

"Are you modulating your voice for effect?" I asked when he dropped back down the ladder a few minutes later.

"Everyone does." He laughed sheepishly. "It's all about holding the microphone a certain distance from your lips. Mind you, some lookouts never get it quite right."

"Very smooth," I remarked. "So, where were we?"

"I'm not getting back with Eileen if that's what you're worried about."

"Okay, but I don't want to be an Eileen substitute, you know." I wanted to feel that there was no one else in the whole world he wanted to be with other than me. Maybe that was adolescent, but I wanted to be his partner by choice, not by default.

"You're not a substitute, come on. But really, think about it. There are any number of people we could be with, right? That doesn't take from our relationship. The Relation Ship. The ship of relations we're sailing together."

I didn't know what to say to all his detachment. Maybe this ship should sail without me? I sulked at the kitchen table, listening to the westerly winds gust outside in the sunshine.

"Did I just make things worse?" His voice was apologetic, kind.

"Sort of. I feel like the generic-brand girlfriend."

I needed to be alone to sort out my thoughts. I headed for the outhouse but no sooner had I stepped outdoors than the wind whipped my hair, seized the heavy door, and knocked the breath out of me. Head bowed, body curved forward, I braced into the wind, crossing the meadow and the helicopter pad to the wooden shack on the edge of the clearing. I shut the door to escape the torment of the winds, but the stench of the deep pit flooded upwards. Gale-force winds and a mound of feces. I had heard lookouts tell stories about porcupines and other rodents that took up residence at the bottom of the outhouse cavity. I had a pee and vacated, the strong wind pushing me back toward the lookout.

Daniel was upstairs pacing around the cupola, scanning the forest. I loathed having to bring up the Eileen photograph again, but the conversation was unfinished.

"It's often windy like this in the afternoon. By evening the winds might calm down." He talked with the binoculars pressed to his head.

I leaned against the fire finder staring out at the Rockies, their jagged snow-covered peaks brilliant white in the spring sunshine. There was so much forest and parkland to watch and scan. The job demanded looking out, gazing, staring, observing—focussing outside the self.

"I put that photograph away," he added, sensing my uncertainty. "I don't want you to worry about Eileen, okay? It's you and me."

"Okay. I just didn't know what to make of that photo."

"Hey, we'll get a place together in the fall. After the fire season, I'll have cash and we'll take a road trip and look for land. There's nothing to be upset about. It's just me and my obsession with beautiful images. It's not personal."

I sighed. "All right." I didn't want to hound him with more questions, but I felt we had glossed over the issue to maintain harmony. The wicker basket held other images from past lookout seasons, too. I had glimpsed Eileen in a red bandana on the catwalk of Carbondale, smiling into the camera. He had intentionally packed the photos along with all his other stuff. She lived far away in Vancouver now, but she felt uncomfortably close.

Sensing my upset, he said, "Just so you know, a couple years ago, the last time I thought we might get back together, we had plans to go out on a Friday night, and she phoned and cancelled because there was a new episode of *Miami Vice* on TV."

"Oooh, that's bad. Stood up for Don Johnson."

"Then she started dating business guys. It's over, we're friends. And honestly, I never found Eileen all *that* beautiful. I'm not so much into classic beauty. She is super photogenic, and it's true, guys always said 'lucky, lucky you' when I was with her, but there are a lot of disadvantages to being with a beautiful woman. For one thing, it's too much competition. Every guy wants a beautiful woman, and every beautiful woman expects to get whatever she wants."

I had never conceived of a beautiful woman as a risk. Eileen was like high fire hazard; sparks could ignite any moment, the potential for loss ever present.

With me, Daniel had set his sights on less perfection and more stability.

As though second-guessing my thoughts, he added, "Comparisons are odious."

"Where did that come from?"

"That's a quote from the poet Gary Snyder, Jack Kerouac's friend. It's good advice."

I wrapped my arm around his waist, looking out at the forest and mountains as he peered through the binoculars. Okay, I'd let it go. We all have a past.

"Do you have a method for scanning the trees?"

Daniel laughed. "I keep thinking I should, but it's more intuitive for me. Maybe this is the year I'll scan more systematically."

He showed me how the manual teaches lookouts to scan, starting on one side of their district and sweeping the binoculars in straight horizontal lines, parsing the landscape in linear chunks. It was a scientific approach, but he couldn't bear the linear routine, the predictability, the boredom.

He said he had no idea whether Tomas or John scanned systematically or in a random pattern like himself. I laughed at the thought of John sweeping the binoculars in straight lines. Tomas might during high hazard, because he seemed extremely conscientious about his job performance.

"Maybe later this season, when things heat up, I'll get more systematic," he said.

For now he was pleased with his own methods; he had developed a gentle, soft-focus way of looking, letting the landscape fill up his field of vision without hard staring, without effort.

I earned a reputation for loyalty, most loyal lookout girlfriend, never missing a weekend from May to October that season. Every Saturday evening after locking up the store, I rolled out of town in the Chevy, anticipating the freedom, and potholes, of the Forestry Trunk Road. From far away on Cline Lookout, John wrote to Daniel: "You're so lucky to have Mary visiting every weekend." Then, he described his own disappointment when the monthly groceries and mail had arrived with no parcel from Dinah. Upset and angry, he had no choice but to wait another month—alone. In a letter dated July 20, 1987, he wrote:

> dinah sent a pkg from home a day after I was serviced—so nothing from home for 2 months. i was pissed off for a couple weeks on that one. nevertheless in aloneness, oneness, isolation the opportunity to examine feelings, emotional patterns, attachments…
>
> but to have detachment is not so easy when a giant squid is on your head sucking your brains out your nose—if you know what i mean. putrefacto as the old alchemist on bluehill might declare. the sweat box is my saving grace.…
>
> my heart is a flower, love, om shanti, John

A giant squid sucking out his brains? We did not know what he meant.

I was surprised by the self-disclosure, because during the winter John had insisted how much he relished his solitude on Cline. But obviously he also struggled and his emotional health seemed to hang precariously on whether or not Dinah made it to the post office.

"He's done ten seasons," said Daniel. "He knows how it goes. He probably gave her a shopping list for stuff the ranger can't get in town, that's all. He'll be okay."

Daniel was lucky, indeed. Each week he radioed his eclectic wish list, which, in addition to supplemental groceries like fresh fruit, might include *Elle* magazine, denim fabric for sewing, or an extra box of clay. I didn't mind running errands, and once at the lookout, I didn't mind listening to the mysterious radio voices that infiltrated his world either. But I had no interest in learning how to cross off a smoke or do the weather. For me, the fire finder was furniture, a place to rest my coffee mug, and the topographic maps, paper wall decor. Daniel never offered to train me, either; it was obvious I had no interest in learning basic fire detection skills to replace him in a pinch.

Despite the gendered history of the job, women did work as fire observers. In fact, Eileen had worked alone on Burnt Timber, a remote wilderness lookout northwest of Mockingbird and Blue Hill, and male rangers were always pleased for a reason to drop by. I pictured her in the cupola, a dark-haired Rapunzel, yearning for a lover-prince. And there was Ingrid, our English friend on Kananaskis Lookout, who had put in as many years as John, although her location kept watch over a golf course, detracting from the romantic image of the wilderness hermit and sage. I couldn't picture myself working on my own fire lookout, getting in bed at night, alone, on top of a mountain, to which the precise directions appeared in thousands of hiking guides.

During my own workweek in the city, I looked forward to the mountain escape. Mockingbird was a time-share retreat for which I had unlimited access. The first time I arrived during a smoke, I was dismayed to find the usual vacation ambience vanquished. Daniel, sequestered in the cupola, stooped over the fire finder, shoulders tense, brow pinched. Topographic maps lay unfurled on the desktop.

"Hey, how's it going?" I expected him to throw his arms around me.

"I need a cross shot, Tomas." Daniel held the microphone to his lips.

"I got a smoke!" he yelled in my direction.

He raced to the fire finder and peered through the scope. "Yup, that's a puff of white all right!"

"XMC26, D58 here, with a Pre-Smoke Report."

"XMC26, go ahead Daniel."

I recognized Karen's calm voice.

"I got a puff of white smoke coming up about sixteen kilometres to the north. Just crossing it off with Tomas." He read off a string of township numbers pinpointing the location.

"Copied that Daniel, XMC26." As soon as Karen signed off, Tomas was back on the air.

"Yeah, Daniel, I can barely make it out from over here. I'd say it's behind a ridge along the Fallentimber Creek." Tomas read his bearings.

"I have to write up the Smoke Report now, hon, I'll be right with you." Daniel scribbled on the government form, and then, after taking another look through the binoculars, radioed Karen again.

"D58 here with a Smoke Report."

"Go ahead, XMD58." Karen answered instantly. After all, it had been only sixty seconds since they last spoke.

Had I heard that correctly? A Pre-Smoke Report and a minute later a Smoke Report? I was baffled, but maybe this was like medical language, precancerous and cancerous skin cells.

Daniel rhymed off the report data: the time of the sighting; the size, colour, and consistency of the smoke; and the exact location. "It's intermittent, puffing up and then disappearing for a bit, but it's there." He put down the mic, squinted through the fire finder, and then swung around, ebullient. "Come on baby, light my fire! We got a smoke tonight! Whoohoo!"

"So, what happens now?" This was my first smoke ever, but I was less enthusiastic, unable to discern the puff. I had become so used to Daniel strolling around with binoculars pressed to his head, I had forgotten the endgame.

"Well, it came up suddenly. There's no burn permit over there, no sawmill, so I'm pretty sure it's the real thing. But it's tricky, puffs up and then dies down."

"So now what?"

"The ranger will decide if they want to action it or not. They'll probably send the chopper pilot over, take a look, maybe dump some retardant, although it's kinda late in the evening to be flying around."

"Are you done, then?"

"I need to stand by and keep an eye on this."

"Okay, how long do you think? I'm starved." As usual I had brought groceries: lettuce, broccoli, fresh fruit, pasta sauce, cheese, and yogourt.

"Go ahead, I'll be down in a bit. I wanna keep an eye on this little smoke and see if it changes."

I went downstairs to hang out and cook dinner. The fire talk inspired me to think Mexican, hot sauce, chilies, and bean tortillas. The difference between a Pre-Smoke Report and a Smoke Report was esoteric to an out-sider like me, but as I spent more time at the lookout, the distinctions became clear.

During the 1950s, Alberta Forestry had hired "efficiency experts" to streamline forest operations and departments. The efficiency experts de-termined that fire observers must report a smoke within three minutes of spotting it. This sounded reasonable, except before an observer could file a Smoke Report, he had to call up a neighbouring lookout, hunch over the fire finder for a cross shot, calculate the bearing, and then radio Calgary with a description of the sighting: colour, consistency, height, and distance. In practice, despite rushing around, fire observers had trouble meeting the three-minute window. Of course, it was always possible to fudge the time, but if your neighbour had fallen asleep or was having sex with a hiker, it could take a few minutes to rouse him over the radio for a cross shot. The most tantalizing female hiker in the Canadian Rockies, invited inside to sign the guest book, could be tagging Daniel around the fire finder, but as soon as he heard his call sign, he'd ditch her faster than you can say D58. His nervous system was programmed at such a deep level, the call "XMD58" over the radio could wake him instantly from REM sleep.

To allow fire observers more time without compromising the ulti-mate goal of forest efficiency, managers designed another reporting form, the Pre-Smoke Report, a rather functional taxonomy. Calling the radio room with a Pre-Smoke Report alerted the rangers and standby crew of possible action, and granted observers the grace of a couple more minutes to refine their smoke data and, depending on the circumstances, grab a pair of pants.

It was the Extra Smoke Report that I found most compelling. In keeping with the theme of functionality, it should have been named the Missed Smoke Report, but administrators chose a more diplomatic title to preserve morale, perhaps. An Extra Smoke sounded like a bonus, as though observers were working more, not less.

Of course everyone missed a smoke at one time or another, and often there were good reasons; sometimes the terrain obscured sightlines, valleys tucked away behind hills created tricky blind spots. But when I heard the words Extra Smoke Report over the radio, it was hard not to wonder if the lookout man had been napping or snuck off for a hike.

There was nothing comparable to missing a smoke in my job. I suppose the closest mishap would be missing an entire vitamin trend. What if I had missed the green chlorella and spirulina craze? It would have been disastrous for sales and made me look incompetent. But a missed smoke could explode into fire and put an entire community on standby for evacuation.

Writing to me from Mockingbird, Daniel described how an observer on Carbondale Lookout had failed to spot a smoke. "McNeal apparently missed a big smoke/fire and supposedly he took it as a sign to resign or something. Honourable fellow?"

An honourable fellow requesting an honourable discharge? Perhaps missed smokes were like missing an advance across enemy lines? In the end McNeal did not resign, but he certainly would have supplied an Extra Smoke Report. The report asked for specific details: *What was the fire hazard at the time? Were you in the cupola at the time of the discovery? Where were you?* The remiss observer had to call in to the district headquarters and read the Extra Smoke Report over the radio. McNeal would have clicked open the microphone saying something like this:

"XMC33 here with an Extra Smoke Report."

"Go ahead, C33," the radio operator would answer, deadpan, without a hint of curiosity.

"Time of incident, 1530 hours; hazard level, medium; *I was not in the cupola at the time.*"

Then where the heck was he? Now everyone in the forest, probably even the wildlife, would listen in for the excuse. I don't know what reason McNeal offered for his miss, but Tomas once told me that he, himself, liked to say, "taking care of metabolic processes." How could a ranger take issue with that excuse? Daniel preferred to report a more productive reason, such as "doing generator maintenance in the engine shed," thereby constructing the image of a busy lookout man, deserving of a paycheque. Many observers simply said, "I was in the outhouse at the time."

There were also unofficial mystery smokes. At Mockingbird that summer, Owen, a ranger in the Ghost district, radioed Daniel with strange news.

"XMD58, are you by, Dan?"

"D58 here, what's up, Owen?" Daniel responded as usual within seconds.

"Dan, I'm east of Black Rock here, maybe fifteen kilometres southwest of Mockingbird, and I'm standing in an area of black charred timber."

"Copy that, Owen," Daniel trained the fire finder on the section of forest Owen had identified. Charred! He prayed the area fell outside his district.

"Dan, I'm standing in the middle of a burn down here. Did you see any smoke over this way lately?"

Holy smokes! He hadn't seen even a wisp of road dust or rain vapour over that way in weeks.

"Uh, no, haven't seen a thing at all. Nothin' at all."

"Yeah, well, Dan, I know we didn't action anything, but there was some kind of forest fire here. I'm going to have to report it."

"Maybe a lightning strike, Owen. I don't think I can see into that valley. Must be a blind spot from Mockingbird."

"Well, okay. Yeah, looks like it could have been a strike."

"D58." Sheesh, he hadn't missed a smoke, he'd missed a whole forest fire!

Sometimes, despite all the risk calculations, aircraft patrols, and lookout hours, fires burned. And after the devastation, a thick layer of ash nourished the forest floor.

In addition to the Smoke Reports, there was other record keeping. I was learning why Daniel said being a fire lookout was a white-collar job. Fire lookouts kept a multitude of records: the daily weather, storm activities—start and end times were especially important—the number of lightning strikes, and other special events, such as hail and snow.

Daniel also kept an eye out for frogs falling from the sky. He insisted that during certain types of storms, frogs got sucked out of ponds and thrown high into the air, and then fell out of the sky in some faraway random place. It sounded plain apocalyptic in the Biblical sense. I was certain frogs would never fall out of the sky at Mockingbird. He insisted he knew someone who had witnessed it.

Regardless of frogs, observers recorded all their weather measurements and observations on government forms, a fresh form for each day. Then the observer transferred all this daily information, by hand, into the Blue Book, a sacred forestry text. The way I saw it, the Forest Service Blue Book, a record of outdoor weather, was the masculine equivalent to Emily Post's *Etiquette: The Blue Book of Social Usage*, a record of indoor manners.

At the end of the season, some rangers checked the quality and legibility of the lookout man's handwriting in the Blue Book, reprimanding fire observers who wrote with a sloppy cursive. In response to this surveillance, Tommy, a neighbouring fire observer in the Bow-Crow Forest, colour-coded all his cloud descriptions one year, transforming pages of black-and-white notes and numbers into splashes of decorative patterns.

During Daniel's first season at Cowpar Lookout in northern Alberta, the whole summer passed before he noticed the empty storm records in the back pages of the Blue Book. Horrified by his mistake, he attempted to reconstruct the entire season's storm activity from memory, guessing start and end times for months of storms, even switching pens now and then to maximize the credibility of his handwritten entries.

The fire detection system in southern Alberta suppressed fire so efficiently, I seldom witnessed a smoke, let alone a real forest fire. To me, the lookout was a place to relax encircled by wild beauty, a mountain retreat in the heart of hearts. In late morning when the winds were calm, we dragged the kitchen chairs outside to drink coffee and eat fruit salad and toast in the sunshine, the radio turned up loud so Daniel could hear his call sign. Grey whisky jacks soared out of the pine trees, plucking a raisin or whole-wheat crust from my outstretched hand.

Jack Kerouac, the patron artist of lookout observers, had described a similar experience on Desolation Lookout.

> Early in the afternoon was the usual time for my kick of the day, instant chocolate pudding with hot coffee. Around two or three I'd lie on my back on the meadowside and watch the clouds float by, or pick blueberries and eat them right there. The radio was on loud enough to hear any calls for Desolation.[1]

I didn't know it at the time, but those days on Mockingbird were some of the best days of my life. How could I have known? As a young educated woman, I expected every summer to blossom into a season of gain; I desired more from life, more adventure, and more purpose. And without much gratitude, I also had my complaints; the list was long and expandable. One morning, I lounged in the sunshine, the magnificence of the Rockies at my back, by now already taken for granted, and I itemized my dissatisfactions, a shopping list of troubles. There was my perpetual job funk, customers and staff members to complain about. There was my contemporary dance teacher, Francine from Montreal, who wanted her students to perform, and I bemoaned our group wasn't ready. Calgary, headquarters for the resource sector, was always a ripe target for my complaints, the logging and oil industries whittling away the east slope of the foothills.

Daniel always listened without interrupting, and when I had exhausted the inventory, he met my gaze for a long moment and slowly shook his head. "You suffer from the grass-is-greener syndrome," he observed.

"It's divine discontent," I quipped, then felt exposed. "Everybody complains."

"Not like you. You're just never satisfied," he insisted. "It's your downfall."

Lightning

I wanted to be at Mockingbird in a lightning storm.

Before a direct hit, Daniel said his tongue tasted like a copper penny. His hair stood up, the air sizzled, and the sky ruptured—boom! The electric flash lit up the room. He wrote to me, "This morning (at 0001 hrs, 0002 hrs, & 0003 hrs) there were 3 direct hits of lightning on the mast—good ones, the kind you taste in your mouth." One season, while he cowered in bed, a lightning bolt cracked twenty feet above his head.

Tomas had ventured outside to practise qigong during a storm on Mockingbird and nearly combusted when lightning struck the ground close by. He scuttled inside, hair bristling, *Oh, the power of Shakti to decimate a man*. Another time, while he was seeking refuge indoors, the metal in his alarm clock glowed red-hot after a direct strike. Lookout folks often told a story about an unknown observer who was knocked unconscious when lightning hit his cupola. The poor fellow must have been watching the light show and forgot to unplug his radio equipment.

I wasn't yearning to get knocked out by lightning, or spontaneously combust, but I hoped to witness a heavenly zap. Busy reading *Beyond Supernature* by Lyall Watson, Daniel was brimming with extraordinary facts about lightning strikes, such as cases of rocks and soil that permanently kept their magnetic charge after being hit. I wondered what the odds were of a lightning storm commencing while I was there during any given weekend. The field of a high-voltage strike might have tremendous health benefits, and as long as I stayed inside, it wasn't risky; the lookout was well grounded to prevent injury. In the early days, it was a different matter. Lightning surged down the transistor-style radio antennas and metal guy cables, destroying equipment and blasting holes in the cabin.

One weekend in late June, I arrived at Mockingbird and found Daniel in the kitchen, agitated, padding around the kitchen in flip-flops, a colourful sarong around his waist, as though he were stationed in Indonesia. A row of empty Jolt Cola cans cluttered the table.

"Are you okay?" I eyed the beverage logo. It depicted a bolt of lightning shooting through the O in *JOLT*.

"Fine, really. I might need to cut back on the cola. I'm drinking so much it's giving me the shakes."

"I'm here to do a caffeine-sugar intervention. Have a beer with me, instead. I brought Big Rock in glass bottles this week."

"Might as well," said Daniel, "join the boys down below; didn't you notice the noise?"

Stepping back outside, I listened. "Oh my God, it's Creedence Clearwater. Is that the campground?"

"Yup, it sure is. It's 'Proud Mary,' rolling down the river. Waiparous campground again. I've never actually heard the campground up here before. They must be monster speakers. I should probably call the ranger before it gets any later."

During the long weekend in May, the campground had made national news when drunken campers drove trailers and off-road vehicles through the woods, destroying trees, and leaving piles of garbage behind.

He grabbed the microphone for the two-way radio, holding it a hair's width from his lips to guarantee a mellifluous broadcast voice.

"D58 here, are you by, Owen?"

"XMD58 go ahead."

"Hey, Owen, just wanted to tell you I'm listening to CCR up here tonight."

"Say again, Dan."

"The Waiparous campground. They're blasting CCR."

"You can hear it at the lookout?"

"That's affirmative."

"We'll get on that right away, thanks, Dan."

"Copied, D58."

He clicked the microphone closed. "Might as well take care of that before the party gets any louder."

We sat around the kitchen table with a beer and mused about our separate lives that week. In the background male radio voices, rangers, pilots, and guardians, streamed into the lookout, a barrage of call signs and forest jargon.

"I have an idea to tell you about," said Daniel, monitoring the radio operations, attention split.

He was stoked to photograph a nighttime lightning strike from the top of Mockingbird Hill, the kind that cracks open the sky with iridescent branches, splitting, forking, and propagating downward from a white-hot centre.

"I can see it in my mind's eye," he said. "A white lightning strike on a black T-shirt. Mail-order business."

"You *could* just look for smoke, make some pots, and play sarod."

"I know, I could, but it's such a fantastic idea. Lightning T-shirts. I'll take a photograph during a real lightning storm, silkscreen it onto a cotton T-shirt, and we'll sell them to lookout people. All the fire lookouts will buy at least one. I'll design an order form and get the secretary to send it to the ranger districts all over the province as an official memo."

Daniel was certain if we offered a selection of colours, T-shirt orders would be unstoppable, a direct cash hit. When the lookout observers received their monthly groceries and mail, they'd receive the notice about our T-shirt promotion. The best part was that we could distribute the shirts free of charge, sending them through the Forestry mail system.

I was on board with the project. Selling was familiar ground; the only downside I could see was the potential ceiling on sales—there were a total of 120 fire lookouts in Alberta. Daniel might have to design a full collection of lightning wear to push sales into a profit margin. Heck, most forest fires were started by lightning; wouldn't everyone want a lightning T-shirt? There were rangers, guardians, radio operators, initial-attack firefighters, helicopter pilots, forest managers, and administrators. On casual Fridays, they could wear their lightning T-shirt to the office. This was obviously an unstoppable commercial venture.

He waited patiently for a high-voltage electrical storm to pass by at night, darted outside, and stood on the hill in the blackness, vulnerable, anticipating the white zigzag bolt to explode the sky, coolly snapping a picture without electrocuting himself. He developed the photograph in a makeshift dark room inside the Volkswagen van. At first, he insisted on screening the shirts by hand at Mockingbird, a plan that made me anxious. If he missed a smoke handcrafting T-shirts, Forestry might ship him up north next year, back to the mosquitoes and thirty-metre towers.

"Let me take your artwork to a shop in Calgary and screen a prototype."

"It looks fantastic," Daniel exclaimed when I brought back the sample from Wheat Buckley the following weekend. "Very striking—let's do it."

On the next servicing, Daniel handed off our lightning memo to the helicopter pilot with instructions to deliver it to the secretary in Calgary. She would photocopy the one-pager and distribute it throughout the province. In a few weeks the orders would rain down.

While we waited for T-shirt orders, we took up boffing on the weekends. Boffing was the closest Daniel and I ever got to fighting. It was also the closest we got to a sports activity, and of course, it involved a craft project. To make boffer bats, Daniel wrapped a wooden baseball bat inside thick layers of foam padding until it swelled to about twenty-five centimetres, and then he stitched the whole bulky thing inside heavy denim fabric. On sunny afternoons, we chased each other around the meadow at the top of Mockingbird Hill, batting each other with the soft weapon. I sprinted across the knoll, cornering Daniel and pounding on him, while he shielded his face from the friendly fire. Then, when he busted an escape, I would flee the other way, his boffer bat clobbering me from behind.

Boffing helped reduce the lassitude that happened every day following the afternoon weather sked. Oddly, an uncontrollable fatigue enveloped us, as though someone had slipped Valium into the water barrel. We often succumbed to the crushing lethargy and stumbled toward the bed, desperate for the relief of sleep, pledging to nap for only thirty minutes. I could enjoy the pleasure of falling deep into the black, but Daniel forced himself to look out the window intermittently. "Nothing burning out there," he'd say and burrow into the pillows for another twenty minutes of bliss.

Whether it was the effects of altitude, the unrelenting wind, or electromagnetic frequencies, afternoon sleepiness was a universal lookout phenomenon. When it rained, the urge to sleep was insurmountable, but at least then the worry of missing a smoke was almost non-existent.

In July, a torrent of rain accompanied the opening of the Calgary Stampede, and when the overcast conditions persisted, I had the presence of mind to make the most of it.

"Let's sneak into town and ride the roller coaster," I challenged. "The fire hazard is low, everything's soaking wet."

"Gee, I don't know." Daniel shrugged. "It's dicey driving a red van around the backcountry. I'm a bit of a mark. If I pass anyone from Forestry, they'll know it's me."

"Come on, it'll be fun. You can drive back late, the rangers will be off the road then."

"Can't you go with a friend?" Daniel resisted.

"But I want to go with you. We can stroll the midway together."

"Okay, but I have to be back for morning weather. Which means I need to leave your place by five thirty tomorrow morning."

"All right, let's go, so we have more time in town."

We had barely passed the Ghost ranger station when a green Forestry truck approached, travelling in the opposite direction. Daniel waved at the driver.

"Shoot, it's probably Owen or Vic."

"Maybe they didn't notice. It's not like you have the only red VW van in the world," I said optimistically.

"Of course, the ranger noticed me! Sheesh. I think it was Owen, shit. Well, it's obvious nothing could be burning in this rain."

"You deserve a rainy day off."

"Yeah, but I get paid for an eight-day week."

"Don't worry, it's still afternoon; maybe you're just running into Cochrane for a few groceries, right?"

"I guess, but if Owen calls me later, I won't be answering, will I?"

I laughed. "I can't believe we just drove by a ranger. I mean, what are the odds?"

"I told you this would happen."

"Everything's fine, it's been raining for days. He won't care."

"You don't know that."

He was right. I didn't know the work culture, or Owen, at all. But sitting up there in the pouring rain seemed lonely and boring, when we could steal away to the bustling midway, surrounded by throngs of strangers and bright lights, and show the whole world how happy we were together.

At the Stampede, I persuaded Daniel to ride the big roller coaster, and we screamed as loud as we could at the crest of each hill, he turning ghostly white.

"It's good for the lymphatic system," I shrieked, hoping he wouldn't throw up.

Next I steered him over to the Himalayan, my second-favourite ride. It was all about speed, a tilted circular track that sucked riders like a giant vacuum into a tiny corner of their seat, the operator yelling *Do you wanna go faster? Yeeesss.* At least I did; by the looks of Daniel, maybe not. Using all my strength, I clawed and gripped the edge of the seat to resist the gravity and suction, but no matter how hard I fought, I crushed Daniel against the metal safety bar. His head bobbed up and down, his body limp, surrendering to the vortex of speed. When the ride ended, we zigzagged, unsteady on our feet, into the crowd. I was rejuvenated; Daniel looked traumatized.

"That's enough for me," he said, breathless.

At my apartment he set the alarm clock for 5:30 a.m.

"I'm going to get up and leave first thing. You won't even hear me go."

Early the next morning, I rolled over, accidentally kicking Daniel, my toes rubbing along his bony, hairy shins.

"It's six thirty," I cried, looking at the clock.

"I know," said Daniel. "I just woke up too."

"What are you going to do? Call Owen and fess up?"

"No, I think I can do the weather from here."

"Do the weather from here? Are you kidding me?"

"I'm serious. I think I can call the phone number for the repeater and it will bounce me into the weather sked. I'm going to try."

"I'm getting up for this show," I said, "but we have an hour to spare." I turned toward him and slid my leg across his hip.

"It isn't like you to be awake so early," he said, pleased.

"How often do I have you in my own bed this summer?"

"I see, this is a reward for risking everything last night."

"For not throwing up on the roller coaster."

"Now there's a sexy image. Come here."

At 7:29 a.m., he punched the number of the Forestry cell repeater into my telephone, waited for three beeps, and then entered a code.

I covered my mouth, astonished.

"Good morning, everyone, this is XMD58 with Mockingbird weather." He recited the weather without a glitch, his voice bright as usual.

"How did you decide what to say?" I marvelled when he hung up.

"After a while, you just know your weather. My relative humidity might be off a tad, but overall I bet it was right on. You can tell by the neighbouring lookout. I listened to Tomas on Blue Hill and altered my numbers slightly. John noticed that pattern years ago. He used to do the weather lying in bed sometimes."

"I wonder if you sound any different without the microphone." His cleverness so impressed me, it raised the spectre of marriage.

"Probably, but they'll just think I was klutzy with the mic. Anyway, I'm gonna get back—back to where I once belonged. See you on the weekend, hon."

And he was gone.

The next weekend I arrived on schedule and discovered Daniel in the kitchen, fidgeting aimlessly.

"Forestry called today. They said they're sending Jack Carter up here to talk to me."

"Jack? What's his position?"

"He's supervisor of all lookouts."

"Uh-oh. Do you think it's because we skipped into town?"

"I don't think that's it, no."

"The weather sked? Did someone figure out you fudged the numbers?"

"No, I don't think anyone suspected that."

"Then what are you worried about?"

"I'm not exactly worried, but Jack's not driving a couple hours to say, 'Great job Daniel, keep up the good work.'"

"Why do you suppose they're sending him, then?"

"Probably because I've been on the radio a bit too much."

"Doing what?"

"Shopping."

"Shopping?"

"Mail order."

He said with the regular paycheques going into the bank, he'd been tempted to shop by mail-order catalogue. First he requested a catalogue from the company, and this required one phone call over the forestry radio. Then, to complete the purchase with his credit card, he needed to make a second call. Both phone calls took place during regular business hours.

"How can a couple phone calls be a problem for Forestry?"

"Well, it was more than a couple. There's so many cool mail-order companies now."

There was the Lee Valley catalogue with nifty, hard-to-find hand tools; the L.L.Bean catalogue with stylish outdoor wear; the Banyen Books catalogue with alluring titles on sustainable architecture; and there was the perennial IKEA catalogue.

"I had to restrain myself when I got the Zola catalogue from the US. They have such a nice kitchen series."

"Okay, what did you order from Zola?"

"Well, the cutlery here is such junk. It's old and mismatched, so I ordered a set of black enamel flatware. That's all. When we leave Mockingbird, we can take the good cutlery and put back the metal relics. It's hard to find cutlery that matches my pottery."

"So you ordered designer cutlery over the forestry radio?"

"I did, just this week. And I'm so glad I squeezed in that last order."

I gave him a look. Even I knew the radio rules.

I found it interesting it was the black cutlery order that incited a cease-and-desist order from Forestry supervisors. If he'd been buying a rifle over the radio, would there have been less fuss? Perhaps the domesticity of cutlery violated the masculine image of the forest service.

"It's not like I don't get it. When I place an order, everyone in the forest has to listen to the whole transaction. The radio is supposed to be kept open for fighting fires. Fortunately, I didn't get put on hold."

On Monday, when we heard Jack's truck on the switchbacks, Daniel dashed around tidying up the lookout.

"You stay down here in the kitchen. We'll go up into the cupola."

Jack was a generation older than us, a big man with a long history in the forest service. A lifer, Daniel called him. He had worked on every mountain and bush lookout in the province, the last generation of lookout men who worked their way up the ranks, becoming a full-time employee without going to college or university to study forest management. Jack had started out as a lookout man in 1955 and now, over thirty years later, held the position of chief fire detection officer in the province. He also had the awkward title of permanent spare lookout, which sounded like an oxymoron to me, but meant that Jack was the spare man should any lookout person in the province need time off to attend a wedding or funeral, or deal with a crisis.

To us he was simply Jack, supervisor-of-all-fire-lookouts.

Startled to see a woman in the lookout kitchen, Jack shook my hand and quickly turned away. "Let's go have a talk upstairs, Dan."

In that brief encounter, I sensed his masculine nature. He was manly in the traditional sense, proud of his physical strength and stoic self-control. I had never found myself attracted to hypermasculine men, regardless of their occupation. It's not that Jack and I were from different planets, Mars and Venus—we were from different galactic sectors.

They must have been up in the cupola for half an hour. I strained to eavesdrop, unable to hear through the ceiling. Jack's voice droned on and on.

At last footsteps clanged down the metal steps outside. When I peeked out, they were shaking hands next to the truck, chatting in buddy mode.

Back inside, Daniel collapsed on a kitchen chair. "What a guy!"

"Is everything all right? You're not getting fired or anything?" I was sure he didn't want to end his lookout career in a dispute over cutlery.

"No, it's okay. As Jack would say, 'That was crazier than a sandwich for breakfast.'"

"What?"

"Never mind, it's one of his favourite sayings, 'crazier than a sandwich for breakfast.' Anyway, I pissed off some bigwigs. He said I have to stay off the radio during the day or else. He kept saying it's different in this forest. He knows up north everyone chats on the radio. Even down south at Carbondale it's a lot more relaxed."

"That's not so bad, right?"

"Yeah, it's fine, at least I got that last mail order in. It's just that he drove all the way up here to tell me. Sheesh, oh well. Guess what else?"

"No idea. What? You want to quit lookouts sooner than later?"

"No, no. Jack's in love with Nana Mouskouri!"

"Nana Mouskouri! Are you kidding?"

"I'm serious. He's president of the Nana Mouskouri official fan club. He goes to every concert. She was just here in May, he said. They met in Greece years ago when he was on an archeology dig. His apartment in Calgary is plastered with photographs of her. He's infatuated, big-time. I guess he can't resist the black, horn-rimmed glasses."

"Is he married?" I asked.

"Jack's not the marrying type. He's the stereotypical backwoods man, isolated and lusting after women. I heard his bedroom walls are a collage of *Playboy* centrefolds, floor to ceiling. Totally unreal."

"Not the best way to impress a date," I said, wondering what motivated an adult man to cut out magazine photos of naked women. Nana Mouskouri was a respectable singer. Perhaps a part of Jack longed for a normal relationship.

"Jack's okay, don't get me wrong. We all like Jack. He's a good guy, knows a lot about the geology of the Rocky Mountains. He's travelled around the world to archeology sites and takes good wilderness photographs. We just ignore the *Playboy* thing."

It was Daniel's defence of Jack that I found memorable; it occurred to me that as a woman I would always be an outsider in such a situation.

I could never sit in a room with a group of men and fully comprehend their perspective, because I would never have access to their embodied experience.

I was confident interacting with men in social situations—because I had confidence in my own intellect. But male culture in its mainstream expression baffled me: emotional restraint unless the home team scored, devotion to technical facts, and earning power as a marker of success.

Throughout the summer, orders and cheques for lightning T-shirts flowed in from all over the province. My apartment transformed into lightning headquarters; stacks of small, medium, and large, black, blue, green, and burgundy T-shirts occupied the living room floor. I assembled and packaged the orders, marvelling at the romantic names of lookout destinations: Flat Top, Ironstone, Raspberry Ridge, Red Earth, Salt Prairie, and Sugarloaf. But only a few rangers and radio operators placed orders. The title *Fire Lookout 1987* emblazoned across the front may have been our commercial undoing. Rangers and initial-attack crew worked the front lines of firefighting; from their perspective they did the manly, exciting jobs. They didn't want a shirt applauding lookout men, who sat on a mountaintop and watched the action from a distance.

I bought an accounting ledger and kept meticulous records to track our profit, which we figured was enough to buy a used truck.

"We're gonna need a truck when we move to the country," Daniel said. "One more lookout season, and we'll be ready."

One more year in the natural foods business—would I be ready?

Secretly, I had been playing with the idea of continuing studies in psychology and applying to graduate school. If we moved to the country I would either have to give up that goal or live apart from Daniel for periods of time while I went to school. Maintaining two residences would be costly. I'd have to get more student loans, and I already had $8,000 of debt from my bachelor's degree, but money and its tangible benefits had never been deciding factors for me. I was motivated by the need for a sense of purpose. When we align with a greater or deeper purpose, we feel energized, as though a tiny zap of lightning has revitalized our soul.

In time, lightning would strike when I was at the lookout, and I would cower in the dark next to Daniel and shudder, a blinding crack splitting open the world, iridescent branches, forking and propagating downward, the negative charge of the bolt fascinated by the positive charge of the soil.

Winter

In September, after our first season on Mockingbird Lookout, Daniel and I bought a tiny bungalow near Rotary Park, close to downtown Calgary, and up the hill from the Centre Street Bridge. The narrow house couldn't have been more than seven hundred square feet, but it had a basement, a backyard large enough for a garden, and renovation potential. The asking price was $49,000, nothing down, with a convoluted history of mortgage liens, which our lawyer admitted were on the sketchy side of the ledger, but legal.

Before we merged our stuff, Daniel vetted the furniture and kitchenware in my old apartment. Flinging open my kitchen cupboards, he pointed at the offending plates.

"Those have to go. I can't live with china dishes. I'm a potter."

I tried to sell Daniel on the idea of the dishes' antique value. He inspected the stamp on the bottom of the plates. "They're run-of-the-mill English china, nothing valuable, and even if they're worth something, it's a dreadful esthetic: light, fragile, and mass-produced. I'll make us new dishes. That stainless steel cutlery should go to the Salvation Army too."

"What's wrong with my cutlery?"

"This old stainless steel doesn't match clay. I have that new black flatware, remember? Much nicer."

He moved on to the living room, flitting around my apartment like an antique dealer. "Not much here really—rattan loveseat, I guess we could take that. But the maple wood table needs to go. I'll find a pine slab table for our kitchen."

So far, I was bringing my clothes and the rattan.

"We have the 1940s couch and armchair from my grandmother," he reminded me. "We're not going to have room for much more."

I didn't mind that Daniel policed the esthetic of every object coming into the house; more importantly, I appreciated his willingness to speak about us as a "we." So, we hauled my stuff back to its source, the thrift store, and took possession of 212 Sixth Avenue NE.

Throughout the fall, Daniel renovated the old house, tearing up three layers of old carpet and underlay on the floors, scrounging a deal on a used hardwood floor in *Bargain Finder Magazine,* nailing down the boards, and then stripping, sanding, and staining the wood. We painted the walls gallery white.

Then, he moved on to the basement to build a pottery studio. The basement was an unfinished cellar, concrete floors and exposed studs on the walls. After hitting his head a few times on low-hanging metal pipes, he took to wearing a bicycle helmet downstairs. It would take months of work to make the studio usable. He built drying racks, a table for kneading the clay, and shelving for his assorted ceramic tools. By the time he finished the studio later that winter, we would be edging toward the next fire lookout season.

Daniel awarded *Tweety Bird*, an assemblage of rusty scrap metal and an old spoon, its own wall in the living room. *Tweety Bird* shone out with rustic simplicity and the hint of a secret, as though the found pieces had magically fallen together. For the longest time, I assumed Daniel had made it, because he handled the piece with such reverence.

"This is your art, isn't it?" I asked, watching as he chose the perfect spot.

"Actually, John made this piece when he was on Livingstone Lookout, years ago. He gave it to me in the fall when he came down."

In response, the next year at Birch Mountain Lookout, Daniel constructed a folk art sculpture using Chinese coins, glass beads, and found materials, and presented it to John. He titled the artwork *Getting to Cry Is Shaped Like a Seahorse*, a poetic phrase borrowed from his guru, Adi Da, in which the spiritual teacher described the opening of his heart chakra, and the awareness of an S-shaped current of energy linking the heart and head chakras. In some ways, the artwork was a statement that Daniel had severed spiritual ties with his first guru, Maharishi Mahesh Yogi. The gift may have been an affront to John, because it diminished his original role in Daniel's life as meditation teacher.

There was friction between them, but to me they were like brothers, connected by invisible threads, sometimes admiring each other, sometimes disappointed.

"He's a really good artist," Daniel said. "And he encouraged me to make art."

John had initiated Daniel into Transcendental Meditation in 1973, whispering the assigned mantra into his ear at a meditation forum in northwest Calgary. Two meditation teachers presided over the public event. After the presentation, the audience was invited to receive their meditation mantra from either one, and for some reason most of the attendees lined up in front of the other teacher. Feeling empathy for the shy-looking hippie in a suit jacket and tie, Daniel gravitated toward John to receive his mantra.

John was older than Daniel and had accumulated more spiritual cachet: he had met the Maharishi in person in 1972, attended advanced teacher-training retreats in Europe, and was once married to a beautiful woman who had been the Maharishi's personal aide. Sheila, John's ex, had travelled internationally with the yogi, assisting him on his mission to spiritually regenerate the world. Like John, Daniel attended an international TM teachers' retreat, and chose a program at Avoriaz, in the Alps of southern France.

Committed to the Maharishi's vision, he still needed to earn a living, so like other TM teachers in Calgary, Daniel had walked door to door delivering hydroelectric bills for the city.

"And then John discovered fire lookout jobs. We were both living in the Anderson Apartments then, you know the one? I still dream about that place."

The Anderson was a red brick, six-storey, H-shaped building off Seventeenth Avenue, the hippest address in Calgary—brass cage elevator, marble floors, even a cupola. Daniel assumed it was here that John first read Jack Kerouac's *The Dharma Bums* and *On the Road*. It occurred to John that if Jack could land a job on Desolation Peak, a fire lookout in Washington state, ten kilometres across the border from British Columbia, a stone's throw away really, then so could he. In the spring of 1977, he contacted Alberta Forestry and put in his application.

John had good fortune in those years; he was hired mid-season, in July 1977, and sent down to the southernmost fire lookout in all of Alberta—Carbondale Lookout.

Jack Kerouac had already died of alcoholism, but, inspired by his wild tales of freedom and altered states in *The Dharma Bums*, John mailed a postcard to Kerouac's good friend, the poet Allen Ginsberg, and invited him to visit Carbondale Lookout. Ginsberg wrote a reply saying, "Thanks, I'm a bit busy right now."

Ginsberg may have turned down the invitation to Carbondale Lookout, but Daniel accepted and cruised south down Highway 2 in his van, riding the eastern edge of the Rocky Mountains to the Crowsnest Pass, almost all the way to Waterton Lakes National Park. That summer he and John sat on the south meadow below the lookout, gazing out at the Whitefish mountain range and the Castle River valley, thanking their lucky stars for this place.

Several months later, at the end of his first season, John signed the Carbondale guest book with the comment *Searching for the perfect mammal*, proclaiming his desire for a marriage partner.

"He spotted Dinah at the soup kitchen across the street from the Anderson Apartments," said Daniel. "She worked there as a server. With Eileen. We used to go there all the time. In fact, it was John who gave me a job reference so I could get hired as a lookout."

More recently, John had given Daniel a yarn painting. After making several trips to Mexico and hanging out with indigenous Huichol people, John had become infatuated with their traditional yarn paintings, psychedelic depictions of altered states made with Day-Glo coloured yarn and beeswax on canvas. He brought some of the art back to Canada with the idea of using the Huichol connection to establish a tribal-art business. When the hallucinogenic paintings failed to sell, John lent them out to friends and presented them as gifts. To Daniel and me, the spiralling neon oranges, yellows, and lime greens appeared out of place in cool, temperate Canada.

We dragged our yarn gift from wall to wall throughout our little house, trying to find the right spot.

"How about here?" I said over and over again. "I'll hold it up while you stand back and look."

"Nope," said Daniel. "Doesn't work. Actually, I really hate that yarn art—and all the shaman crap that goes with it."

Eventually we stored the yarn painting in a closet.

I joked that we might need protection from a shaman's ritual if John found out. Once, after a trip to Mexico, he had crowed about battling with the dark forces on the subtle plane.

After all the found objects had found walls, Daniel approached me about hanging a photograph.

"I have a slide I want to develop into a large photograph for this space," he said, gesturing at a wall in the living room. "It's a photograph I took."

"Of what?"

"Well, actually, it's of Eileen, Eileen outside the art museum in San Francisco. Eileen's in the photo, but it's not because of her that I love this image. How can I explain?"

I searched his face; he was serious. I thought we had put the ghost of Eileen to rest at Mockingbird.

"So, you thought you'd hang a supersize image of Eileen—in our new house?"

"Hon, it's not about her personally, you have to believe me. It's one of the best photographs I've ever taken."

"Maybe we should put it in the bedroom," I said.

"Hon, come on."

I stared at the blank wall, considering it for about two seconds. Friends would visit and we'd sit next to the image and they'd say, *Daniel, what a gorgeous photograph, who is that, anyway? Oh, no one,* he'd say, *just my ex-wife.*

I didn't want to be mean-spirited, but neither did I want to live in a gallery with a permanent collection featuring Daniel's ex-wife.

I vetoed the photograph, no more discussion, just flat out "No."

That winter I quit my job at Community Natural Foods and accepted a position at Earth Harvest Co-op, a horizontal job change, much like swapping one mountain fire lookout for another. Lee, the accountant, recruited me as store manager, luring me from Community Natural with promises of more flexible working conditions and bold opportunities for skill development. She wrapped the negotiations with the offer of a winter, all-expense-paid sales trip to the leading trade show and convention in Anaheim, California. I was easily persuaded by a small raise and Lee's assertions that Earth Harvest was destined to become the Wild Oats Market of Calgary. She flashed a trade magazine, glossy photographs of the mega natural foods retailer in Boulder, Colorado. "Wild Oats and Whole Foods are opening stores across the entire USA," she said. We could catch the edge of the organics wave all the way north in Canada.

Lee also intimated that we would revive and nurture food politics. That was the hook. For me and many others, the natural foods movement was essentially a social movement, a critique of pesticide-based agriculture, processed foods, and food distribution systems that imposed malnutrition and hunger in our own communities and in many other parts of the world. Buying and growing food was about more than improving our personal health; it was about sustainable agriculture and the health of the planet. If there was going to be a food fight in the eighties, we would show up and stand up to Big Food. No one had even heard of fair-trade coffee in the eighties, but Lee flaunted the fact that social-justice activists were warehousing fair-trade coffee in the basement of Earth Harvest, further proof of the store's hipness.

I felt giddy being headhunted by food radicals. I mean, we weren't monkeywrenching farmers' tractors to stop pesticide use, or reclaiming food from dumpsters, but we were committed to reforming industrial agriculture, one sack of organic flour at a time.

Lee neglected to mention that Earth Harvest, located in a rundown building at the corner of Memorial Drive and Tenth Street, a congested intersection where traffic crossed the Louise Bridge into downtown, had only one parking spot, a situation that challenged many co-op members to buy only what they could carry on foot. Gummi fruit bears were a hot seller.

On my first day, Doug, a stock clerk with long blond hair, who was well versed in the ideas of Buckminster Fuller, motioned from the row of bulk beans and whispered, "Save us, Mary, save us!" In addition to his knowledge of geodesic domes, Doug could toss his blond locks with the poetic defiance of rock singer Tom Petty.

"What do you mean, 'save us'?" I asked, checking to see who might be within earshot.

"The inventory situation—it's outa control. I can't possibly stash any more bags of rice or cases of juice."

I had thought the massive back stock was a calibration error, a few wholesale deals needing to be pushed out the door.

"I'll work on it," I promised and surveyed the narrow aisles, shelving crammed so tight that customers twisted sideways to shop.

"We're counting on you, Mary," said my lead guitarist. "There are enough dry beans in the basement to last into the nineties."

"Hang in and don't worry," I said. "Things will get better." As store manager, I felt obligated to build team spirit. Then, forced to jump over a burlap bag of mung beans to get out of the cramped space, I added, "And try not to block the aisles, Doug."

Lee informed me that she and I would meet weekly to resolve any staffing problems that arose and to brainstorm ideas for the expansion of Earth Harvest. We walked across the street, fair-trade coffee in hand, and strolled along the Bow River, making plans, big plans.

"I think we should open up a food kiosk at the University of Calgary. We'd be the only natural foods deli and bakery on campus," said Lee. She spoke in a reserved manner, as though we were in a Canfor boardroom. "And we need to start thinking about a second location."

"With parking," I suggested.

"That's right, the second location will need parking."

I thought the one and only first location needed parking too, but I could tell Lee was in denial.

"I have noticed most customers don't purchase more than one small bag of groceries," I said, matching her grave demeanour.

"It's about foot traffic and merchandising. I want you to focus on better end displays and a few lost leaders, soy milk, rice cakes maybe. We need to boost sales and improve our cash flow to expand."

"The parking situation is a bit of a problem," I countered. How could she not see it was a humongous problem?

"We *have* parking," Lee pressed her lips tightly. "It's minimal, but we do have parking. I want you to do some volume purchasing for better wholesale discounts. Think about how Safeway merchandises. Case lots. We'll never compete buying six items at a time."

I panicked at the words "case lot." I could have pointed out that Safeway provided parking the size of wheat fields, but I didn't want to come off as a know-it-all, being the new employee. I let Lee carry on with her grand vision.

She put me in charge of purchasing, a task I preferred to call inventory control. I decided "fasting" was a good buying policy until we cleared out some of the excess stock. The basement of the store contained more inventory than the retail floor; Lee and I threaded a path around the sacks of grain and case lots of chips, soup, hot sauce, and falafel mix to get to our office. I kept wondering how she couldn't notice the state of overabundance, since she was tripping over it every day, not to mention that from a financial perspective, we had no cash reserves: it was all in food. We were like survivalists pretending to be in the food business.

I accepted the challenges, got a feel for the sales levels, and moved out the excess juice and chips. Red lentils and white beans would take more time, but no matter, as co-op folks pointed out, dried beans and grains stored well—especially in pyramids. Didn't Egyptian wheat kernels sprout after centuries of storage?

Soy milk in Tetra Paks emerged on the market. I purchased case lots, plain, vanilla, and chocolate; we could barely keep enough in stock. Doug frowned at the six-foot stack of product.

"It's impossible to recycle a package with three different materials. Look, aluminum, plastic, and cardboard, what a disaster."

I agreed, plus the cost of the packaging must be more than the milk, but if I pulled a hot seller like soy milk, Lee would combust.

This was the strange thing about the eighties: as the natural foods industry ballooned in sales, the corporate sector invested, and products were delinked from social issues, shrink-wrapped into individual consumer bargains. The social discourse, one healthy planet, was devoured by "my organic purchase."

I coped, optimistically, until the ski season opened in Banff and Lake Louise.

"There's fresh powder in the mountains, Mary, just can't pass it up. You should be okay without me tomorrow." Apparently, Doug of the domes was also a downhill skier.

I froze next to a tower of puffed rice cereal that tilted precariously. "Doug, come on, are you kidding? We might have a big shipment arrive tomorrow."

I could insist he come to work, but if I put the kibosh on skiing, he might quit altogether and go work for Mountain Equipment Co-op.

"I doubt Porter Trucking will get here tomorrow. I gotta take the powder when it comes. Besides, you can handle it. You'll be fine."

I stared into his glassy, euphoric eyes. He was already primed for the slopes.

I conceded. "I guess we need someone to work on call—for situations like this."

"Good idea," agreed Doug. "But not many guys will do heavy lifting for seven dollars an hour. Plus we need a man who knows the difference between a chickpea and a soybean."

Yes, we did, and preferably a non-skier.

The next day I was in the aisles inspecting the Garden of Eatin' tortilla chips, salted, unsalted, blue, yellow, spiced; it was impossible to keep the right flavour in stock. Invariably, customers wanted the flavour we had run short on. Sometimes I longed to throw a salt shaker at the foodies and yell, *Salt it yourself.*

The back door buzzer interrupted my revenge fantasy. I was greeted by a driver, who handed me a freight waybill and said, "One hundred and eight pieces from Lifestream Natural Foods. I'll back in and move it to the tail."

I freaked at the sight of a semi-trailer truck. "I'm going to get some help, I'll be right back." This would be a good time to quit, I thought, running up front to the checkouts, but both cashiers were ringing through customers.

When I got back to the truck, which was now blocking the alley, there was a wall of boxes and fifty-pound bags at the end of the deck.

"It's all yours," said the driver, wheeling his dolly back into the cavernous shell.

I cursed Doug. He was probably flying through pockets of powder on Paradise Trail at Lake Louise, his long hair flowing free, his mind flowing freer still, swirling with BC bud.

If only Lee were here. She was lean, strong, and could heave boxes like the boys. The one day I needed her, she was off scouting new locations.

Damn it! I marched back and forth between the truck and the back door, hurling boxes inside on the landing. The driver sucked on a cigarette beside the truck, annoyed at the slow pace.

"My guy is off," I yelled over at him.

He did the stoic man thing and said nothing. Then he tossed the cigarette butt into the alley, put his filthy gloves back on, and came round to my side of the truck.

"I don't normally do this," he said. "But I got a schedule to keep. Don't expect this as a regular thing." He grabbed a couple of boxes, double the weight I could carry.

"Hey man, of course not," I said, relieved.

We shoved the 108 pieces into the small area inside the back door. I signed the waybill and sat down on a box to rest. Now the whole delivery had to be moved downstairs into the basement warehouse. There was no elevator at Earth Harvest; the long flight of stairs was the descent into the underworld.

Someone, maybe Doug, had built a wooden slide that folded down the stairs. Basically he'd built a bobsled run to access the warehouse. I needed someone to get in position at the bottom, so I could push each bag, box, and case lot down the slide into the basement. *Fifty pounds of brown rice coming at you!*

I decided to pull a cashier and together we would deal with the shipment. It had become Margaritaville up front since I disappeared. Because she was married to Doug, our hardest-working cashier, Diane, was also away, apparently a skier—or designated driver. The part-time cashiers had opened a bag of Garden of Eatin' blue tortilla chips and a jar of Pure & Simple salsa, and were busy mashing an avocado for guacamole.

"Lee likes us to put out samplers," one cashier explained, her mouth full of chips and salsa.

"Brilliant idea," I answered, "but save some dip for the customers. I need one of you to help me get the shipment into the warehouse."

"You mean slide everything downstairs?" She reached for another chip and plunged it into the guacamole.

"Unless you want to walk it all down."

"It's too garlicky," she said, ignoring my sarcasm.

"Come on, gals, let's go." Earth Harvest employees thought arriving on time for their shift deserved a raise or promotion.

The two of them looked at each other.

"Do you want to go?"

"Do *you* want to go?"

"Let's flip a coin." The cashier with avocado fingers opened the cash drawer.

"Heads or tails?"

It was excruciating. Finally one cashier agreed to the task without consulting an astrology chart or intuitive counsellor first.

"I'll stay at the top of the stairs," she said. "I don't think I have your strength to catch fifty-pound bags."

"Sure. Let me get in position and then we'll pull down the slide."

I had seen Doug's technique for catching stock, so I crouched low, engaged my abs to protect my back, and nodded up at the cashier. "Okay, let's do this."

A case of aloe vera juice hurtled down the slide; I blocked, clutched, and lifted it off. Then a case of apple juice, gallon-sized glass jugs, rocketed toward me, building momentum on the way. Stopping it with my whole body, I wrestled it to the ground.

"Don't push," I screamed as the cashier shunted a fifty-pound bag of basmati rice. "Just release it gently. You're not bowling."

Over one hundred boxes later, the warehouse was mayhem, a tangled heap of inventory. Doug could reorganize things tomorrow. I probably needed a chiropractic adjustment to realign my lumbar spine, but it was done.

And that was the easy part. To stock the retail bins and shelves on the sales floor, the product had to be hauled back upstairs, a Sisyphean labour. But there was a solution. The existential philosopher Camus argued we must respond to the absurd and futile by imagining poor Sisyphus happy and content in the present moment. Earth Harvest employees certainly tried to embody a happy Sisyphus by enjoying a toke before they hoisted their rock up the warehouse stairs.

While I dealt with über-relaxed, pot-smoking employees in a natural foods store that resembled a flea market, Daniel signed up for a career-counselling workshop, a winter activity he had done several times before.

"Do you think you're going to get a different outcome this year?" I asked, puzzled.

"It's a good workshop," he countered, "writing about early memories, passions, past jobs. And I love the group discussion, learning about everyone's work history, and getting feedback from the group."

I wondered if social deprivation at the lookout was cumulative and he was unconsciously offsetting the isolation. Storing up social interactions for the next lookout season.

"What career did the group suggest for you last year?"

"Ceramic artist."

"Really. Now there's a surprise."

"You know, instead of criticizing, you might want to read *What Colour Is Your Parachute?* Stop complaining about Earth Harvest and go out and do some career interviewing."

At the end of the nine-week workshop, Daniel returned home with fresh-baked muffins from admiring female participants and tiny slips of paper with words like "deep," "peaceful," and "creative." One slip simply read "potter."

"What's all this about?" I asked.

"It's how the group sees me," said Daniel. "We wrote them up for everyone."

"I like the one that says 'potter,'" I said. "Here's one from me. How about 'mud'? Your name is mud if you don't make pots soon."

I had my own methods of career counselling. The psychic Lance Regan shopped at Community Natural Foods and Earth Harvest and often left his business cards on the counter. He provided a service that he called a life reading. The rumours about Lance were all good; even a Calgary psychiatrist had consulted him for a life reading. I persuaded Daniel to come to a public event at the Calgary Public Library.

Inside the theatre, Lance lay on a couch, eyes closed, in front of an audience of hundreds. A man sat next to Lance on the stage. He introduced himself as a scientist, a professional geologist, and facilitator for the evening. The geologist protected Lance when he was in trance, and regulated the order of questions from folks: questions about health problems, relationship issues, finding purpose in life, and resolving conflicts. Like a modern-day Edgar Cayce, Lance claimed to read from the Akashic Records, the repository of history archived on the inner planes containing all the information about a soul's evolution.

Impressed by Lance's performance, we consulted him by telephone and arranged for individual readings at his home. An assistant ushered Daniel and me into a private room where Lance was stretched out on a couch, eyes closed. The assistant prayed for protection and then Lance cleared his throat. "Ahem, yes, do we have permission to read from your book?" The voice of Lance-in-trance deepened, with different intonation patterns from the voice of Lance-awake.

For an hour, Lance fielded our questions. We taped the session on cassette, and Daniel later transcribed the recording, word for word. We asked Lance about previous incarnations that may have influence on our present-day qualities. He said Daniel had a "thick book" of past lives and his soul was part of an ancient time on earth, a pre-Atlantis period on the continent Lemuria, when humanity evolved from anthropoid consciousness into early *Homo sapiens* forms. He also spoke about a more recent lifetime in Malaysia, an experience that fuelled Daniel's resentment toward Western culture.

This is one incarnation of 1500 AD approximately, Malaysia, of yourself being of a sea merchant plying the trade in your boat. That of taking goods of the area which is now Cambodia, South Vietnam etc. and trading them to that of the Philippines, that of the mid and northern China. Your trade routes were quite long, and on one occasion, towards the end of this incarnation, running into Europeans that at times were filled with disease, ego, and blood-lust, which indeed did create much damage to your own environment as well as your family and friends. But this plays itself out for a particular purpose of this incarnation that you would choose to understand and be flexible to all different lifestyles, that each individual is to a degree an entity unto themselves and cannot be judged by the values, morally or socially, that you were brought up in.

Daniel expressed such contempt for all things European, we were thumbs-up for the Malaysia explanation. Lance also said we had lived a series of indigenous lifetimes together and this was the basis of our desire to own land. As clichéd as that might sound, years before we met, Daniel and I had, independently, lived in teepees. Apparently, I had also been a pioneer in the early 1800s, a Loyalist in a male body, and operated a successful grocery business, trusted by European colonialists and indigenous peoples. (I bet those shelves were never overstocked.)

I asked about psychology as a career direction, and he advised me to connect my business skills with good artistic judgment and deal in art and antiques.

Psychology here is simply just for the sake that you desire to understand yourself. Psychology is the working of the motivations of core beliefs....There are fields in the future that will open themselves up to income....This includes medical practitioners as well as those providing services for the simple reason they are needed for compassion, of these humanitarian elements, etc., etc., here is useful means for certification. But yet here to be strained of your own individuality again, we say strained, this means rather, deprived. How to deal with this is to realize your purpose....A certificate indeed wouldn't deprive you of any system you would develop on your own, communication, sociology, this is just a stepping stone.

Of your own abilities as an artist—there be a list here we can gather of your talents. One is that involved in embroidery, the fineness of needle and thread—

There was a scuffle as Daniel flipped over the cassette and Lance cleared his throat and proceeded:

—not just necessarily doing all the artworks yourself, as well as being musical, but being here that of a business person, a dealer of artworks. You will find it a most profitable area to go into and it doesn't need that much cash. It can work on a consignment basis. In any case, there be a whole list of talents you possess. Yes.

Unfortunately, I failed to ask for more details and Daniel seized the pause to ask about his artistic block with ceramics. The answer filled four pages of text, including advice to use the daily affirmation "I approve of myself" and information about a successful lifetime in Japan when Daniel concocted herbal preparations in clay jars, healing many people, but feeling self-critical when an herbal cure did not work.

As a couple, Lance encouraged us to build a model farm, a retreat-like place where others could learn about nature, a sustainable lifestyle, and spiritual development.

At times the two of you, indeed, are like two innocents that are lost in this artificial structured society when indeed it would be far better if you had your own lands, of your own environment… not a commune as in the '60s and '70s, but a model existence that is representative of humanitarianism…where a balance between male and female is so expressed.

Daniel and I pondered and mused over the transcription of our session, exhilarated by the notion that we had a purpose in moving to the country.

Enamoured with the soul hotline, we shared our reading with the Supper Club. Christos and Alice were excited by the idea of a model farm. They had speculated about buying land to create an intentional community for years. Maybe the right group had finally emerged. Afterwards, on the drive home from Dinah and John's, we admitted our mutual reticence to merge fortunes with the Supper Club, our dearest friends.

"I don't know how we would ever agree on things, on the design of buildings, fences, on the grid, off the grid," ventured Daniel. "I wonder what Lance would say?"

"Another reading?"

"Yeah," said Daniel. "I think it's worth it to find out. A men's reading."

Without much of a sales pitch, the men agreed, curious to explore the meaning of their friendships, according to Lance-in-trance. As the instigator, Daniel posed questions on behalf of the group.

"Hmm, yes, there is a higher purpose to which the group of four could fulfil if they so choose. This is not necessary of course, you having free will at all times, but there is a best possible means by which you could proceed."

Lance likened the relationship of the four men to the four arms of a Celtic cross, each with a unique gift to contribute. He portrayed Christos as the most balanced, in terms of masculine-feminine energies, and assigned him the role of seer and communication facilitator. Tomas, the philosopher, bore responsibility for the moral compass of the group. He named Daniel the artist, saying Daniel would design and construct beautiful spaces and buildings. That left John. He designated John as the fundraiser, the financial wizard who could make the endeavour happen. We were flabbergasted. How could John not be handed any creative or priestly roles? Did the Akashic Records need an update?

After the round describing each man's individual purpose, Lance spoke about the soul work for the whole Lookout Supper Club. Our highest group purpose, he stated, would be to create a healing centre, a hospital of the future, in which all aspects of an individual's health would be treated: body, mind, soul, and spirit. There was no mention of fire lookout jobs, art shows, or trips to Mexico.

The men were puzzled, especially about John's fundraising role; but unknown to Lance, John—or David—did come from a money-based lineage. His father had worked in finance, a branch manager at the Royal Bank of Canada in Ontario. And John had often strategized offbeat money-making schemes. There were the heaps of soft, silver jewellery he and Christos brought back from Mexico, and of course, the dozens of psychedelic yarn paintings. Both ventures had failed miserably.

Inspired by Lance's reading, Christos and Alice urged us to collectively purchase a rural property in the Okanagan. It became a major topic at our dinner parties.

"I could live in the Okanagan again," John swooned. "It's beautiful there, fruit-growing country." A move to the country suited him; he could leave home for the lookout job from almost anywhere.

Daniel and I had concerns a joint investment with the Supper Club could translate into a joint lineup at the food bank. Especially if John was in charge of the finances.

"How will we all make a living in the country?" Daniel worried. "I can set up a pottery studio and sell to tourists, but what's everyone else gonna do?"

Dinah was lukewarm on the land idea, more dedicated to the Waldorf School. "I don't know if I want my kids going to a public school with rednecks and right-wing Christians," she said.

She had a point, albeit a politically incorrect one. Interior British Columbia was Bible country and working class. She envisioned rural kids climbing out of their father's logging semi-trailer to get to school. What if her boys grew up to be rednecks and rode around on dirt bikes?

Tomas and Athena were quiet on the land front, but, like John, Tomas could probably live anywhere; and now that he was a father, he had no intention of quitting fire lookouts.

Christos and Alice had no children to support, but they faced the unappealing prospect of returning to an isolated tower in northern Alberta. They had been sent to Bitumont tower near Fort McMurray and the tar sands the previous summer. The flares from burning oil dotted their horizon, and flecks of an unknown substance fell from the sky at times. On weekends the whine of quad bikes infiltrated their refuge; camp workers from oil and logging operations partied nearby in the bush late into the night. Christos and Alice could request a different lookout, but there was no guarantee of a better outcome. Even if someone quit or took a season off, Forestry might give a more desirable lookout to someone with more seniority.

We waffled about buying land together, fearful of the risk, unsure if we trusted each other enough to get entangled legally and financially.

On New Year's Day, 1988, unable to inspire the Supper Club to buy land and form an intentional community, Christos and Alice left Calgary, friends, and northern fire lookouts and headed to Mexico in their sturdy Volvo.

Later that winter two things happened. One afternoon during a minus-thirty-degree blast of Arctic temperatures, I was startled by banging at the front door. Thud! I opened the door and was met by a big black-and-white cat braced to hurl itself against the aluminum screen again. It met my gaze as though to say, "Have mercy, please let me in!" I named the cat Sylvester because he had such a quirky personality with strange markings. Then, not long after the addition of Sylvester to the household, Joe, the older shih tzu, got sick and was diagnosed with cancer. Daniel held the dog for hours, rocking him like a baby and feeding him drops of wheat grass juice as therapy. In several weeks, the dog passed away in his arms.

"I want to leave his body in the basement for three days," Daniel said. "Then I'll cremate him in the backyard."

"How will you do a cremation in the backyard?" I asked, picturing funeral pyres along the banks of the Ganges River.

"Easy," said Daniel. "I'll use propane and the insulated barrel for firing raku pottery. I can get it hot enough. I'm going to wait until after dark so the neighbours don't get curious."

The loud hissing of propane lasted for hours. Now and then he would come back inside to warm up and I would ask, "How much longer?"

"It takes a long time for all the bones to burn to ash," he said matter-of-factly. "Longer than I expected, actually."

Finally, he reappeared with a clay jug. "Look, you can almost see pieces of his spine, but it's clean, pure ash."

I peered into the container; a mound of white-grey powder and fragments of bone were all that remained.

"He's gone," said Daniel.

So far in my life, I had been remarkably protected from death and dying. But now, thanks to Daniel and his DIY ethic, the backyard cremation served as tangible proof of the impermanence of all physical forms.

Despite the noble fight to reclaim control over the food chain, I felt stymied as a buyer at Earth Harvest. I had a talent for memorizing the per-kilogram retail price of hundreds of bulk foods, along with their wholesale source and price. I scanned wholesale catalogues the way Daniel scanned the forest, searching for a puff, a lower price on raw almonds, brown rice, or sunflower seeds. At the end of the day, I stared at more numbers to balance the cash tills and prepare the bank deposit. I could find a cashier's over or short within minutes. *There's an error in your cheque total. You forgot to subtract your void receipts.* I had an instinct, a nose for accounting errors. I worked with numbers the way other women worked with cooking ingredients: a dash of this, a spoonful of that, and the bank deposit was perfectly balanced. My natural affinity for numbers made the job easy to perform, but it left a bad aftertaste. I was an imposter, playing with sales numbers and inventory sheets, uninspired by business, soured by my job predicament.

Lee kept an eye on my buying patterns, querying me now and then about whether licorice ropes were on order, but letting me manage on my own, or so I thought.

"I want you to bring in canned tuna fish," she announced one day. A sales rep had come by on Monday, my day off, and done business with Lee. "We'll make an end display," she said. "Twenty cases to get the best price."

I was flummoxed. Because dolphins became entangled in commercial fishing nets, environmentally minded consumers supported a ban on tuna, a protest to force change in fishing practices.

"Make an end display, and stack it high," she said. "It's a way to bring in more foot traffic."

I braced for complaints rather than sales. After several days, I pointed out that the tuna was not moving.

"We stacked it high, way over my head," I said. "You can't miss it; in fact, shoppers are crashing into it. But it's not selling."

Lee frowned. "Give it time; it's a good buy."

"Yeah, well, the vegans are complaining we brought in fish. And the environmentalists are complaining we're killing dolphins." This was true; I had entertained many irate comments from shoppers offended by the presence of canned fish.

Lee dug in. "The strict vegetarians are in the minority. We need to broaden our customer base."

Maybe, I thought, but not before I get flogged with *Diet for a Small Planet* by an angry mob of vegetarians. Then again, on a low-protein diet with high THC intake, they might be perpetually chill; perhaps I'd be spared.

Fortunately, during the tuna controversy, I had to fly to LAX to attend the biggest-ever natural foods trade show in Anaheim. Like everything in California, the floor of the trade show was supersized; it would take three days to make the rounds of all the booths. In the evening and late afternoon, the food wholesalers booked suites in the hotel rooms above the show and courted retailers, like rock stars partying with fans. I avoided these gatherings, too embarrassed to let industry big shots know I had put Earth Harvest on a cleansing fast. If my resolve weakened over an organic microbrew and I signed off on a super special deal, I'd wake up the next morning disappointed with myself. Whenever I was tempted to splurge on new products, I visualized myself at the bottom of the basement food slide; the craving would pass.

I shunned a new line of organic baby food in cute resealable jars, the Paul Newman organic salsas, and instant ramen noodles in microwave-friendly Styrofoam cups. There was spirulina, blue-green algae, the newest supplement on the scene, which was possibly a winner, but Earth Harvest had no vitamin or supplement section, so how could I merchandise it? As Wendell Berry said, there were limits to growth, and we had straddled them. Americans spend less of their annual income on food than any other nation in the world. For instance, in parts of Asia people spend over forty-five percent of their household incomes on food; in America folks spend less than seven percent.

On the third and final day, I wandered from booth to booth and realized I had not placed even one convention order. Wholesalers offered discounts of ten to fifteen percent when you purchased at the show, but if we stored the product in the basement for months, the discount was hardly worth it. I trekked around the great hall, observing the labyrinth of food fads, organic packaged foods, herbal capsules, vitamin pills, and weight loss products.

There was no food fight going on in America; it was a food fest, and the natural foods industry was being slowly appropriated, folded into the mainstream food industry like homogenized milk. *Sure, I'd love a sample of chlorella*, I said, tossing the green tablets into my plastic shopping bag. *A multivitamin and mineral supplement for dogs, why not? Ginkgo, for a better memory; mine's pretty good, but yeah, I'll take a sample.*

I would buy nothing.

Liberated, I renewed my fasting vows.

When I returned to work, Lee was waiting to hear about the Anaheim show. Had I gone to the evening parties with the national wholesalers, CRS Workers Co-op, Wild West Co-op, and Purity Life?

"I rested, laid low in the evening. The show is exhausting," I feigned.

"Well, what about the specials, the big deals, what's coming in?"

When I confessed I hadn't purchased any megaorders, she halted her reckonings on the desktop calculator, the roll of white paper uncoiling in serpentine fashion over the edge of the desk, dragging to the floor.

"It's where all the deals are," she said with tight lips. "That was the whole point of sending you."

"The deals weren't so good this year—and I don't believe we're short-stocked on much of anything really."

Lee grimaced, refusing to admit there was any problem with our inventory levels. If we could stick to my lean purchasing plan, I could get us into the black, but I couldn't say that to her directly.

"I checked out the new products and trends," I said, hoping to appease. "Protein powder with spirulina, it's gonna be the next big thing."

I hauled out my bag of samples. "See, here it is. You can try it and let me know what you think."

She accepted the envelope. "Mary, we need to offer new products to keep shoppers coming back."

"Right. Whole foods aren't enough of a reason to shop here? We need fun food, is that what you mean? I brought in Kettle Chips. They'll fly outa here."

"I'm just saying, we need to stock the most popular products for our members, or they'll go somewhere else. The industry is growing."

She was realistic. It was me who wanted to go somewhere else, somewhere far away from the number crunching and the flashy new supplements that promised longevity, vitality, or a smarter brain. Moving to the country appealed more and more as a way to live in accord with how we wanted the world to be. If the world wasn't changing fast enough, then we would leave the city and create our own world. We would grow our own food, build a house with natural materials, and earn a right livelihood. Daniel would make pots full-time. And me, well, the specifics of work were vague, but something would come my way. What was that saying? You have to close one door before another one opens.

On April 29, 1988, Jack Carter opened Mockingbird Lookout for Daniel, his last fire season, we said. Within days, Tomas and Athena were back in position on Blue Hill. On May 10 John said goodbye to Dinah and the kids and commenced another season on Cline Lookout.

The fire lookout world was in order, except we were missing Christos and Alice.

Three Years on a Rock

I renewed my commute to Mockingbird, rattling back and forth along the trunk road every weekend. On Monday night I'd return home, unlock the front door and stop, flooded by the emptiness of the house. I felt split between two realities: working and living alone in the city versus being a couple in a government building on top of a mountain. Of course, I savoured my time at Mockingbird and the privilege of relaxing high in the sky, beyond the reach of ordinary life, but the primary experience, for me, was not freedom. Tethered to the commute, I was beginning to feel as though I had a boyfriend doing time. A seasonal life sentence. When he returned in the fall, I would be there waiting; he simply walked in the door and recovered a home and relational life.

For Daniel, the landscape he watched over at Mockingbird had become so familiar he said it was like looking at wallpaper. He had zoomed in and stared at every acre of forest, all the ridges, valleys, and meadows for hundreds of hours, converting the natural world to the lines on a topographic map.

Sometimes, in the cupola, surrounded by breathless hikers impressed by the mountain vista, he dangled the metaphor of the view as wallpaper, affronting many who expected him to double as a tour guide. Male hikers, in particular, were eager to know the name of every peak and its precise altitude.

"Devil's Head, now what's the altitude of the summit there?"

"Geez, I forget, it's all wallpaper to me," Daniel would respond.

"What's the distance of the farthest peak we can see in the southwest?"

"Ya got me; it's probably in Banff National Park, outside my boundaries."

"Male hikers are relentless in their pursuit of facts," Daniel complained. "Why do they always want numbers, measurements, and degrees?"

I had watched him feign busyness, dog-ear paperwork, and fidget with the binoculars, politely sabotaging a male hiker's fact-finding mission.

The fact gathering started as soon as they were inside the cupola door, as though someone had flipped a gender switch. Not all men, of course; a variety of hikers presented at Mockingbird, but the guys in spandex or the ones sporting expensive watches to time their hike couldn't resist a quest for facts.

Sometimes I vetted hikers. "That guy looks interesting," I'd say. "Let's invite him inside."

"I dunno, he's wearing a Nike-brand vest, maybe not." Daniel could assess a hiker's potential for a good quirky conversation before I even noticed the guy hanging around on the catwalk, hoping for an invitation to come inside.

In early summer, a group of schoolchildren hiked up with their teacher and crowded around the fire finder, watching how Daniel located an imaginary smoke on the horizon.

After the demonstration, one of the little boys blurted, "Where's your wife? Doesn't she live here too?"

The kids giggled when he told them he didn't have a wife. "Lookout men often aren't married," he explained, an idea that struck the children as more interesting than anything he had told them about fire detection.

Somewhere between elementary school and adulthood, males learned to focus a conversation on technical facts or measurements, such as the volume of fire retardant a bomber could drop in one flyover.

"The men always ask about the precise altitude of the highest mountains," said Daniel, "and the women always ask if I get lonely."

"Men never ask about loneliness and isolation?" I was surprised.

"Never. It's not something a guy mentions."

The Alberta government, however, played up the isolation in its recruitment information, portraying the job as a dreary experience. "Only highly self-motivated individuals can overcome the loneliness and often monotonous routines associated with the lookout observers' way of life."[2] There was a government handbook at every station that contained helpful hints to alleviate the loneliness and monotony. It advised observers that once a week they should cook a full-course meal, prepare an elegant table setting, dress up in good clothes, and "dine out" as though in a five-star restaurant. I mocked that section of the handbook, especially the illustration that pictured a man wearing a shirt and tie, seated alone at his little table, happily serving himself from platters of food, spruce forest in the background.

"Oh, come on, do you know anyone who does that?" I laughed. "Brings a tie and good clothes to the lookout?"

Daniel wrinkled his brow. "I doubt it, but it might be a good idea round about August. I've scared myself looking in a hand mirror after a few months alone."

There seemed to be a masculine code of stoicism that prevented most men from probing into another man's experience of loneliness or depression. Kerouac resolved the sensitive issue by invoking the term "bleakness." His lookout job was bleak, the world was bleak, and his mood was bleak. Bleakness did not violate the male stoicism rule. In *Lonesome Traveler* he described his time as a fire lookout man.

> Sixty-three sunsets I saw revolve on that perpendicular hill— mad raging sunsets pouring in sea foams of cloud through unimaginable crags like the crags you grayly drew in pencil as a child, with every rose-tint of hope beyond, making you feel just like them, brilliant and bleak beyond words.[3]

And not once did he reckon the numeric altitude of those craggy peaks. Despite feeling bleak and lonesome, Kerouac extolled the rewards that wilderness isolation brought a man.

> No man should go through life without once experiencing healthy, even bored solitude in the wilderness, finding himself depending solely on himself and thereby learning his true and hidden strength.[4]

Hidden strength, indeed. Kerouac spent two months, exactly sixty-three days, on Desolation Peak. Daniel and most other Alberta fire observers spent about five months, or 150 to 160 days, on the lookout, a situation demanding considerably more hidden strength. According to the memoir of Kerouac's girlfriend, Joyce Johnson, he used the isolation of the fire lookout as a self-imposed intervention, attempting to rescue his booze-soaked cells from alcohol.

I wondered if being a lookout man made the guys feel like Jack Kerouac. It was Tomas's regular use of the word "madcap" that first alerted me. I told Daniel I found it synchronistic that Tomas should describe his friend McNeal as a "madcap," using the same term Kerouac did in *On the Road*.

"Well, Tomas read Kerouac too," said Daniel. "That's probably where he got it. We all read Kerouac, we loved Kerouac; he was the model for all of us."

"Do you admire Kerouac, personally?" I asked Daniel, surprised by the admission.

"Of course," he said. "We all wanted to be like Kerouac."

I was stumped. Putting aside for the moment that Kerouac was indeed a major literary figure, in terms of masculinity, he didn't bring anything new to gender relations. I was puzzled by the power of his legacy among my own male friends. What was it about Kerouac that held so much appeal?

In one section of *On the Road*, Kerouac asserts that he identified more as a black man, laying personal claim to the social marginalization experienced by black Americans. His discontent is with other men; women barely figure in his mental schema. When he recounts his temporary relationship with a Mexican migrant worker, a woman who works the cotton fields in southern California with her children, and whose home consists of a tent, he presents the experience as some kind of exotic freedom, until the sheer drudgery and hard work end the romance for him. In leaving her and the migrant community, he expresses a small measure of guilt, the awareness that he has another future and she does not.

When men valorize Kerouac as an icon of male freedom, creativity, and sexual liberation, they tend to overlook that he died from alcoholism at forty-seven years of age. He lived the last years of his life with his mother, in her house in Florida, far from the art scenes of New York and San Francisco.

Maybe for Daniel, John, and Tomas, Kerouac had poetically captured their personal experience being alone on a mountaintop. But it was more than that—they spoke about *On the Road* with a kind of reverence. Kerouac, a working-class maverick and self-taught writer, had broken into New York literary and art circles on his own merit, a talented outsider who challenged social and literary conventions. He wrote about homeless men, drunks, bums, vagabonds, and outcasts and romanticized their lives with a stream of flourishes about the Void, as though contemplative mysticism was practised with a shot glass. He championed invisible men, outsiders, and idealists who refused to conform to commercial society.

This was Kerouac's appeal.

❀

Now that we had decided to leave Calgary next spring, we marked time at Mockingbird, and the lookout became a stopover on the way to a new life. Daniel's letters that summer recounted vivid dreams about male rank, leaving the lookout job, and building a house.

> Mockingbird Lookout
> August 11, 1988
>
> Last night a falling star, I read about thatching. In my dreams I saw a thatched house. I was a soldier coming home, after the war, crossing a l-o-n-g 6 foot wide floating bridge over a wide river. It was the same height as the river, which just skimmed over it and it was tippy. I followed an officer of higher rank, British fellow. On the other side was a house, and I was so excited and went to look at it…wake up.
>
> Thatch would be perfect for our home, if we could find the right half acre of grain (rye) to cut.

As romantic as a thatched house might be, we decided on a yurt, a more sensible and pragmatic choice, the perfect housing solution until we had the funds for a cabin. Inexpensive to construct, a yurt was circular, and its architecture complemented the natural environment. Determined to make it himself, Daniel ordered a brochure from Pacific Yurt Inc. in Oregon, the original yurt manufacturer, and studied the detail and design information for weeks, slowly figuring out the measurements for a building plan. The walls of a traditional Mongolian yurt were made from animal skins, but we would buy white tent canvas for the walls. By grace and luck, the skinny, straight pine trees on top of Mockingbird Hill were the perfect radial spokes for the ceiling framework of a yurt. "I went and cut more poles for the yurt today," Daniel wrote, "They are pretty easy to find. I really should cut a bunch…could make a quick studio/workshop building too…will see."

In the fall, he could load the poles into the van and bring them home to our backyard in Calgary.

Feeling the need for company one overcast evening, and knowing Tomas was alone on Blue Hill, Daniel ventured out to pay him a surprise visit. For the first time ever, Athena had taken a pass on living at the fire lookout and was spending the summer in the city with Willow. She had become involved with the Arusha Centre and volunteered for social causes, especially women's issues.

The weather had turned cool and rainy, and a low-pressure system hung over southern Alberta.

August 1988
Mockingbird Lookout

Couple nights ago I thought I should "visit" Tomas, but I've been so-o-o-o lethargic. Started off but didn't make it past the berry patch....Tomas is hiking down the trail now to meet Athena in the rain....This weather is doing weird things to people. Even Tomas has been working on stained glass and enjoying its "tangible result-ness." I'm sure Rose [another lookout] will be shutdown on the 15th, like last year, and I'm suspecting, unless a Sahara heat wave blows steady for a few weeks, we all might be politely excused from our needless duties at the end of the core period.

Then, after Athena departed Blue Hill, Tomas migrated over to Mockingbird for companionship.

Tomas passed by last night. Polka dot bandana like a Mexican Hutterite. Serious driven fellow, big hands, bandaged finger... Tomas's Lament. He was starving but lost his appetite when he looked in the fridge. I have to admit, it does take imagination to eat. That's good enough for me. We munched almonds, raisins and sipped Ovaltine, philosophizing about the limits of words and such. Brief comments on Catholicism...

We should all get polka dot bandanas and visit Tomas wearing them!

The expansive sense of freedom at the start of the season had dissolved into the bleakness of captivity and an interminable stalemate on the conditions of release. By the end of August, Daniel and I were counting the weeks, if not days, until the lookout closed. Because the hazard was low and the days shorter, sometimes he would call in the evening.

The last couple of phone calls you didn't sound happy. As usual, I wondered if I did something wrong or what. Frustrating set-up,

this. That's probably what you feel too. A few more weeks…
"three years on a rock."

It's driving me nuts.

At the time, I had missed the reference, *three years on a rock*, unaware it was part of a Japanese meditation proverb: cultivate patience, three years on a rock.

He had cultivated patience, accruing eleven years on lookout rocks: Cowpar, Burnstick, Birch Mountain, Moose Mountain, Carbondale, and now Mockingbird.

There would be no third season on Mockingbird.

Before the fire lookout closed that fall, I bought a black-and-white striped jumpsuit and delivered it on my last weekend. It fit perfectly.

Daniel photographed himself in stripes on Mockingbird Hill, an inmate awaiting release.

Drumming on the Edge of Magic

Every fall the sockeye swim upstream from the Pacific Ocean on the coast of British Columbia to the Adams River in the Shuswap, near Salmon Arm. Every fourth year the reunion is grand: a couple of million fish return home to one of the largest salmon spawning grounds in North America.

Two years ago, Daniel had seen the big run. The river churned crimson red with the strange homecoming: exhausted fish mating, laying eggs in the gravelly waters, and then dying.

"We could look for a place in the Shuswap," he said. "I have a friend up there, Chris; she's a potter and she might know of land for sale."

Ready for a vacation, an autumn road trip after the lookout season, I agreed. "I can probably book off work. I have a few holidays I haven't taken yet."

Daniel said Chris had built a wood kiln and fired pots in the same tradition he admired. Then he added, "If I was a woman, I'd be just like Chris."

"If you were a woman? What do you mean?" I asked.

"Chris is the female version of myself—her clay work, the Japanese kiln, it's uncanny, her whole esthetic is totally me."

"I'd love to meet the female you," I said, perplexed by this disclosure.

Chris was like a Hindu warrior goddess, swarthy complexion, thick, black hair wrapped in yellow silk, her clothes brightly dyed Indian cottons from her many trips to Asia, semi-precious jewellery coiled around her wrists and neck. Like Daniel's, her features, eyes, lips, and cheekbones, were prominent and sensual; she was Italian ethnicity and he, Scottish. I felt like an Irish scullery maid alongside these two ceramic artists, my small green eyes, large teeth, and mousy brown hair so ordinary in comparison.

"Come in, come in," Chris said, warm and effusive, guiding us into her sunny kitchen. Heavy clay pots, vases, and ceramic sculptures were displayed on wooden shelves; beaded and embroidered tribal cloth from Afghanistan and India adorned doorways and cupboards.

"So, tell me, what is *your* passion in life?" Chris enunciated her words, sizing me up.

I stammered, nervous in the presence of so much panache.

"Well, what is it you do then?" She persevered, studying me intently.

"I manage a natural foods co-op, but that's not my passion." What was my passion? "I do a lot of dancing, contemporary dance."

"Well, there are lots of actors, dancers, and performers in these woods." She waited a beat. "My pottery store down on the highway could use a good manager, too."

"We're looking for land to buy out here," said Daniel. "Do you happen to know of anything?"

Chris inhaled a puff from a cigarette, her fingertips stained yellow from rolling her own tobacco.

"The acreage next door is for sale. The old fellow who owns it is selling, no real estate agent. It's forty acres, a nice piece of land. No buildings, no water, a bad road, but I would give you road access through my property. To the north it's all Crown forest, no development or neighbours on that side."

Daniel squirmed. "Can we take a walk over there now?"

"Go ahead, no one's over there. You'll see a big meadow on the other side of my fenceline, just past the kiln. That meadow would make a nice sunny house site. The property extends all the way south to the cliff overhanging the road, and west through the woods to a neighbour way over on the other side, who you'd never hear. Go on, I'll find the owner's phone number."

Excited, we bushwhacked through the trees and brush, emerging onto the meadow Chris had described; it was about five acres, overgrown with high grass and a weedy perennial with yellow flowers. The rest of the property was mixed forest, cedar, spruce, pine, and aspen trees.

"Let's go for it!" exclaimed Daniel.

"But it's the first piece of property we've looked at it."

"I know, but it's amazing. Someone else is going to snap it up if we don't act fast."

Chris hooked us up with the owner and Daniel phoned, asking how much down payment he wanted and whether he would finance a mortgage.

We didn't think a bank would approve us, given our precarious financial situation, but maybe this older man would finance us, if we showed him we cared for the land.

"Do you have a cash down payment to offer?" asked Chris, when Daniel got off the phone.

"Not really," I said. "We could take cash advances on our credit cards if we had to."

"He wants at least $5,000 down," sighed Daniel.

Chris pinched tobacco into another rolling paper. "My brother Martin and his wife Hannah would share this parcel of land with you. I think they might be able to make the down payment, and then you could work out a business arrangement with them."

"Let's go down to the Adams River and talk about it," said Daniel, nudging my arm.

The mouth of the river was a grotesque scene, misshapen dead sockeye scattered and bleeding across the smooth pebble banks. The gravelly waters glinted with the bodies of thousands of salmon, propelled by instinct to navigate the rapids of the Fraser and Thompson Rivers, migrating all the way from the coastal waters of the Pacific Ocean. Battered by the journey, their scales transformed from a blue-grey to an orange-red colour as they reached their final destination.

"I'd like to collect salmon vertebrae and see how they fire in clay. I could make fish pottery for the tourists. Or even salmon oven mitts, how about that!"

The presence of so many fish laying eggs had unleashed Daniel's imagination. "The timing is unbelievable too. If we buy now, we'll have two years to get ready for the next big salmon run in 1990. People come from all over the world for that event, and it could be right here, in our backyard. Think about all the pots I could sell."

I was less inspired by the dead fish. Notwithstanding the power and awe of nature, the salmon carcasses didn't help me picture what I would be doing here to make a living. "I can't make a decision right away, Daniel. I need to think about it."

"Oh, come on, hon, you'll love it here, it's quiet and beautiful. We're not gonna find a better piece of property. Don't do the grass-is-greener thing now."

"I don't know. I need more time." I thought about Chris's garden, the watermelons, cantaloupe, and tomatoes thriving on that hot, sunny slope.

She piped water up the hill from the lake and never worried about water table shortages or summer droughts. What would we do? Drilling a well was expensive, and there were no guarantees we'd find water at any reasonable depth. I wanted to grow as much of our food as possible, and gardens required plentiful amounts of water in the hot Shuswap summers.

And then there was Chris herself, Daniel's doppelgänger. I was uncomfortable becoming her neighbour—she and Daniel appeared to be the only members of the Clay Mutual Admiration Society.

From Calgary, Daniel talked to the seller and Martin by phone, and negotiated a tentative deal that worked for everyone—as long as I agreed. Martin would handle the cash down payment and we would be responsible for higher mortgage payments.

"Just think, hon, next spring we could move to the country. It's what we want. Why wait for something else to come along?"

I was the only obstacle holding back the sale. "What about the mortgage on this house? We can't carry two mortgages, and if we rent this house, it could be a headache managing things from a distance."

"Then we'll sell the house." Daniel was unequivocal.

"Just like that, sell, after all the work you've done on this place?"

"Yeah, let's sell. The guy who owns the apartment building next door will buy our house."

I sighed. "Okay, I don't want to stand in the way any longer. Let's sign the sale agreement."

Daniel leaped up and encircled me in a tight hug, lifting me off the floor.

"Things as They Are Pottery, that's what I'll call it. Things as They Are."

While salmon inspired us to buy land in the Shuswap that fall, Native rights inspired John to conceive his own brilliant plan, although it was more a stunt than a coherent strategy. A supporter of the Lubicon Lake Nation in northern Alberta, he had been following their struggle to stop Shell's oil and gas exploration on their territories. To help publicize their legal fight, John decided to drag a large wooden cross along Highway 2 from Calgary to Edmonton. I say "drag" because he wasn't planning to carry it, the way Jesus Christ shouldered the cross—he planned to rest the end of his cross on a trailer with wheels and pull it.

The Lubicon issue had been gaining publicity and support. A UN Human Rights Committee had reviewed the Lubicon claims and accused

Canada of human rights violations, pending hearings. During the Calgary Olympics the previous winter, thirty museums from around the world refused to lend cultural artifacts to the Shell-sponsored exhibit, *The Spirit Sings*. More recently, the Lubicon had blockaded roads throughout their territories to prevent Shell from drilling, and when the RCMP moved in and tore down the blockades, the likelihood of conflict escalated.

"This is the winter for my walk," John said not long after he arrived home from Cline Lookout. "I'm going to need a pair of new heavy-duty boots."

Dinah was ambivalent about the walk, because, like us, she wanted to buy property. John's creative activism would siphon their cash reserves, and she didn't want to see the down payment for a house get poured into a wooden cross.

John confided to Daniel that as soon as the thermometer dipped, he would be on his way. In the meantime, the cross needed some finishing touches. Most important, he had to build a compartment in the cross to hold a Thermos of hot coffee. This idea got Daniel brainstorming and he said, "Hey, why not build speakers into the horizontal arms of the cross and enjoy the music of Laurie Anderson on the long cold walk?"

We imagined John on the evening news, interviewed by a reporter at the side of the highway, the cross resting on his shoulder. After all, it had been only a few years since Steve Fonyo ran across Canada on one leg. Surely John could make it to Edmonton with two good legs and a cross.

Raised Catholic, I knew the stations of the cross by heart, and I failed to see how the symbolism of the Christian cross connected with the Lubicon land struggle. The only gas stations John would be stopping at were Husky and Petro-Canada. He had warmed up to Christianity after learning that Jung embraced Catholicism, and somehow to him it made sense, but I couldn't figure out how he expected the media to make the leap from a fire lookout man dragging a cross on Highway 2 to the Lubicon legal case. What if the news story made a link to marginalized men and mental health issues instead?

It seemed that maybe John was smoking way too much pot.

To celebrate New Year's Eve and our last winter in Calgary, Daniel and I gathered together the Transcendental Supper Club for a party and drum jam. With Alice and Christos far away in the Okanagan Valley, we had befriended another lookout couple, Jim and Ingrid. Ingrid worked at one of the few drive-in locations, Kananaskis Lookout, and Jim drove up every weekend to see her. They had a set-up like Daniel's and mine.

Jim was a postal carrier, a writer, and a comic improviser. He and Ingrid had met during a stint in TheatreSports, an improvisational comedy group. Jim performed with TheatreSports because he was a funny guy, Ingrid because she was married to the creator, Keith Johnstone. But life with Keith was not full of laughs, and Ingrid had divorced Keith, abandoned theatre with no regrets, and discovered the fire lookout lifestyle.

A few years back, she and Daniel had worked on neighbouring towers up north. Sometimes late at night, they impersonated Monty Python characters over the forestry radio. Ingrid had a marked English accent, which made everything she said sound funny. We figured Ingrid and Jim, being improvisers, would be a good addition to an evening of drumming. And since Tomas's lookout friend McNeal had flown in from Toronto, we invited him too.

Daniel kept telling me how Tomas wanted to get John and McNeal in the same room. The two lookout men had never met, and the rest of us figured it was better that way. John, the shaman, in conversation with McNeal, the academic, didn't sound like a promising social event. The difference in their world views might produce a violent storm; except, according to Tomas, McNeal had experimented with LSD back in the day, and this was the kind of resumé that would impress John, ethnographic research in the tradition of Carlos Castaneda.

Tomas had first met McNeal in 1979 at the Hinton Training Centre, a facility three hours west of Edmonton where Alberta Forestry trained forest officers, firefighters, and fire observers. Like all new hires that spring, Tomas and McNeal would have attended the mandatory, one-week program, which taught the basics of radio communications, collecting weather data, and detecting smoke and fire.

Tomas and McNeal gravitated to each other, Tomas impressed by McNeal's ferocious intellect and biting wit, McNeal impressed by Tomas's investigations of Jung and the notion of *mysterium coniunctionis*, the alchemical union of opposites. After learning how to calculate the dew point and relative humidity, they became twentieth-century men of letters, sending long, philosophical treatises back and forth, debating Gnostic beliefs and the place of sexuality in spirituality. It was a small miracle they ever found each other in the small Alberta logging town, surrounded by men who would have assumed that *Alchemy* was the name of a microbrew. (Note to self: copyright that name.)

Daniel had described their friendship to me in such detail I could imagine them inhaling cigars and exhaling retorts, like the reincarnation of Jung and Freud, their friendship thorny and, over the years, at times vitriolic.

"It's probably just a projection of my own psyche," Tomas would say, referring to his desire to witness John and McNeal in dialogue. "Those two cats are different aspects of my own psyche struggling to integrate."

"Sheesh, Tomas," Daniel said in response to Tomas's musings. "Analysis paralysis, I say."

Daniel had a drum from India that he wanted to play in a group, and he asked John to bring instruments to the party, any kind of drums. He knew Tomas wouldn't be caught pounding on a drum unless it was therapy, but if we found a groove, he hoped Tomas would stop analyzing and drop into the zone. We had no idea how McNeal would respond to drumming, because we didn't know him well enough, but we didn't worry about such things; we'd let them unfold or, as Tomas said, "untwirl."

We bought beer, wine, tortilla chips, and salsa, cleaned the house, and lit a dozen white IKEA candles outside on our front walkway. The candles stood up in brown paper bags weighted with sand and created the welcoming effect of Japanese-style paper lanterns. At eight o'clock the Supper Club folks arrived, John more outgoing than usual, ebullient. He walked into the house clutching a bag.

"We need tea bowls, Daniel. I'm making us mushroom tea."

"Really, mushroom tea?" Daniel had rarely taken any recreational drug.

"It's the new year man, let's do some mushrooms and drum."

If mushrooms would facilitate a music jam, Daniel was willing. John grabbed the kettle to boil water and lined up tea bowls on the counter. "This Is the Picture," from the Peter Gabriel *So* album, streamed from a cheap boom box.

> Sitting by the window, watching the snow fall...
> Looking out...watching out...
> This is the picture.

Athena and Tomas skulked in, a bit sullen, as though they'd put aside an unresolved argument and were unable to reckon the new year.

Jim and Ingrid phoned to say they were running late, and Daniel assured them they wouldn't want to miss the drumming. The party was off to a slow start, in need of a little kindling.

"Where's McNeal? Isn't he coming?" Daniel looked at Tomas.

"He's coming. He almost changed his mind, but he said he'll be here soon."

"Well, I better save him a tea," said John. "Which lookout did Mc-Neal do last season?"

"He's on Carbondale." Daniel and Tomas spoke on top of each other.

"Then I better make it an extra good cup," said John.

At six feet three inches in height, McNeal ducked through the front door of our small house, like a giant visiting hobbit friends. Daniel found him a chair and McNeal pulled it next to the kitchen doorway, his back against the wall, facing the group. John had positioned his chair on the far side of the narrow living room, and quietly sipped the mushroom tea. It was awkward, and I wasn't sure how to put people at ease.

Ever polite, Tomas attempted to start a conversation. "McNeal's on Christmas break at the University of Toronto."

"What is it you're studying?" I asked, doing my part to keep the conversation rolling.

"Finishing up a master's degree in religious studies, and then I'm applying to a doctoral program. I plan to research the origins of Gnostic thought."

"Ah, a dualist." Tomas smiled. "You're in a room full of monists."

McNeal scoffed. "Of course, it's part of the New Age shtick. All is one."

From a TM and yogic perspective, there is only one awareness and one Self, but no one wanted to argue with McNeal. Tomas changed course, making an obscure reference to the anima and animus in Jungian psychology. Jung and his notion of the shadow was Tomas's best hook, an irresistible topic for both McNeal and John. But here, the intellectual morsel dangled in space and the conversation floundered.

When the Peter Gabriel tape ended, Daniel pushed a drum toward McNeal. "Let's give it a try."

Daniel started with a simple rhythm. McNeal listened, and gently patted out a syncopated response. He kept his wrists down, tapping with relaxed fingertips in the style of tabla players. I was impressed by the sensitivity in his playing. As they improvised, John disappeared into the kitchen and returned with a steaming cup of tea. Strolling by McNeal, he passed him the tea bowl.

"We're all drinking this tea." He padded back to the other side of the room, stealthy in his thick wool socks.

"What is this?" McNeal inspected the muddy liquid, inhaling the hot vapour.

"It's tea, mushroom tea. We're all having some." Tomas spoke in a soothing tone.

"Magic mushrooms? Are you crazy?" McNeal shoved the tea bowl aside. "You just gave me a drug without informing me!"

He snatched his coat and addressed the party like a lawyer giving a closing argument. How dare we! Tomas and Athena tried to coax him to stay with a glass of red wine, but he stalked outside into the cold night.

His sudden exit, like a local squall, dissipated quickly. John could have said more, but it seemed obvious we were not drinking ordinary tea. McNeal may have been a veteran of hallucinogens, but he wasn't prepared to trip with us spontaneously. Whatever his reasons, I found McNeal's spitfire response overly dramatic and out of proportion to the deed.

Daniel eyed the full tea bowl. "No point in wasting this," he said, tilting back his head and swallowing the contents. John laughed in approval, picked up a drum, and moved closer into the circle.

The effect of the mushrooms enveloped the room like rhizomes spreading out underneath the surface of the earth. We could feel the energetic quality of each individual in the room, as well as a "we" presence, an invisible field of group connection. There was no need to speak; words felt clumsy and redundant. Because there were only three drums, Daniel rounded up some pots and large spoons from the kitchen, so everyone had a percussion voice. I passed on the makeshift instruments and danced outside the circle of drummers.

Finally around midnight Jim and Ingrid showed up, so we took a break from the drumming to catch them up on the happenings.

"He actually stormed off?" said Ingrid, incredulous. "Didn't fancy any mushrooms? I'm sorry we missed him. I hear he's very intelligent."

Jim and Ingrid slid into the ambience of the circle without a glitch. Hearing about McNeal, a scholar and writer, prompted Jim to tell us about his book, *Nothing So Natural*, which had won the Three-Day Novel Contest. The book was a story about a young boy growing up in an eccentric family in small-town Ontario.

"My family and friends weren't thrilled with the story. Unfortunately, they thought they could identify the characters. I can pretty much never go back there." Jim cackled, remembering his book tour.

Daniel interrupted the wry humour, directing us back to the rhythm. "Okay, you guys, grab an instrument or a pot and let's drum."

We beat, rapped, tapped, and slapped out rhythms, suspending and syncopating the beats, rotating the drums and pots around the circle. Every rhythm choice felt like the perfect call to the universe. We had bypassed language; there was only rhythmic sound. Every thought, laugh, and gesture manifested as sound. We were no longer separate from the rhythm; we were one unified field.

At least that's how it felt in the moment.

After several rounds, Daniel found his vocal cords and spoke, stopping the drumming to pop a blank cassette in the tape deck.

"This is good, I want to record it, we're in a groove."

In the interlude, Athena and Tomas made motions to leave, apologizing for their exit. "We have a sitter," explained Athena. "We need to get home."

Dinah snored, crumpled in an armchair, her head wobbling up and down; she could fall asleep anywhere. John would rouse her when he was ready to go home.

"Come on, you guys, don't anyone else leave. Let's go another round," said Daniel, pressing record.

The mushroom chorus resumed, thumping and pulsating into the early morning.

We slept late the next day. I had never seen Daniel hungover—on alcohol or drugs. When he crawled out of the bedroom in the early afternoon, he headed straight for the tape deck.

"I'm so excited to hear this—I can't believe how good we were last night."

"It was okay. I mean, for a group who's never drummed together, I guess it was pretty good." Having drunk far less of the shrooms than Daniel, I had lower expectations for the recorded performance.

The replay of the drum party crashed out of the two small speakers. Where was the free-flow, ecstatic feeling of rhythm that had overcome us? The drumming sounded amateurish and stilted at times. The crescendos were too brash, the mellow sections sloppy.

"You guys just need to practise more." I wanted to be positive about the mushroom cacophony.

Daniel fast-forwarded through the tape, stopping to listen here and there, convinced he would rediscover a few moments of musical brilliance.

"There was one point when I was laughing and I couldn't laugh with my mouth—the whole drum laughed for me. It was revelatory; I've never experienced sound in that way."

"Yeah, well, it's kind of hard to capture that on a cassette."

"Really, last night, I swear, we were good. It wasn't just the mushrooms. Our drumming was amazing."

Whatever the mushroom fairies had brought that night, any evidence of rhythmic ecstasy had evanesced from the tape.

In the following days, we ventured over to Tomas and Athena's one afternoon to see how things were going with the men of letters. We received a warm welcome from Tomas and McNeal, who were engaged in an intense conversation in the living room.

"Sorry about the other night, you guys," said McNeal. "I can't believe that shaman clown gave me mushrooms without asking. Duhhh. What's with that! I was jet-lagged too. End of a semester, just really burnt."

McNeal struck me as gracious and conciliatory, rather unlike the opinionated and sharp-tongued man who had stormed out of the party.

"Where's Athena today?" I asked, moving on from the mushroom debacle.

"She's working," said Tomas. "Anybody for tea?" He hurried away into the kitchen.

"Okay, what's going on with him?" I looked at McNeal.

"Athena and Tomas are fighting," he said.

"Really? What's happening?" This was the first I'd heard of any conflict in their marriage.

"Well, I'm sure she's having an affair," he whispered. "Tomas suspects, but he's not certain. He's upset."

"An affair? No!"

"Oh, I'm sure of it." He laughed heartily.

"Why are you so sure?" I was intrigued the lookout scholar claimed insight into a woman's motivations. We were seated side by side on the IKEA futon couch.

"Oh, all the signs are there," he said mischievously.

"You sound so sure. I have to ask, specifically, what signs?" I whispered.

Before I could extract the details, Tomas and Daniel returned with tea brewed in one of Daniel's pots and a tray of tea bowls.

"Hey, Binky, are you really leaving fire lookouts or what? Come on, you'll be back." McNeal goaded Daniel, abandoning the affair exposé.

"We're moving to the Shuswap in the spring. I'm done with lookouts."

McNeal looked unimpressed. "I'm hanging on to Carbondale until I'm done this academic gig. Feel free to swing by the lookout if you get tired of life in paradise."

"I'm going to be busy setting up a pottery studio and stuff. But who knows."

"Daniel, you're such a gregarious creature for the isolation, but in other ways you're a perfect fit for the lookout job." Tomas spoke with quiet authority.

"Except for the shitload of cargo he hauls up there every year," chided McNeal.

"I tend to take more than a box of books, you're right. I'd say you guys are more suited. It's easier for writers than artists to fit into the small space."

I listened to the three men kid each other in a way that women never do, almost trading insults in a competitive and brotherly fashion.

On the walk home, I relayed what McNeal had said about the affair, but Daniel stopped me.

"Hold on, we don't know what's going on with those guys and I don't want to gossip. I didn't notice anything funny with Tomas, but you know me, I miss these cues."

"That's for sure. He was so tense, something is going on. And 'Binky,' what's with that name? What did *I* miss?"

"Yeah, he calls me Binky, the depressed rabbit from the *Life in Hell* cartoon."

"And you don't mind?" I asked, mystified by the innuendo.

"Not at all," said Daniel. "Sometimes, I am—depressed a little."

It was time for John to bundle up in the arctic parka and new boots and set off on the long cold highway. But just when he'd finished work on the cross, the terms of the Lubicon and government dispute radically altered. After fourteen years of protest, Premier Getty promised Chief Ominayak and the Lubicon people a 243-square-kilometre reserve area, de-escalating the conflict and initiating talks that led to an accord—in principle.

Suddenly, John's protest plans were redundant.

"I would have done it," he insisted. "I was ready to walk to Edmonton for the Lubicon, but they have a deal now."

It had been a fine idea, especially the Thermos compartment in the arm of the cross. He kept the new boots; after all, they'd be good to have for walking out to the Dragon during the winter.

In the coming years, John would have learned that the promised Lubicon deal never materialized because governments, once again, stalled. He could have resurrected his plan to drag the cross along Highway 2, but his path would never lead to Edmonton.

Soon, he would have a heavier cross to bear, and it would have nothing to do with the struggle for Lubicon land rights.

That winter Jack Carter died of pancreatic cancer. He was fifty-three years old. Daniel, John, and Tomas went to the funeral, which was attended by about one hundred folks from the Alberta Forest Service who had worked with Jack over the years.

Nana Mouskouri did not make an appearance.

Not knowing Jack personally, I didn't go either.

It was hard for me to fathom, but Daniel and the lookout guys were deeply touched by Jack's life and death. As Tomas said, "he was a rare specimen."

To honour Jack's life, John made an outdoor fire and performed a sweat lodge ritual on the back forty behind his farmhouse.

There was another side of Jack that I would uncover. After his death, the Whyte Museum of the Canadian Rockies in Banff archived his photographs and journals.

Despite his infatuation with pornography and Nana Mouskouri, Jack's diaries proved he had been touched by an ordinary woman. In the summer of 1968, when he was thirty-two years old, he met Olwen, an Englishwoman, who was on vacation in Alberta. One weekend in mid-July, Jack took her camping in the Rockies. Setting out in his VW van, the couple had a picnic lunch along the Red Deer River. Then they drove north to Wildhorse Lake, a remote campground in the foothills east of Jasper, and spent the night there. The next day, after a light rain cleared off, they drove on the gravel back roads to visit Ya Ha Tinda, a well-known horse ranch. Because Olwen taught equestrian skills in England, Jack wanted to show her these magnificent Alberta horses. In the afternoon, on the way home, they stopped to rest and fell asleep in a sunny meadow somewhere along the Forestry Trunk Road.

Jack's diary said this was their only camping trip together. At the end of the summer, she returned home to England, leaving him heartbroken. Even though he was employed with a good income and loved to travel, he never, to my knowledge, took the risk and went to England. He stuck with what he knew best, working in fire protection as permanent spare lookout until his death, twenty years later.

Jack never saw Olwen again.

Around the same time as Jack's death, give or take a few weeks, we received an unusual evening phone call.

"I've got to go down to Tomas and Athena's place for a bit," Daniel said, hanging up the receiver. He pulled jeans over his sweatpants and grabbed a heavy sweater. "I think I'll just walk down the hill; I don't want to drive on the icy roads."

"Right now? What's going on?"

"Athena asked me to come over and mediate. I think they're fighting."

"Did she ask for me too?"

"Well, not really, but I'm sure it's all right if you want to come along."

"No, I'll stay here. It's too cold out."

He pulled the Afghani wool hat down over his forehead, wrapped a thick scarf around his neck, and set out, crossing Centre Street and slipping his way down the Crescent Heights slope to the Sunnyhill Housing Co-op. Tomas answered the door, ushering him into a room on the lower level of the townhouse, where he was working on a stained-glass project, a mandala design.

"Ah, Daniel, come in," he said in his soft, courteous manner.

Tomas showed Daniel how he wrapped each cut piece of glass in foil before soldering the pieces together; there was no mention of Athena. Then he stared at Daniel's face. "You look angry. What are you angry about?"

"I'm not angry. What do you mean?"

"Daniel, your face is red. Your nostrils are flaring."

"It's cold out, Tomas. My face is red from the cold."

"No, I can see it in you. Your breathing is shallow. You want to fight, Daniel, don't you?"

"Fight! Why would I want to fight? I don't want to fight. What's going on, Tomas?"

"If you want to go outside and fight, let's go."

"Don't be silly."

Daniel had never been in a fist fight, but each time he said no, Tomas dredged up another reason why Daniel, surely, wanted to pick a fight. They argued until Daniel, exasperated and worn down, said, "Okay then, yeah, I do want to fight!"

"Outside then!" said Tomas. "I'll get my coat."

The two men stood in the bitter cold driveway, and Tomas said, "Maybe we should go for a walk along the river."

"Okay, sure, but what's going on?"

"Men and women, Daniel, the marriage of opposites—there's nothing like jumping into the alchemical fire."

"Which men and women, Tomas? You and Athena?"

"What's a man to do, Daniel?"

They walked briskly, footsteps crunching on the icy snow, and Tomas, in his arcane fashion, disclosed the financial strife he and Athena were embroiled in.

"I don't know what to say, Tomas, except I'm not the best person to talk to about money. I always go into the lookout season with my credit cards maxed out."

Back at home, baffled by the incident, Daniel described what had happened.

I had my own angle. "Athena wants to major in women's studies, you know. A feminist analysis of gender and patriarchy doesn't mesh well with Jung."

"Or with Tomas." Daniel smirked. "Really, I don't want to take sides. It's not fair; we're friends with both of them."

Whatever the real nature of their conflict, it surprised me because over the years I had pieced together the romantic lookout tale of how they met. Independently, Athena and Tomas, on several occasions, had shared with me the details of their first encounter.

Tomas first set eyes on Athena at Mockingbird Lookout during the summer of 1982. Athena was Beverly then. She and a girlfriend had driven out from Calgary to hike up the fire lookout road, well supplied with food and drink for a day in the foothills.

Wanting to picnic at the summit, Beverly had loaded her backpack with avocado and cheese sandwiches, tortilla chips, sweets, wine, and other treats. As the women emerged from the trees at the top of the hill, flushed from the climb, Tomas scoped them in the binoculars and bounded down the stairs, guest book in hand. They were willing to share their goods with the man on the hill, and for Tomas, a long-legged, sensuous woman offering him wine constituted the last temptation.

Within the hour he was satiated; within two he was smitten.

For Beverly, everything about Tomas was mythic in the beginning—from his dramatic childhood to his explorations into Jungian psychology. Born in Hungary, Tomas had learned English as a child immigrant, obtained a university degree, and taught school on a First Nations reserve in the North. He left a teaching career in 1979 for the freedom of working as a fire lookout observer, after befriending John, who shared his philosophical interests. Weighty ideas he tackled in solitude. The fire lookout was a refuge from the banal, a place where he could study and write without interruption, notwithstanding the radio chatter, or worrying about mundane things like housing for the next winter.

Beverly had never met a man with such an intelligent, probing mind. Her last boyfriend had been a rock musician; it was Tomas who rocked her world. The following week she hiked up to the lookout again, this time alone. She had a serving job at a Calgary restaurant, Fourth Street Rose, and for the duration of the summer she spent her days off serving Tomas at Mockingbird.

High above the valley, Tomas and Beverly would have discovered each other in all weather conditions: thunder and lightning storms; cloudless, pristine crispness; and grey, drizzling overcast. They sexed on top of the world, a masculine deity and his consort, until Tomas would excuse himself from their intimacy, apologizing that he must look for smoke—or fires brought on by lightning.

"Such a Dionysian existence," he probably sighed, admiring Beverly as she dressed.

It was a union of opposites; she would laugh and leave him to his work, drive into town, and shop for more brie, chocolate, or a carton of cigarettes—his weakness. With a partner, Tomas no longer had to stretch his meagre groceries until the monthly service day. By nature, he was self-disciplined, eating boiled lentils or rice for weeks at a time, but Beverly's sensuality revitalized the lookout, and the refrigerator, changing forever Tomas's quest for transcendence.

Despite the breach of austerity, I am sure Tomas felt freer and more uplifted with Beverly in his life. The divine feminine had ascended, or rather descended, on Mockingbird Lookout. He bestowed on Beverly the name Athena, in honour of the Greek goddess of wisdom, learning, and strategy, and the epithet stuck.

Their lives were blessed, and in October 1983, love child Willow was born. In November 1984, they married in Hawaii at a Zen Buddhist temple.

Now, after spending several years at home caring for her family, Athena chose to go back to school and pursue gender studies at the University of Calgary. That decision would change the course of her life as much as her meeting with Tomas on top of the world.

Firebricks

We had 1,300 firebricks stacked on wooden pallets in our backyard, bricks Daniel had been buying from the Bargain Finder over the last two years, many stamped with the names of the old brickyards, Brickburn and Calgary Pressed Brick.

"They're firebricks, not patio bricks," he kept saying, as though I would understand the distinction. "Firebrick is dense and heavy, and it's fired to a really high temperature. You can't build a kiln with patio brick."

I hadn't paid much attention to the growing pile of bricks, but now that we were moving over the Rocky Mountains, their dense, heavy qualities seized my interest. When I expressed reservations about moving bricks, Daniel waved aside my concerns.

"I'll hire a flatbed truck and driver to come for them all," he said. "If we don't have to worry about the bricks, this move will be easy."

In preparation, we acted on a naive impulse to sell our house to the real estate tycoon next door for $49,000, the same price we had paid for it two years previous. Why deal with renters and taxes when we could so easily unburden ourselves? It did feel weird staying on as renters for the last few months in our own house, but responsibility for the mortgage was like a tether to Calgary we promptly severed. The weight of bricks was a far more reasonable burden to assume than a house mortgage.

Our delusion was mutual; in the future, we would practically bang our heads against the wall recalling that decision to become lighter and freer.

During our last few weeks in Calgary, Jim and Ingrid invited us over for dinner. They owned a classic three-storey home in northwest Calgary with a kitchen that sported an island countertop, the latest trend in home renovations. Jim paced around the island, buzzing with nervous energy; he was particularly edgy that night because word had leaked out that Athena and Tomas might be splitting up.

"I can't believe those two are separating," said Jim. "What will happen to the Supper Club without Athena and Tomas?" Though he laughed, the rumours clearly agitated him.

"They might sort things out and get back together after the lookout season. It's just a separation. I don't think they're filing for divorce." I thought Jim was overreacting, especially given that he and Tomas weren't buddies. Jim, the stand-up comic, and Tomas, the reclining Jungian. Ingrid was more connected to both Tomas and Athena. Not only did she work on a fire lookout neighbouring Tomas's, but, like Athena, she also studied part-time at the University of Calgary.

But Jim escalated the doom; he was weirdly compelled by relationship catastrophe.

"Okay, let's take bets, who's next? Who's splitting up next? I've seen how these things go. It's like a virus. First, it's Athena and Tomas. Then, who? Which of the four couples is next?"

"Jim, sit down and relax! Have a glass of wine." Ingrid chopped vegetables as she tracked her husband around the island. She appeared untroubled by the news.

"Where did you get your information, Jim?" I couldn't figure out how he would know before Daniel and me.

"John. Ingy and I saw John a few days ago and he told us."

Of course, it was the pot connection. I was so out of the loop, I didn't even know who was selling and who was buying.

"Athena and I were in a women's studies class together," said Ingrid. "Tomas won't do better than Athena. She's such a lovely woman. And she always shows up in such beautiful outfits."

"I know, but how can she afford it?" I instantly regretted my comment. I had no right to infer judgments about Tomas and Athena's finances. Daniel flashed me a do-not-go-there look.

"Do you think she's really having an affair?" This wasn't any subtler than the spendy jab, but we were all thinking the same thing. Who was she having an affair with?

Jim turned pale, unable to grapple with this possibility.

"Did John name any names?" I mentally flipped through our male friends.

Athena had such a large social network, it was impossible to guess. She hadn't confessed to me, but then we hadn't seen each other much lately.

"I didn't ask," said Jim. "I doubt it's anyone we know. God, I hope she's gone outside the Supper Club."

"Of course she's gone outside the Supper Club," I retorted. "We know it's not either of you two, right? I stared at Jim and Daniel and, oddly, answered for them. "Of course we do. And as for John, she regards him as one of the original patriarchs, so there you have it."

I had no idea who Athena was involved with, but I was confident she'd tell me soon.

Daniel had already made six trips across the mountains, each trip taking three or four days, loading the Ford pickup truck with kilns, tools, and art supplies. Because we were moving near a lake, he had bought a sailboat, a real deal, he said, and the boat had to be pulled over the mountains, too. He hitched it to the back of the truck and away he and his dog, Zip, went on another journey. The other big purchase he made was a used gas kiln. He explained that as much as he loved wood-fired pottery, it would be smart to produce work that was less rustic and had a more contemporary smooth surface; wood-fired pots burned hot with bumpy, drippy deposits of ash, not a good match for modern kitchens. In addition to these large items, Daniel's basement studio was like the miracle of the loaves and fishes; after two years in our house, no matter how much stuff he dragged upstairs and into the truck, there was always more left to pack.

One day toward the end of the month, when I was at work, Daniel paid a truck driver $800 to load up the bricks, drawing him a map and directions to the BC acreage, and warning him about the long, hilly driveway he would have to bump up to make the delivery. When the driver began loading, he discovered some of the pallets were so frozen into the icy mud in our yard that the forklift was useless. The driver was forced to give up, leaving some of the bricks to thaw in the Calgary spring.

"That's okay," Daniel said cheerily, as he told me about it that evening. "I'll come back in May and get the last of those bricks." He would talk to the new owner of our house and arrange to store the bricks for another month. "They're bricks and they're heavy. They're not going anywhere."

We had to be out of the house by midnight on March 31, 1989. I finished my last day of work and rushed home to help Daniel pack up the last of our belongings, expecting to find the house mostly empty. Each room had an assortment of boxes in disarray, as he attempted to make everything fit into one last load. I descended the basement stairs, calling out his name, disappointed to find pottery equipment, buckets, boxes, and found objects he'd been stashing down there.

"What can I do to help? What can I take up?" I asked, eyeing the chaos.

"I guess you can start carrying up clay, if you want. Just put it on the ground next to the truck."

I looked at the clay lined up against the basement wall. "How heavy is each box, Daniel?"

"About forty-five pounds."

I groaned, lifted a box, and wobbled up the stairs, crossed the living room, the front yard, and dropped it at the curb. I retraced my steps, grabbing box after box of clay, cursing as I heaved them up the stairs. It was like carrying bags of rice up the basement stairs at Earth Harvest.

"I can't believe you still have this much crap to move," I yelled. At this rate, it would take until midnight to finish packing and clean the house.

"Sorry, hon, I know, sorry." He was genuine, but his remorse didn't change the weight of the clay.

I worked in silence for a while, steadfast in my desire to clear out the basement. Finally, the boxes of clay gone, I assessed the room, feeling more optimistic.

"What's next?" I asked.

"Maybe you should just start cleaning," said Daniel. "This is all pretty heavy stuff."

"No, I can keep helping you down here. Let's get this done."

"Well, there are buckets of wet clay that need to go up."

"Wet clay?"

"Yeah, I've got clay soaking in those white buckets over there, but I don't know if you can lift those." He gestured toward a collection of five-gallon plastic buckets, lids closed tight, concealing the primordial, watery contents.

"You gotta be kidding me. Wet clay!"

"I know, hon, sorry, but I want that clay to come with us. Those plastic buckets are the good kind, too."

I seized the handle of a bucket and dragged it along the concrete floor. Even with anger and adrenaline pumping through my bloodstream, I wasn't strong enough to budge wet clay. Conceding defeat, I stomped up the stairs and banged my head on the low ceiling beam at the top. "Ouch! Damn it!" Dazed, I stumbled out the kitchen door into the darkness of the backyard. Time was running out; it must have been 9:00 p.m. by now.

My breath drifted upwards in the brisk spring air. I screamed out in frustration, charged through the backyard and out into the alley, angry nonsense syllables streaming from my throat and chest. Maybe I should disappear right now, run away, check into a motel, and abandon Daniel to his mounds of art supplies and his love affair with heavy, awkward things.

I circled the block until the waves of frustration subsided. As the tightness in my chest melted, I admitted to myself that I had only one choice: to go back and finish packing. I would never really leave Daniel—what a ridiculous idea. We would stagger through this move if it took all night.

By the time I returned, Daniel had dragged the buckets of wet clay outside and hid them alongside the house next to a hedge.

"No one will even notice them here," he said, "and if they do, they're so heavy, who would want them?"

"Well, that's a given," I retorted. "Unless Bret Hart comes by looking for something to wrestle."

"I'll get them in May when I come back to pick up the last of the firebricks." Daniel ignored my sarcasm. "I know this is frustrating, but hang in, it's almost done."

I was almost done, that was certain.

At 11:00 p.m. the porch light shone across the front lawn, revealing a collection of cardboard boxes, rubber storage containers, furniture, and the unpacked contents of closets and cupboards.

"Don't waste time taking clothes off hangers and folding them. We're running out of time. Just stuff everything into a garbage bag," said Daniel.

In one swipe I emptied the closet and tossed the bags onto the front lawn. My life was an episode of *The Beverly Hillbillies*, except my Jed Clampett had struck clay instead of oil.

The pickup truck was loaded so high Daniel fastened it down with a meshwork of ropes and tarps. Just before midnight we cheered, finally loading the last item, our futon mattress, which Daniel heaved over his head, the white cotton draping his body—"It's easier to carry it this way," he insisted—tottering like a headless ghost to the truck. We drove out to Bearspaw Road and stayed overnight at John and Dinah's farmhouse, throwing the futon down on their floor and sleeping until late the next morning.

When we got up, Dinah had already left for work and dropped the boys at school. John scuffed around the kitchen in his socks, making strong coffee, which he and I drank leisurely, while Daniel bundled up the bedding, lashed it onto the truck, and waited for the caffeine to jolt me into action.

"It's a long drive," said Daniel, meaning it was time to hit the road.

John drawled, "Yeah, yeah," smiling at our impending adventure, swearing that as soon as the fire lookout season was over in the fall, he and Dinah would drive out to British Columbia.

"Another season on Cline, eh?" Daniel said.

A redundant comment, but it seemed like the right thing to say. In their separate worlds, Daniel and John had each worked over ten seasons on mountaintops.

"I love Cline," John answered. "Can't wait to get back. I'm going to be painting more this season, I can feel it."

"Here's a map to our place, in case Dinah wants to come out with the boys this summer. You guys are welcome any time."

We exchanged hugs, climbed into the green truck, and drove west on the Trans-Canada Highway, steering straight into the mountains. Zip snoozed at my feet and Sylvester paced around the perimeter of the cab.

"I can't drive with a cat on the dashboard." Daniel shoved the animal toward me. "We should have put him in a cage."

"He'll yowl the whole way if he's confined. Don't worry, he'll settle down in a bit."

Daniel swatted him with the back of his hand and the cat slunk away, only to return in a moment to the smooth leather on the dash.

He pulled over on the Trans-Canada. "Okay, that's it. He's going into a cage and riding in the back. I'll find a safe spot out of the wind." He found the travel cage, scooped up the cat, and gently but firmly pushed the black-and-white furry body inside the door. "He sounds like he's being tortured, but he'll be fine."

We crossed over the Continental Divide at the top of the Kicking Horse Pass, the creeks and rivers flowing westward out of the mountains now. Blasted from the mountainsides, the highway curved in and out of dark avalanche tunnels. Then we coasted down the long steep hill into Golden, the abyss of the Columbia River valley far below.

"I can't believe you drove this route six times this spring," I said.

"I stopped and dug clay near Golden too," said Daniel.

Of course he did. That's why we were hauling buckets of earth across the Rocky Mountains.

"Maybe let's not talk about clay," I suggested. "I might get angry all over again just thinking about those buckets."

"Sure, hon. But we're okay, right? We're moving to the country!" He slid one hand along the bench seat, massaging my legs. "Thunder thighs, yay! We made it out of the city."

"Barely," I said, taking his hand.

We stopped in Golden to gas up, buy a coffee, and check on the yowling cat. Then we headed for Revelstoke and stopped again briefly to stretch. Breathing deeply, I noticed how softness pervaded the air here, moist and gentle, so different from the brisk dry air on the east side of the Rockies.

In another hour we had entered Shuswap Lake country and passed by Salmon Arm. It was dark by the time we crossed over the Squilax Bridge and pulled into our meadow. I could see the outline of the yurt walls in the moonlight and piles of belongings sprawled across the meadow. We had no outbuilding or shed, so Daniel had done the best he could, storing things under tarps. As I hopped out of the truck I felt a large presence and heard rustling in the tall grass.

I called out to Daniel, "What is that? There's an animal over here."

He shone the flashlight in an arc, revealing not one animal but a herd of horses, standing in the tall grass, munching. The horses moved in closer, brushing up against the truck and the yurt, snorting, pawing, and sensing their new neighbours in the meadow. Heaps of fresh horse manure spotted the ground.

"Whose horses are these?" I was exhausted, but irritation welled up again.

"I'll find out tomorrow, hon. Let's just go to bed."

We carried the futon inside the yurt and set it up on a wooden frame, a few inches off the ground. We were so tired we didn't bother to light a fire. We fell asleep to the sound of horses breathing against the canvas walls.

In the morning Daniel went next door to ask Chris about the horses. She said they belonged to folks in the Lee Creek community who needed pasture. They hoped we didn't mind having a few horses around.

"Yes, I do!" I said. "We don't have fencing to keep them out of our living space. We shouldn't have to live inside a giant horse corral."

Daniel went back and relayed the decision in softer language, and within several days the horses were rounded up and removed. Chris told Daniel that the Lee Creek folks figured we would be glad to have all that horse manure. It was excellent for growing pot plants, and even a few plants, say about fifteen, they suggested, carefully tended, would provide us with all the income we needed to live summers on the land and travel in Thailand in the winter.

"We're not growing pot to make a living, Daniel!"

"I know, I know. I'm just the messenger. I don't want to grow pot either."

Our first week and I was already annoyed with the community. Chris was our conduit to the locals, and she said everyone here was a grower. If we didn't start growing a few plants, we'd always be suspect, and never become true insiders. Just mix a few plants in with your tomatoes, she said. No one will ever notice. The horse owners suggested we plant marijuana here and there in the woods, tucked out of sight, watering by hand during the hot spells. It seemed everybody in British Columbia had an opinion about growing pot. We stood our ground, politely declining the invitation to become illegal marijuana farmers. I understood their point; it was far more lucrative to grow marijuana than mint, but I had visions of police helicopters tracking us from the sky, their infrared lights exposing our hideout.

The next day we received a phone message, via Chris, that the semi truck hauling the firebricks had gotten a flat in Revelstoke and the driver had to remove some of the bricks to change the tire. The driver said he was on his way again, but without a forklift we were on our own to get that last heap of bricks from Revelstoke to Lee Creek. That evening, as promised, the massive truck inched its way along the perimeter of the meadow, depositing the bricks in the grass, under the direction of Daniel's waving arms.

Within the week, Daniel drove back to Revelstoke, relieved to find his firebricks near a service station, just as the driver said, and hand-loaded them brick by brick into the pickup truck.

I wanted to grow a large vegetable garden with basil, tomatoes, squash, and watermelon. Daniel rented a Rototiller and plowed a corner of the meadow, and then I shook out the hunks of sod, dug in manure, and built raised beds. By the beginning of May, I had seeded a good-sized vegetable garden. One day when I was gardening, Daniel returned from town with a load of flooring in the back of the truck. "I bought spruce planks for the floor," he said. He had paid a lot of money, on his credit card, more than I even wanted to know, he said, but we should get the yurt off the grass and onto a raised floor with proper joists.

He chose a spot on the edge of the meadow, partially sheltered by a canopy of tall poplar trees. Over the next few weeks, he cut and peeled spruce trees for the joists, painstakingly levelled the main support beams, and nailed down the flooring in a circular shape, extending the floor boards beyond the canvas diameter, so the entire yurt sat dry and protected, thirty centimetres above the ground. It felt more like a house than a tent now. We moved furniture inside, a table, wooden chairs, clothes closet, and a bookshelf, arranging it around the perimeter of the expandable gate-wall and canvas. Since the weather was getting warmer, we decided we could live without the airtight stove for the summer. Daniel scrounged a used screen door, painted the frame yellow, and installed it in the canvas door opening.

On my birthday in May, he bought me a young willow tree and we planted it on the edge of the meadow, hoping its thirsty roots would grow deep enough to find the water table. Then he decided to dash back to Calgary and rescue the frozen firebricks from our old backyard. When he got there he was horrified to find someone had stolen half the bricks. A neighbour told Daniel that just the day before a guy had pulled up in a truck, helping himself to a stack of bricks, for a patio, he said, you know how these bricks make a nice patio. Daniel groaned, elucidating once again the difference between patio brick and firebrick. He recovered the few remaining bricks and, when he got back to the Shuswap, promptly consulted a Bargain Finder and tracked down more firebricks for sale in Kamloops. We rushed to Kamloops to buy them up, and this time we moved them without a forklift, by hand, brick by brick, on and off the truck.

I stood in the tall grass at the edge of the meadow, the aspen and spruce trees at my back, the spring air warm and gentle. Daniel kneeled at the back of the pickup, passing bricks one by one into my outstretched hands, and I stacked them neatly, bending over the pallet, surrounded by blooming chicory. We fell into a steady rhythm, and the weight of the bricks barely registered in the pulse of our movement.

There was no creek or well on our acreage, and the locals said the water table was deep. We might drill down hundreds of feet without finding water. Daniel located a public water tap in town and filled up a fifty-gallon plastic rain barrel, lookout-style, on the back of the truck, drove it up the long bumpy road, attached a long garden hose, and sucked on the end to stimulate the flow of water, letting gravity take over to fill up smaller containers. That exercise took care of water.

We didn't worry about refrigeration because we didn't eat meat or fish; milk and cheese preserved well floating in cold water in a picnic cooler. I cooked on the propane stove and stored perishables in the cooler in the shade.

The yurt suited us. At night we lay in bed, gazing at the darkness through the clear plastic cone in the centre of the canvas roof. In the morning, light streamed in, the white canvas walls suffused with sunlight. We were pleased with our simple lifestyle.

So pleased that one day, out of the blue, Daniel said we should get married this summer.

"This summer! How will my family come out from Toronto with so little notice?"

"I was thinking about something simple, maybe just you and me, and a few friends," he said.

"I can't get married and tell my mother after it's all over, Daniel. My family would freak out. Besides, I want my brothers to be here and play music. Let's plan a wedding and have a ceremony in the meadow when we can afford a celebration."

"So you don't want to get married now?"

"It's not that I don't want to get married. I do, but we don't have electricity for amps and microphones and stuff. We would need to rent equipment and tents, and we're maxed out. We can't afford to get married right now."

"I wasn't picturing a big deal. Something more simple."

"Getting married is a big deal. I want to have a celebration and invite our family and friends."

"You really want to rent generators so your brothers can perform music?"

"Yeah, of course, it'll be beautiful, outside in the meadow on a sunny day."

"Different from what I had in mind. Will your family really travel all the way from Toronto?"

"Of course they will, if we're getting married. How about next summer? We'll be more set up then."

"Maybe. That's a ways off."

I thought Daniel would be on board with a wedding party, since he had broached the marriage conversation. Unresolved, we dropped the marriage plans as a serious discussion. Every now and then, I would say, "When we get married, let's write our own vows." Or, "When we get married, let's have my sister make spanakopita." He would nod in agreement and say, "Sure, if you like, when we get married."

Every evening we listened to CBC News on the boom-box radio powered by batteries. At the beginning of June, the media were reporting on student demonstrations in Bejing, China. Hundreds of thousands of students had converged in Bejing from all over the country to protest the government, demanding democratic reforms. The Chinese leaders referred to the students as terrorists and counter-revolutionaries, as a danger to be halted. On June 2, Communist Party leaders announced Tiananmen Square would be cleared to restore order, and army troops would use force if the students refused to disperse.

Feeling the tension all the way from China, I wanted to see the news images.

"Can you hook up the TV to the car battery, so we can watch the news, Daniel?" I was confident he could get the TV operating with direct current off the battery. I hauled the TV out of storage in the wall tent. Daniel parked the truck close to the yurt and ran a cable from the car battery under the canvas to the TV set. On June 4, from inside the yurt, we watched television coverage of the Tiananmen Square massacre, horrified by the reports the army had shot and killed students for peacefully demonstrating.

In comparison with Chinese youth, we had so much political and social freedom, and we wanted more, much more. We wanted freedom from meaningless jobs; from environmental degradation and the clear-cutting of old-growth forests; from consumerism and soulless communities constructed around big-box stores. We had come of age during the immense social changes of the 1970s, and the continuation of that social transformation felt like a birthright.

For those reasons and more, we were happy to live in a yurt, grow organic vegetables, and make pottery, music, and dance. This was absolute freedom, the expression of our ideals—and it was also naive. We each had a Mastercard and a Visa card. We had maxed out all four credit cards to make our move to the country. Now we were accruing daily compounding interest. I had no job, not even a meaningless one. Daniel's intention was to sell pottery to tourists and art shops, after he built the hill-climbing brick kiln. We would move into town for the winter months, rent a house nearby.

But it soon became apparent that even with that caveat, Daniel could not build a kiln and a house at the same time. I had no building skills; in fact, I was not handy in the least. It would take years and a lot of money before we could upgrade our living conditions from the canvas yurt to a small cabin. In our enthusiasm we had not thought this through.

Now that we had escaped the city and landed in the meadow, the implications of our situation became real. As sublime as life could be in the summer, our debt mounted daily, and I had no idea where to find work here. The last thing I wanted to do was live in the country and commute to work on the Trans-Canada Highway. This was a high-unemployment region, and most jobs were connected to the resource sector, logging, pulp and paper, farming, or tourism and the service sector. There were tree-planting jobs in the summer, but I didn't see myself climbing over slash piles in mosquito netting and sleeping in motels. I had tried tree planting in my early twenties, and I was no highballer, barely earning enough to buy groceries. In the city my problem had always been a meaningful career versus a job; now, in the country, my problem had simply become survival.

Chris offered Daniel a shelf to sell his work in her gift shop down at the roadside. But it would be six months to a year before he had a studio and could produce work. In the meantime, he would need to spend more money on building supplies. If he worked out at a job, he wouldn't have time to build the pottery studio and kiln. Chris needed a manager for the gift shop. Never mind the gift store was really a shack on a back road across the lake from the hordes of tourists zooming by on the highway. Maybe I could source pottery and artwork from across western Canada and turn it into a tourist destination? On the other side of the ledger, Chris wanted me to work for commission or minimum wage. I would spend my days sitting at the side of the road, hoping for a tourist to pull over and buy a twenty-dollar tea bowl, while the two ceramic artists nurtured their creativity on the hill above.

I didn't want to play assistant to the artist or dreary accountant. Stubborn, I turned down Chris's job offer.

What I didn't know was that the widespread recession of the late eighties would continue for several more years. Interest rates and unemployment levels were on the rise.

At the end of June, after school ended, Athena, Dinah, and their kids rolled into the meadow on summer vacation. Hosting guests allowed me to push my employment and money problems aside, and I elected to enjoy the summer instead. I refused to worry about the credit card debt. In the tradition of Scarlett O'Hara, I told myself, "After all, tomorrow is another day."

Tomas and John had gone back to their fire lookouts, leaving Athena and Dinah a couple of modern grass widows. Athena worked at Community Natural Foods, my former employer, and was chipping away at her degree while she raised her daughter on her own. She and Tomas had not repaired the breach in their marriage. Dinah was off for the summer from her job at the Waldorf School, caring for the two boys on her own. She planned to fly in and visit John at some point, but for now, she and Athena were happy to camp out with their kids on our land. Daniel pitched a brown wall tent in a secluded clearing on the other side of the meadow, giving them some privacy.

The days were clear and sunny, the lake a short ride down the hill, and every night we cooked dinner together outside the yurt, lighting a campfire at dusk. I picked salad greens from my garden, which also produced a constant supply of basil that thrived in the hot Shuswap climate. Night after night, Daniel made fresh pesto in a huge Thai mortar, so large he ground the pine nuts, olive oil, and basil with the end of a baseball bat. Buckwheat noodles and pesto with lettuce and arugula salad became a regular meal. We drank Olympia beer in cans, and sat on logs and stumps around the outdoor fire, ducking from the smoke, swatting mosquitoes, and squeezing out every last taste from each day. It was like endless summer from childhood, evenings filled with the singing of cicadas, the quaking of aspens, and the stain of grass on muddy, bare feet.

We sat around the fire and talked about Tomas and John and how they always missed out on a real summer, alone on their mountaintops, listening to the forestry radio, the wind, and the thunder. Were they thinking about their family and friends down in the valley, and wondering who, if anyone, might visit that season?

There was a pay phone on the road down below our property, and on a few evenings Athena disappeared from the firepit to make a call. She said she was checking in with Tomas on Mockingbird. She would come back to the fire anxious and upset. I wondered if maybe they were reconciling, but she shook her head vigorously no, not a chance, she said.

One of those summer nights, I leaned over and said, "Who did you have an affair with, anyway?"

Athena looked mortified. "Oh, that. That's over. It was nothing."

I waited, leaving space for her to confide what happened, but she skirted my question, choosing a diplomatic response.

"It was stupid on my part, but Tomas won't let it go. That's not even the real issue. We're just not right for each other. He's not a feminist at all. I'm an evil woman these days, according to Tomas."

"Evil, really? Well, face it, Athena, maybe your middle name is Eve. You're thrown out of the garden now."

She laughed, blocking the drifting smoke. I tossed some kindling on the waning fire and poked at the smoky logs. I wanted to hear more about the affair, but I could tell Athena was not, at that moment, willing to share more details.

After several weeks, rested and well tanned, Athena and Dinah begrudgingly ended their holiday, driving off to Calgary in their used Volvos.

"We want to stay and live here with you," they teased, appreciative of the break from their routine in the city.

Once our friends were gone, Daniel and I imposed a more structured rhythm on our new life, each day striving to make progress on a long list of work projects.

I had anticipated living in the country would mean falling asleep to the delicious sounds of owl and coyote calls. But in the middle of the summer, I started waking up at 3:00 or 4:00 a.m. to the sound of barking dogs. Each night, the incessant barking jarred me out of deep sleep, and the cacophony lasted for hours.

One night, exasperated, I got dressed, found a flashlight, and thrashed a path through the bushes, tracking the sound of the barking dogs. I walked beyond Chris's property, making my way to ground zero, a house on the next acreage. Two big dogs were chained to the veranda, barking feverishly. I marched up to the house, circumventing the dogs, and banged on the front door. I pounded and pounded; no one answered. Furious, I made my way back to the yurt and fell asleep at dawn.

The next day Daniel consulted with Chris, and she advised us that the neighbours with the chained dogs slept through the barking, as did she, undisturbed, a benefit of the relaxing effects of marijuana. The barking kept away pesky coyotes, Chris pointed out, and if only we would try a little toke, life might be better. We were full circle with the marijuana issue again. But it wasn't only barking dogs that tormented my sleep. Freight trains rattled through the valley at night, whistles blowing, and a parade of semi trucks rumbled along the Trans-Canada Highway in the wee hours, brakes screeching on the hilly, winding road. The echo reverberated across Shuswap Lake and up the cliff to our meadow.

I longed for deep silence and had expected by moving to the country I would hear only the birds chirping, frogs croaking, and leaves rustling. Here I was in the middle of nowhere, shielding myself from a barrage of uncontrolled and unregulated noise. Daniel said once we were living in a real house, I wouldn't notice the dogs and trains. I needed to be patient. All in good time.

I bought earplugs. Each night I took the kettle off the stove to prevent any rattling when the trains passed.

The other impending issue we faced had to do with our road access. In winter, it would take a four-wheel-drive truck with chains, something we couldn't afford, to make it up the long steep road that was our driveway, and even with that luxury, the perils of negotiating the road would be a constant feature of life. Daniel and I had decided we didn't want to winter in the yurt. Compared with Alberta, the winter was mild, but it was also cloudy and rainy at times, and we'd burn cords of wood to stay dry and warm.

But it was still July and the summer glorious. Why worry about winter now? Chris planned to fire her anagama kiln, and Daniel would help throughout the three-day event. He would spell her off so she could sleep, and in return she would give him kiln space in the firing. "I'll have work for sale sooner than you think," he said, excited by the prospect. He set up a makeshift studio in a grove of giant cedars and began throwing pots for the firing.

Then one day he came back to the yurt after a meeting with Chris, distressed and discouraged.

"She wants to give me one-eighth of the kiln space. One-eighth! I told her I thought we had a fifty-fifty deal."

"I guess she's testing you to make sure you keep your end of the promise."

"It's an awful lot of work for one-eighth of the space."

Chris was our closest neighbour. We had to get along if we were to live here. Our land partners, Martin and Hannah, were her family.

"I'm going to do the firing. I wouldn't back out now, but I'm pissed off."

It was one of the only times I'd ever seen him angry.

Daniel kept his word and fired the kiln with Chris, packing in her pots, splitting wood, feeding the fire, boosting the temperature hotter and hotter. After three days he staggered back to the yurt, smudged with black soot and sweat, half delirious from the heat and exhaustion.

"I'm going to focus on getting my own kiln built now and not worry about Chris. I'm so sick of listening to Tom Waits," he added, peeling off his grimy clothes. "Kiln firings need a nice raga for concentration."

He had burned through the infatuation with his female self.

On August 24, in the late morning, Daniel pushed open the yellow screen door of the yurt. He had been scouting the land to select a building site for the kiln. There was a spot near the cliff edge in a small clearing, which he thought would be perfect. The secluded spot was protected from the wind, and if you looked through the filter of spruce and poplar trees, you could see the surface of Shuswap Lake glimmering below. For days he had been cutting back the underbrush so he could drive in the truck. Next, while the weather stayed dry, he planned to build a large open-shed roof to shelter the kiln site.

"I'm about to pour concrete for the main posts that will support the kiln shed roof. I was standing in the clearing and I thought about concrete, how permanent it is, really permanent."

"Okay." I wasn't sure where this was going.

"What I mean is, once I pour this concrete and start building, that's it. I won't be moving again."

"Oh, come on, ever?"

"Ever. Either this is home or not. I need to know—and quick, because I'm about to add water to the dry mix."

I was on my second Bodum of coffee, considering the day. Stunned by his forthrightness, I held the coffee bowl with both hands and reflected on the dilemma. Barking dogs, unemployment, and debt.

I felt trapped and isolated, as though we were living on a remote fire lookout, the chance for social connections and job opportunities out of reach in the valley below. I was afraid to tell Daniel this. He had already put in months of hard work here. He was committed to realizing his dream of a rural pottery, and I wanted to support it, be part of it. But I had little vested here, and the pot growers were not my people. I would not be happy growing mint or echinacea, always wondering what I might have become somewhere else.

"I can't do it, Daniel. This isn't where I can live my whole life."

"Is there any such place you can live? I mean, really, where is it, we'll go there. There's always something wrong."

My lip twitched. "I'm sorry, I can't do it. I didn't know how noisy it would be in the country. And it will be years before we build a cabin."

"Okay, good to know. Let's get on with it, then. I'll talk to Chris about a buyer." He didn't argue or try to coerce me into staying. He accommodated, accepting my point of view. "It means we have to move everything all over again," he added, walking away.

"We'll find a place." I trailed after him as the screen door caught the latch. It was like telling someone who's just lost their dream job that everything will be fine, good things are around the bend.

I stared through the screen door as the back of his blue denim shirt receded across the meadow. What was wrong with me? Why couldn't I relax and simply accept things as they were unfolding? For some reason, the reality of life never measured up to my expectations, never felt complete. I could go after him, swear I had changed my mind, and say, "Yes, I could live here!" But it wouldn't be authentic. I would be faking it to maintain harmony. Either way the choice was beset with a mixture of guilt, sadness, and relief.

Wherever we moved, the two tons of firebricks would come with us.

Our life changed rapidly after that decision in the yurt. Chris had a sister who would gladly buy our twenty acres. The legal transfer could be completed by October, which meant we needed to find a new home. We drove down to Vernon in the north Okanagan; Daniel said he could look up some folks he'd known in the early 80's to get a lead on a place. I was ecstatic with the thought of living in a cabin after months in the yurt.

We pulled in to Partly Dave's Neighbourhood Garage, and Daniel jumped out to chat with Dave, who ran a business doing car repairs. In ten minutes, he reappeared.

"Dave's got an empty cabin on Silver Star Mountain. He said it's not much, but the rent's only a hundred bucks a month."

"Whoo-hoo! Let's go."

"Don't get too excited. He said we probably won't be able to drive in during the winter; we might have to walk in, and the neighbour's really particular because technically the road's on her property, but she has to grant right-of-way access."

We drove up Silver Star Mountain toward the ski resort, and halfway up the mountain turned left on Keddleston Road. A few kilometres along,

Daniel found the dirt road leading through the bush to the cabin. We bumped up the road a short distance until we saw the tall, ranch-style gateposts Dave said marked the entrance. On the other side of the gate an old VW bus had been abandoned in the trees, a relic from the 1970s back-to-the-land movement.

"This vehicle must belong to the owner; he's back in California," said Daniel.

A few hundred metres farther up the driveway, the cedar-shake cabin stood in a clearing. High on the south wall, the original hippie builder had cut a window in the shape of a Celtic cross.

"It's not built to code," said Daniel. "I guess that's obvious. Inspectors noticed it in an aerial photograph, but they let it go. They could have come in and demolished it."

We pushed open the wooden door and went inside. The mice had taken over, their droppings everywhere, on the kitchen counter and along the perimeters of the walls. In the main living area, a large picture window provided a lovely view of Swan Lake and the north end of the Okanagan Valley, if one could ignore the horizontal crack running across the pane. Wooden stairs led to a small loft for sleeping, just big enough for a queen-sized futon.

"I love it," I said. "Let's take it."

"Really? Just like that, it's okay?"

"It's a whole cabin. I'm so relieved we've found it. And we're fairly close to town. Tell Dave we're in."

"Okay, long as you realize it's totally off the grid. We'll have to buy an efficient wood stove. The airtight won't heat this place. We'll still have to haul water from town, but I know where there's another public tap where we can fill the water barrel."

Maybe now I was home.

That fall we moved the yurt and all our stuff from the Shuswap to the cabin on Silver Star Mountain. Daniel must have made ten trips, the pickup truck piled high on each run. We had already accumulated more heavy stuff, such as the yurt floor. Daniel dismantled the planks, marking each floor-board for reassembly on a level spot of ground next to the cabin. We wanted the yurt close by—its round simplicity and beauty were comforting, and re-minded us of our original goal to build a sustainable lifestyle in the country.

The Silver Star property was an eighty-acre strata, owned jointly by four partners, which meant we had acres and acres of quiet forest around us.

At night the coyotes yipped and I fell asleep to their singing. Sometimes we could hear Donna, our neighbour, splitting wood or banging around through the trees, but overall it was quiet in the way I had hoped.

It felt strange that we were no longer landowners. "We'll find something else," I said, "a beautiful, quiet piece of property." We had received a tiny amount of cash back from the land sale and I could not bear to put it toward our credit card debt.

"Maybe we will," said Daniel. "But I'm not waiting for that to happen. I'm going to build the kiln right here. This is where we live and this is where I'll build. I've found a spot a few yards off the driveway. There's a natural pool of water and the right slope for a kiln."

I thought it was a crazy idea. "Why don't you wait until we buy property again? Why would you build a permanent structure on someone else's land?"

"Hon, I don't want to think like that, always counting on the future. I'll work out a legal caveat or access agreement. I'm not going to keep dragging bricks around the country."

With that declaration, he called up a local driver and paid several hundred dollars to have the firebricks transferred one last time from the meadow in the Shuswap to the cabin on Silver Star Mountain.

Then he dug out the Things as They Are Pottery sign and hung it on the post at the bottom of the driveway.

I longed for that same sense of purpose in my life.

1,300 Degrees

By the time we finished moving into the cabin, the maple, poplar, and birch trees had shed their leaves and heaps of brilliant oranges, yellows, and reds concealed the forest floor. Invigorated by the brisk fall days, Daniel jumped up early each morning and lit a fire in the wood stove. By the time I climbed down from the loft, he was outside in the yard splitting wood, setting up rain barrels, or tramping around in the woods imagining the kiln.

While Daniel concentrated on kiln-building plans, I spent hours immersed in metaphysical books about the soul and intuition. This was not practical, I know, but I was compelled by a mystical hunger or longing to study. After a day of reading indoors, I would drive to town to take a dance class in the evening, another impractical pursuit given I was thirty-five years old and living in a small town. I auditioned for a community dance production of *The Velveteen Rabbit* and joined the cast, filling my week with rehearsals and more classes. Of course, there was no remuneration in community theatre, but I was never motivated by money or financial gain. Unfortunately, Daniel and I had the same disposition toward money, preferring to scrape by each month rather than work at a dull job.

Back from travels in Mexico, Christos and Alice rented a cottage in an old orchard outside town and were versed in local employment possibilities. They told us that seasonal jobs would be coming up soon with Weyerhaeuser.

"Go put in your application and you'll get a month of good work sorting spruce seedlings," Christos told us. "We've done it for a few seasons now."

Daniel was keen; I was leery. I couldn't imagine myself on an assembly line, but the unemployment rate was high in the Okanagan Valley, and once winter set in, there would be few jobs.

The reforestation-logging company hired us, just as Christos said it would, and we all reported for work at eight o'clock one chilly morning in

November. It was piecework; we were paid cents per tree. Alice was one of the fastest workers on the line; her small nimble hands sorted hundreds, maybe thousands, of trees a day. I felt more like Lucille Ball in the chocolate factory episode of *I Love Lucy*, except I couldn't eat the seedlings to dispose of them.

We worked in two lines on either side of a conveyer belt, and the spruce trees moved along in bundles continuously. The task was to grab a bundle of trees and determine which seedlings had the correct growth specifications for planting on reforestation blocks, and which could be tossed out. The workstation provided measuring tools and we were given precise instructions about root length, width, and overall size of the seedling. I took too much time to assess my seedlings, fumbling with the fine, hair-like roots, and the conveyor belt on my side stalled with a backlog of trees.

The time crawled; our first coffee break came at 10:00 a.m. The two hours felt like a day.

"I hate it!" I said to Daniel on the break. "I really hate it. I knew I would. We're not even allowed coffee at our workstation—that's so unfair."

"You'll get faster, just give it time. It's just a temporary job. You expect so much, Mary."

I did. I expected more from life than a seasonal job handling seedlings doused with insecticide. At thirty-five, the thought of returning to Weyerhaeuser every fall aroused panic in my soul. I stuck it out for three or four days and then gave my notice. Daniel, Christos, and Alice, shocked I would walk away from a paying job in the Okanagan Valley, put in four more weeks, working 8:00 a.m. to 4:00 p.m. until they were laid off.

Just before Christmas, I found a job in a health food store at the Village Green Mall, a small retail outlet that sold vitamins, and due to my years of experience, the owner hired me full-time. It was similar to the job I'd quit in Calgary, minus the aisles of organic bulk foods and the company of hip co-workers, but after the stint with Weyerhaeuser, I felt defeated and told myself to make the best of the opportunity.

I didn't tell my boss we lived without electricity or running water, or that I bathed in a plastic tub filled with hot water from cooking pots on the propane stove. I worried my clothes might smell of woodsmoke and I'd offend customers, but none of that proved to be a concern. It was the astonishing boredom of selling vitamins in a mall and the tedium of standing under fluorescent lights that wore on my spirit. I had moved to the country to create a new life, and somehow things had gotten worse.

By synchronicity, one day Doug, beautiful, long-haired Doug from Earth Harvest, appeared at the vitamin counter with his wife, Diane. They were travelling through the Okanagan on a road trip. After gushing hellos and exchanging news, he cast a look around my vitamin prison and said, "We're so sorry, Mary."

I was hurt. Did my life look that bad?

"Jobs are scarce here," I explained. "It's just temporary."

"You must miss Earth Harvest and working in a real food store," Doug said.

I didn't miss Earth Harvest in the least, or working in a bulk food store, but I liked Doug and Di, and their presence in the mall accentuated my plight, as though I had been hiding from myself, and they had shone a light straight into my heart.

"I miss all you guys, for sure," I said.

After they left, I popped a couple of chewable vitamin C tablets, letting the zing of the orange flavour obliterate any doubts that I could find a way out of this conundrum.

The driveway into our cabin was a long and winding dirt road. Technically, most of the road was on the property strata owned by our neighbour, Donna. Because we were renters and not owners, Donna controlled the road rules, and she issued unambiguous warnings. Under no circumstances were we to ice up the road or spin our tires, making attempts to drive up this winter. Donna drove an eight-cylinder Dodge pickup truck and she did not want to get stuck on her own road.

She instructed us in the backwoods method of winter driving. The trick, she said, was to sprinkle wood ash behind the tires as we drove; if we screwed up, she'd be plenty mad. Daniel didn't want to jeopardize our sweet rental deal, so he heeded Donna's advice, scooping wood ash from the cold stove into a bucket one morning after the first snowfall. Up until December, the wood ash technique worked well. As soon as we turned off the main road, I swung open the passenger door and leaned out like a stuntwoman, tilting the bucket of ash under the frame of the car, praying the ashes would coat our tracks, appeasing Donna.

"More! More ash," Daniel would yell. "I can feel the tires slipping!"

One night Daniel answered the phone, and recognizing his concilia-tory tone, my stomach fluttered. It was Donna.

"We're really sorry," he said gently. "We've been putting down ash, every trip. Every trip, one hundred percent. I had a bit of trouble tonight, but we really didn't mean to ice things up."

Donna did not give second chances.

"Sorry, hon," said Daniel, quietly hanging up the receiver. "We're gon-na have to park at the main road and walk in till spring."

For the rest of that winter, I trudged up the road in the dark, the coyotes howling nearby in the trees when I came home late after work and dance class. I kept a backpack in the car and carried in small amounts of groceries on each walk. There were nights, especially when the moon was full, when the walk was pristine, my footsteps crunching on the cold snow, the stars lighting my way. The blackness of the spruce trees and whiteness of the aspens surrounded me like mysterious companions. When I round-ed the last bend in the road, I was always met by a light glowing through the Celtic-cross window of the cabin. Daniel was home, stoking the fire, sketching designs for his kiln, Zip snoozing at his feet.

The next spring, Daniel began construction of a massive shed roof to shel-ter the kiln. It was the spot he had first chosen, a hill slope a couple of hundred metres from the cabin at the edge of the forest. He devised clever ways to manipulate huge logs on his own, setting up pulleys, and inventing strange methods of dragging the posts and beams into place. On my days off, I heard the rip of the chainsaw, the clink of hand tools, and thrashing in the bushes.

The finished roof was airy and elegant. Six vertical peeled posts, sacrificed from mature twelve-foot fir trees, supported the horizontal crossbeams, and above the massive rectangular structure, he had built an A-shaped plywood roof that sloped gently downward, criss-crossed by smaller beams underneath. The roof was large enough to shelter the kiln along with ten cords of split firewood needed for each firing.

Earth, fire, and ash, the primary elements of high-fired pottery. The process was alchemical, the transformation of base elements.

As Daniel inched closer to realizing his dream, I withered behind the counter in the vitamin store. One weekend at home, I blurted out my feelings when he came inside for lunch.

"Maybe you should take a turn working for a while? I'm sick of my job in the mall."

"What is it you want to do?" he sighed.

"I don't think it's fair that I'm the only one bringing in money. I don't know exactly what I want to do, but it's not selling vitamins."

"What makes you think I can just go out there and get a job? I might end up collecting bottles."

"Ha ha. I'm serious, Daniel."

"I'm serious too. It's hard. I'm planning on applying for one of those community employment grants. You know, the program for self-employed people to launch a business. Now that the shed roof is built, I was thinking I could pitch building the kiln as part of the whole business plan."

"Well, that's a great idea. I can help you with writing the proposal, figure out a budget and all that, but you could still get a job for now."

"I've been a fire lookout for twelve years. Who's going to hire me?"

"Maybe the BC fire protection service will hire you? The province is all forest, they must have fire lookouts."

"I've already checked into that possibility and I don't qualify."

"What do you mean, you don't qualify? Get out! With all your experience?"

"Yeah, I went in and they told me the first step was an eye exam and I failed. My eyesight isn't good enough." Daniel poked at a stinkbug on the windowsill. The insects lived in the cedar boards and clung to the windowsills in the summer heat. "The stinkbugs sure are out of control, eh?"

"Our finances are out of control. We have four credit cards we're making minimum payments on."

"Geez, hon. We're okay. I really did go in and do that eye exam, but fire protection services are different in British Columbia. They want twenty-twenty vision here, and you know my eyes, soft focus."

I wanted to squash the stinkbug.

"You mean Alberta Forestry never made you do an eye exam?"

"Well, when I went to the Hinton fire school, the first year I got hired, I did an eye test back then. I squinted and barely passed without my glasses. But it never affected my ability to spot a fire. Looking for smoke is about texture and colour and noticing subtle changes in the landscape. You don't need twenty-twenty vision."

"Except in BC," I said. "There must be something else you can do to make money here."

"I don't know what that would be."

"Well, how would you know if you've never done a job search?" I was exasperated.

"Okay, okay, I'll get a job then."

Two days later Daniel had a full-time job as a cook's helper at the army cadet camp.

"The army cadets!" I was aghast. "That's the military. What do they do there?"

"It's summer training for young guys who want to join the army. They do a lot of marching around and skills training, and they eat three meals a day in the mess hall. I start tomorrow at 5:30 a.m."

He rose at 4:30 a.m. the next day, humming cheerfully as he got himself ready for work. He returned home about 2:00 p.m.

"How was it?" I asked.

"I made a vat of scrambled eggs for three hundred guys this morning. It was great."

"So it's going to be okay. You don't hate it?"

"No, I enjoy it, it's fine. The head cook is a friendly guy and he's training me. Ever peeled potatoes for three hundred guests? Made gravy in a cauldron? I'm beat, though, gonna take a nap. You might want to run the generator and charge the battery so we have lights tonight."

"Okay. I forget how to start the generator."

"Really, you don't know how?" Daniel met my gaze. "I guess I usually do all that stuff, don't I?"

It was true. I had never learned how to use the chainsaw, maintain the generator, or do any of the other fix-it chores that were necessary to country living. I could split wood, except we bought split wood by the cord now. Daniel had built a beautiful Japanese-style outhouse, framed up garden beds, installed kitchen shelving, and hooked up two storeys of stovepipe. He hauled water from town on the flat-deck truck and syphoned it from the barrel into smaller, usable containers. He did more than the manly chores in the relationship. He had rolled out a fresh coat of paint on all the interior walls of the cabin, cooked delicious meals when we had friends over for dinner, and maintained a social network he had cultivated on his own. Maybe I had taken things for granted.

I vowed to become more practical, do more of the chores, and take swift action on my career. But I wasn't handy and I had no interest in manual work for pay. I felt suited to an advanced degree. I would go back to university and get a master's degree in psychology or counselling and work with people. Surely with a bachelor's degree in psychology I could get into a graduate program. I fired off an application to the University of Victoria because it had a summer intensive M.Ed. program, only to discover I was competing with hundreds of teachers who wanted out of the classroom and into the guidance office. It had been four years since I graduated, and my work experience was unrelated to psychology. How could I connect wheat grass juice and B vitamins to a profession in psychology? I bought a used, portable typewriter and a bottle of whiteout, and crafted cover letters, reinventing my resumé with transferable people skills and volunteer work in the arts.

I languished with a growing stack of rejection letters.

Cline Lookout—as it is june '90
birthday greetings
    fine june weather. 3 days socked in fog & snowing, blowing
    record rainfall…no lookin out—all lookin in
    have begun work towards establishing christian hospice
    foundation. asked elisabeth
    kubler-ross to come to calgary in this regard. good feelings
    on the issue (prog. moon
    conjunct north node), 5 degrees Taurus
    time for manifesting
    made some fine art so far. carved a crucifix—rodin-like (in
    all immodesty)
    archetypal, <u>beautiful</u>, yellow cedar. further work on red
    hat—now a work of art w/ red-
    tail feather, hawk feathers, mucho embroidery thread, red
    cloth—fine hat.
    some mandalas, of course—very beautiful. and a lookout
    collage celebrating full moon
    june 8. some nice polaroids as well. even poesie flowing.
    wheat grass growing in window, lettuce in a hot box on cat-
    walk. made friends with a
    hummingbird. good time in sweatlodge. holy mountain
    darshan.
    God is great.   good medicine to ya, for now,
                                    love john

The prose poem was hand-printed on the back of a postcard John made for Daniel's birthday, a photograph he had snapped of the interior of Cline Lookout. On display in the Kodak photo were antler bones, rocks, and feathers; a red Hudson's Bay wool blanket, a Mexican design carpet, woven fabrics and silk-covered pillows; and the red felt hat, mandala painting, and numerous other ritualistic, New Age objects. In the centre of the photograph, the prize: a large, handmade bearskin drum rested against the edge of the bed.

"John knows how much I'd envy that drum," said Daniel, gazing at the photo. "It's a one-of-a-kind object that you can't go out and buy."

Daniel had been making African-style djembe drums with goat hide and old wooden olive barrels. He hosted drumming circles in the yurt, and the drum jams attracted a small group of eager musicians, men and women from the local Okanagan area, who loved to improvise music. John's drum was ceremonial, reserved for prayer circles and rituals, too sacred to be brought out at a jam.

Maybe John positioned himself as the high priest and artisan on the mountaintop, and maybe wild bearskin trumped domestic goat, but soon Daniel would fire clay in his hand-built anagama kiln and he would present John with a wabi-sabi, ash-scorched tea bowl.

That fall Daniel and I organized a reunion of the Lookout Supper Club to celebrate Thanksgiving. We invited John and Dinah, Alice and Christos, Jim and Ingrid, and Athena and Tomas. Mired in divorce proceedings, we expected Tomas and Athena wouldn't attend the same social event, but we invited them both anyway, in case one wanted to join in. Tomas would be down from Mockingbird and had to find a place to live for the winter. Athena, like Ingrid, was back in classes at the university. In the end we were six for Thanksgiving: John and Dinah, Christos and Alice, and Daniel and me.

John had recently finished his fifth isolated season on Cline Lookout. He was euphoric that weekend, expounding on the good vibes at Gardom Lake, a nearby community in the north Okanagan.

"Yeah," John drawled, "eagles circled above lot number two when we were out here in the spring. Dinah and I are thinking we should buy. I could live in the Okanagan for sure."

Dinah laughed. "John forgets about where I would work if we lived at Gardom Lake."

"Come on, Dinah, you thought it was beautiful, you did." John had tied his hair back under a Tibetan-style burgundy woven hat, an odd contrast with his green rain jacket.

"It is, it's really beautiful, but I think we should buy a house in Vernon. It makes more financial sense right now. We can rent it out to pay the mortgage until we move here."

"I still think we should all buy land together," said Christos. He wore a colourful woven headband and jean jacket, his short beard and moustache the same length as John's. Christos and Alice had just returned from a trip to Guatemala, and their van was awash in turquoise and red: hats, bags, purses, and shirts they had bought as a business venture.

"We have some land we want to show you guys," said Daniel. He had finally taken off his blue work coveralls and donned a red flannel shirt and jeans for company. "This acreage is humongous. It's out past Lumby, on the way to Cherryville. They call it Bear Valley."

"All right, let's go tomorrow." Christos, like John, was more interested in country living than a bungalow in town.

"And after Bear Valley, we'll sweat. Gotta sweat our thanks for dinner." John smiled.

The next day we drove in caravan to Bear Valley, two hundred acres of rural land Daniel had discovered less than an hour east of Vernon. The acreage was a mix of open fields, rolling hills, and deciduous and evergreen forest, the wilderness of the Monashee Mountains on the eastern horizon. The property had been a commune in the seventies and eighties, and the dreams of the former owners lingered in the monstrous slash piles of brush and unfinished log buildings. We hiked around the property, exploring the abandoned buildings and visualizing all the projects we might create. There was so much space it was overwhelming; we imagined a retreat centre, workshops, an organic farm. John was obsessed with the Christian hospice idea and attracting big workshop names. He seemed influenced by the Lance reading, and he envisioned Bear Valley as a healing centre and rural hospice. But Dinah was more concerned about where her kids would go to school.

Daniel said if we bought this property, he could move the kiln from Silver Star brick by brick.

"It's totally possible," he explained. "You just carefully mark each brick as you dismantle it."

I groaned at the thought of moving bricks again.

Back at Silver Star, we built an outdoor fire to heat the sweat rocks, and when they were red-hot, we crawled inside the small willow frame under plastic and blankets, steam rising off the sizzling hot rocks, our heads bowed to protect our faces from the heat. When we couldn't endure another second, we bolted outside and drenched ourselves with cold water from five-gallon buckets.

Famished after the sweat, I prepared a vegetarian dinner, baked acorn squash, sweet potatoes, a vegetable salad, and pie, and we feasted late into the evening. We talked about owning land together at Bear Valley, as though the retreat centre was already on the edge of manifestation, about to be born.

How did the weekend pass without anyone saying, "Let's make an offer"? We had come together, sweated, and feasted, and then we hesitated, letting the portal close and the cloud of potentiality drift by.

The next spring Daniel completed construction of the kiln, figuring out how to build a sloping arch with bricks. He scheduled the inaugural firing for June. First, he had to crawl in and out of the brick mouth for three or four days, packing the unglazed pots together as tightly as possible, envisioning the path of the fire and keeping his best work toward the front where the temperature would stay hottest. After the fire was lit, it would burn for three days and nights, slowly coaxed to hotter temperatures until the kiln hummed at 1,300 degrees Fahrenheit for half a day.

I was not attracted to fire. I elected to look after food and refreshments for the three days, rather than tend the kiln. Daniel had attracted a crew of artisans and friends to help out, and after working through the first day without sleep, he organized a roster of shifts so he could at least catnap at times. Local studio potters Burt Cohen and Don and Isao Morrill, along with folks from the drum circle, showed up to sit with the kiln. The potters understood how to gauge the pyrometer reading and interpret the crackle of the fire. Daniel arranged old armchairs on the hard-packed ground in front of the kiln, and people sat in clusters, sipping tea and munching sandwiches that I carried down the hill every few hours on a serving tray.

I tried to sleep as usual, but the energy of the kiln fire intensified during nighttime hours, and I lay in bed and listened to embers sparking out the kiln chimney, praying we wouldn't start a wildfire. Daniel patrolled the area around the kiln and had cleared out the underbrush, but this was his first firing, and we had no hose with running water. As the kiln sitters pushed the temperature higher and higher, I was overcome by uneasiness.

By the third day he was exhausted, careening around the site in a layer of black soot and sweat, eyeing the pyrometer constantly, and calling out instructions to the crew. At a certain point, the heat plateaued and it became challenging to push the kiln hotter. Then it was time to feed the fire continuously with smaller pieces of kindling. It was like watching the final stages of a home birth; everyone was spent, but the contractions would become more frequent and more intense before the mother pushed out the baby. As an onlooker, I was no help, so I left the potters to it.

Up at the cabin, I relaxed in a lawn chair with a book and a can of Rainier beer. It was a relief to escape from the brick furnace on such a sunny June day. Then I gasped. Above the treetops, a thick cloud of black smoke billowed from the chimney. This must be what potters called reduction. When the kiln burned at the desired temperature, the mouth and dampers were shut tight and the sudden oxygen starvation caused smoke to rush down the kiln's length and swirl around the pots, baking and transforming the clay, and depositing a unique residue on their surfaces.

This was definitely the sixteenth-century part of the tradition. Black smoke drifted toward our neighbours to the northwest, and I desperately hoped they were not at home. Surely we could get fined for this kind of pollution. Sooty plumes of exhaust floated over the meadow, as the kiln was repeatedly shut down and starved of oxygen. Daniel had prepared me ahead of time for the industrial-style climax, but witnessing the black outpouring of smoke first-hand was disturbing.

Finally, at the end of the third night, Daniel called time and allowed the fire to die out. At last we could rest. As the eastern sky got light at 4:00 a.m., we lay in bed watching stinkbugs on the windowpane, whispering about the experience and wondering how many times a year we could survive the process.

"That smoke was like something out of a documentary on China or Russia. It's a bit much. Even for an artistic cause." I was so tired, but couldn't fall asleep.

"I know, it bothers me too, but it's how you get the special effects. Sure is a lot of work, eh?"

"I mean, how often do you think you could do this, realistically?" I was thinking sales numbers and how many pots Daniel could produce using this traditional firing method.

"I know what you're thinking. It's not really feasible for production. It's more an art thing. The amount of wood I burned is obscene. But I was thinking, maybe the kiln could double as a pet crematorium," said Daniel. "Animals wouldn't need that much wood to burn to ash. I think we reached the right temperature for cremation."

I laughed. "Yeah, maybe we could offer a pet memorial service. It might be a good part-time business."

"We'd probably need a special licence, though."

We lay silent in the dawn. Daniel lowered his voice. "You know, I don't think I'll live to be that old. I'll probably get cancer or something by the time I'm sixty."

"Why do you say that? Don't think like that." I had always felt I would get really old, and I wanted Daniel to live into his nineties with me.

"It's just a feeling I have about life, that's all."

I was too tired to answer. We fell into the void of deep sleep, our bodies slumped against each other in dreamtime, motionless, while Zip kept guard downstairs.

The kiln rested for seven days. At the end of the week, Daniel slipped away to open the sleeping dragon and inspect the effects. "I need to do this on my own," he said.

A few hours later he came back, quietly removing his shoes at the door, while I practically held my breath, afraid to know.

Then, he smiled. "It's beautiful! The firing worked, and I got some nice effects from the ash."

"Let's have a sale right away," I suggested. "A solstice pottery sale."

"I don't know what to charge for things. It's awkward putting a fair price on pieces I love."

"I could do that if you want. Photograph the best work for your portfolio and then we'll have a sale." I thought Daniel would be excited about selling the pots, but oddly, he was ambivalent. "Come on, we'll buy some Japanese saké and do an art opening. It will be fun."

"Okay. I just hate to part with the pots so soon."

I eyed Daniel; he was serious. "Are we starting a ceramic museum or a ceramic business?"

"I know, I know. It's just how I feel about the pots. But you're right, I need cash to buy more clay. I guess we should have a sale. The pots have to go somewhere."

He got on the phone and invited all our friends and acquaintances in the valley. We displayed the pots on wooden boards in the yard, and I milled around conjuring up prices as folks selected their favourite pieces.

"Ask Mary," Daniel kept saying, refusing to put a price on anything, other than simple tea bowls, for which he choked out the words "twenty dollars" and then looked forlorn as people fished for their wallets. I threaded my way among the crowd, listening to fragments of fire talk and pouring rice wine in tiny Japanese bowls. I felt in my element, mingling and selling, making change, and wrapping up purchases. By the end of the afternoon most of the firing had sold, certainly the most unusual pieces: the thick slab plates, teapots with wisteria handles, and the wide fruit and pasta bowls, imprinted with carbon designs from leaves or seashells. Gone.

"We did well," I said, counting bills. "Almost a thousand dollars in one afternoon." I was ecstatic. "I'll go to the bank tomorrow."

Daniel sorted the remaining collection of tea bowls, cradling each piece with both hands, touching the surface of the clay like a person without sight.

"I should never have agreed to this sale."

I spun around. "What? Are you kidding?"

"I'm serious. I'll never do it like this again. I need to live with the pots before I sell them. For at least six months. I can barely remember what I made and now it's all gone. How will I study the way the fire scorched the best pieces? I wanted to think about things without rushing. Make notes. Live with the pots."

His words scorched.

Carbondale Clay

Daniel said Carbondale Lookout had the best pottery clay in the whole world. It was pink, the colour of warm, exposed flesh. He wanted to find out how it fired in the anagama wood kiln.

"We'll bring a shovel and fill up a few burlap bags with that clay," Daniel said, knowing I would agree to a road trip. "I'm not sure how the pink colour will take the ash of a three-day firing. It might produce something really special."

"Carbondale? Who's doing that lookout these days?" I asked.

"McNeal's still on Carbondale. We'll surprise him. I was thinking we could go tomorrow morning."

It was the middle of August 1991. Daniel had been lookout-free for three years. He had last worked on Carbondale in 1986, the summer before we met. Carbondale was a trophy lookout: the drive-in mountain access made it possible to have friends visit; the location was so far south it was not overrun by hikers; and the beauty of the surrounding country, Waterton Lakes National Park and the Castle River valley, rivalled places like Banff and Jasper National Parks.

I had quit my job at Lifestyle Vitamins after Daniel got hired as the cook's helper. The owner had offered me a promotion to store manager, tempting me to stay, and I declined, terrified that in a few years I would turn forty and find myself behind the vitamin counter, a retail clerk, at Village Green Mall.

Since the "ransom" pottery sale, I had resigned from playing manager, and now envisioned a new direction for myself, along with an action plan for success.

For the first time ever, the University of Victoria was offering the prerequisite courses for a master's program in counselling psychology in Kelowna, a short commute within the Okanagan Valley. I had registered, knowing that if I did well in these courses and was accepted into the graduate program, I would then spend two summers doing coursework in Victoria and complete the practicum components during the winters in Vernon. I could earn a master's degree without a disruptive move, become a registered counsellor, and work as a professional. For the first time in five years, I felt optimistic about my work future. The classes in Kelowna started in mid-September; until then, I was on vacation. As for Daniel, he had pitched a pottery business to the local self-employment program and was receiving benefits for one year to make the business profitable. Hunting for clay was all in a day's work.

The next morning we drove south to Penticton, turned east on Highway 3, cruised through Grand Forks, Creston, and Cranbrook, and finally, hours later, reached the Crowsnest Pass, a giant wind tunnel, on the British Columbia–Alberta border. Here, the westerly winds blow over the Rocky Mountains, rocket through the pass, trumpeting across the prairie toward Pincher Creek and Lethbridge.

This was my first trip to the Crowsnest Pass. The small towns here, Coleman, Blairmore, Frank, and Bellevue, former coal-mining communities, were familiar places to Daniel. He said at the start and end of the fire season the lookout folks often met up in one of the local cowboy bars. They would gawk at the locals, working-class men with rough hands who had made a living picking coal or felling trees. One year, the night before the lookouts opened, he rode with McNeal on the back of his motorcycle to get a beer on the British Columbia side of the border.

"I don't know why he wanted to drive all that way for a beer," Daniel laughed.

I could not picture Daniel on the back of a motorcycle going out for a beer like one of the working guys.

He gestured toward an immense limestone mount on the horizon.

"Turtle Mountain."

To me, this part of Alberta was beautiful, but because I had never spent time here, it was also emotionally neutral. For Daniel, the landscape was connected to memories and major events in his life. He had stared at these mountains for years, fallen in love, gotten married and then divorced, always coming back to Carbondale. Over the years, Daniel had recounted many off-the-record stories related to jobs down here: secret lookout affairs, drunken parties with rangers in the Forestry bunkhouse, and sketchy flirtations with junior forest rangers. He had also read up on the early history of the lookout and firefighting.

The first cabin on Carbondale Hill had been built in 1928 and manned in 1929. A lookout observer had worked there throughout the Depression and had been especially valuable during the great wildfires of 1934 and 1936. In those days, when the lookout man spotted a lightning strike or smoke, he radioed the ranger, who saddled up and rode into the mountains on horseback to hopefully extinguish the smouldering tree. To combat large forest fires, the ranger had to get permission from the Calgary office to hire men and round up firefighting equipment.

In August 1934, a campfire sparked a wildfire on the BC side of the border and, fuelled by gale-force winds, raged east toward the Castle River valley south of the town of Blairmore. Ranger Frankish and Assistant Ranger Kovach received permission to mobilize men from the nearby Depression relief camps.

On August 7, two days after the fire was spotted, 145 men were assembled and trucked to the Castlemount ranger station, and from there they hiked for twenty-four hours to the fire line. The men packed in shovels, hoes, axes, pumps, water pails, and other supplies, such as blankets for sleeping at night. They would often take lunch at the fire line, devouring a tin of meat with some tomato and water. The original government fire report that the ranger completed stated, "What class of men were obtained? Relief men from camps at Coleman and Bellevue, some poor and others very good." The men were paid fifteen to twenty-five cents an hour, far better than the rate provided in the relief work camps.

Over the following days, the "relief men" constructed a fireguard nine kilometres long to control a wall of fire estimated to be eighty-four kilometres long. It would be three weeks before the fire was under control. It would be three months until the fire was fully extinguished.

As we drove toward his old lookout haunt, Daniel free-associated memories. He said he and McNeal had sparred over a few things at Carbondale in the past. One summer, McNeal discovered a 1926 survey stake near the lookout, half-buried in the ground. Pleased with his find, he hammered it onto a cupboard door with a good-enough-for-this-place attitude. The next year, Daniel was posted to Carbondale, and he pried the stake off the cupboard, planning to restore and frame it in a wooden display box, bestowing more dignity on the artifact. With many projects in various stages of incompletion, when the season closed, Daniel laid the stake aside to finish the next year. That fall the artifact was accidentally thrown out or picked up by Forestry employees who drove up Carbondale Hill to check on the lookout building.

The next year, Forestry sent McNeal, not Daniel, back to Carbondale, and McNeal fumed when he noticed the stake missing. Angry, he accused Daniel of purposely throwing it away, refusing to believe it was an accident.

"I absolutely did not throw away that stake," said Daniel, scanning the mountains as he drove.

I believed him; an old survey stake was exactly the kind of object he would treasure.

When we arrived at Blairmore, we pulled into the ranger station and Daniel asked the radio operator to call up McNeal and check whether he needed groceries.

"Bring libations—and curry paste" was the only request.

I scooted into the liquor store and picked up some beer. The local grocery store didn't stock curry paste.

From Blairmore we drove south on the 774, passed Burmis and the gas station and store at the hamlet of Beaver Mines. We followed the signs to Westcastle Park and the ski hill, before turning off the pavement and bouncing along a dusty gravel forestry road. We were probably driving over deep seams of coal and carbon; after all, our destination was Carbondale Hill.

I thought about all the men who had spent their lives underground, sweating in dark caverns, hauling out lumps of coal for which they were paid by the ton. The coal seams in southern Alberta were angled on steep inclines and full of pockets of sulphurous gas, making the work complicated and dangerous. The men hacked at the black seams with picks, installed timber cribbing underground to keep the mine from caving, and blasted the rock face with explosives to loosen up the coal. Year after year, workers had inhaled the black dust, until their lungs quit. Miner's lung.

I couldn't imagine any of the men I knew lighting explosives underground to pick coal or digging trenches in the bush to hold back a fire.

The key to the green forestry gate was hidden where McNeal said it would be. The road was washed out in places from annual spring runoffs, and rangers had thrown boards across the worst of it. Daniel geared down, and we crept uphill, the forest becoming sparse as we climbed higher, until finally we emerged out of the forest, the only surviving trees now a few scruffy pines, short and bent sideways in the wind, their roots clamped into the hillside. On each traverse of the hillside, the valley receded farther away, and the Rockies came closer into view.

The last three switchbacks were 180-degree turns around the embankment. Relaxed, Daniel coaxed the gas pedal, eyes moving between rocks on the road and the open space surrounding us. On the second-to-last switchback, he grasped the steering wheel tightly and accelerated.

"Hang on!"

He twisted the steering wheel to the far right, and the car made a wide arc, tires rolling off the gravel onto wildflowers at the edge of the cliff.

"If I don't get that one just right, I'd have to do a three-point turn on the incline, and that's no fun."

"Okay, but let's not drive over the cliff searching for clay." I unclenched my hands as we took the last switchback and the dirt road opened onto a clearing at the summit.

There was the orange-and-white Forestry building, a modern-day monk's cabin fastened to its concrete foundations, planted in the centre of a 360-degree view. As we parked outside the lookout, Daniel squinted to protect his eyes from a beam of intense, focussed light. McNeal stood upstairs in the cupola, tilting a mirror toward the sun and reflecting the light directly at Daniel.

"Got ya, didn't I!" McNeal flung open the lookout door, chortling, his large, burly frame wrapping Daniel in a bear hug. "Come on in, you guys."

The building had a similar floor plan to that of Mockingbird Lookout. Accustomed to Daniel's artistic flair, I half expected to find the same interior design elements, but McNeal was living more of a bachelor-style life. He kept things clean, tidy, and functional.

Within the confines of the small building, he looked taller than I remembered him at the drum party, his build larger, more muscular. His dark hair was cut short, a square conventional style, without any stray strands at the collar that might convey softness. I was immediately struck by his eyes—they were narrow and almond-shaped like the eyes of Pan, the mythological goat-man.

"Good timing, you guys. I just got serviced this week. Would you like to have curried chicken with rice for dinner? I make a good curry."

"We tried to buy curry paste, but we couldn't find any, sorry about that," I apologized.

McNeal pulled open a kitchen cupboard, revealing an impressive collection of Patak's curry paste. "No problem. I repeat the same grocery list with different visitors, just to make sure I never run out," he laughed. He dragged out some worn, blackened pots and pans, eager to entertain and show off his culinary skills.

I was curious about this man; there were so many lookout tales about his exploits. I trailed around the kitchen after him to form my own opinion. So far, he seemed friendly, generous, and witty. And he appeared to be a good cook, sprinkling whole cashews into the curry dish.

Daniel prowled around the lookout as though searching for traces of his life from five years ago. In the corner of the room, across from the kitchen table, an unusual painting was mounted in a framed box. The Japanese-style image depicted a deer reclining on the ground next to bare tree branches, and above, a white bird, wings spread, took flight. Black brush strokes on a tan background.

"You kept the deer?" said Daniel.

"Oh yes, I wouldn't take that down. It's a unique piece."

The deer had kept watch inside the lookout for about fifteen years. I could sense Daniel had a little art envy. If McNeal showed any inclination to get rid of the artwork, Daniel was poised to rescue the deer. John had originally brought the piece of art to Carbondale in the 1970s, framing and installing it in that corner of the room.

Daniel climbed the ladder into the cupola and was probably snooping around for lost and found objects, checking off a mental inventory of rare things left behind at Carbondale five years ago.

I stayed downstairs, feeling at home in the lookout, chatting with McNeal, watching him prepare food. He looked comfortable in his body, kinesthetic by nature, well coordinated in the small space. Animated by unexpected company, he conversed openly, sketching a mini autobiographical account of his life and decision to pursue English literature and religious studies at the University of Toronto. At one point in the conversation, as though to clarify his manliness, and counter any lambent impression of his intellectual proclivities, he bragged that he was akin to Heathcliff, the dark, mysterious, and unattainable character from the novel *Wuthering Heights*.

"I'm like Everywoman's Heathcliff," he said, watching my face for reaction.

I had read the novel and seen the film as a teenager, but I had never pursued studies in nineteenth-century English literature. When I heard the name Heathcliff, I naively imagined romance and intrigue.

He unpacked his life history, as though to convince me of the resemblance. Like Heathcliff, McNeal had grown up in a working-class family. Although he wasn't orphaned like the Brontë character, he said his mother had run off with another man, leaving the family home. He despised his father for allowing this to happen, referring to him as a "weak man." In an odd way, he was like an orphan, resentful of his familial past.

Eventually, in his thirties, McNeal discovered his scholastic ability and committed to academic studies. "I got through my oral comprehensives this spring," he confided, chopping peppers and onions.

"You're doing a Ph.D., right?" I had heard Tomas praise McNeal's academic achievements, proclaiming him to be a genius.

"That's right. I've been working on the dissertation all summer—in between looking for smokes!" McNeal laughed. "Being up here is very conducive to writing. I brought a laptop computer with all my files, and scanned in tons of research documents before I left Toronto, so I have everything I need."

"What's your Ph.D. about—something to do with Gnosticism, isn't it?"

"Yeah, I'm doing research to prove that Gnosticism wasn't a Christian renegade sect, the way religious studies scholars claim. I believe it originated in Egypt and evolved out of Egyptian thought."

"Wow, pretty big claim." I knew that most religious scholars believed Gnosticism was simply an unorthodox arm of Christianity.

"It is a big claim," he said, appreciating my interest, "that's right, big enough for a dissertation. Academia is such a minefield. The Christianity scholars have exiled me, they're such uptight purists, and the philosophy department is a boys' club of narrow rational thinking, so I found a place for myself in—well, overall I would describe it as comparative religious studies. My supervisor is an Egyptologist, famous in his field."

I could feel his passion for knowledge, his desire to be recognized for intellectual achievements. Already, he looked down on the world. Physically, he stood six inches taller than the average male, and intellectually, I could tell he scorned the academics writing uninspired theses on some obscure but safe aspect of religion.

"I have to read a language called Demotic," he said, "because a lot of the texts I'm dealing with are written in this script. Weird, eh, like demonic! That's what Catherine and I call it. Demonic."

"Catherine? Is that your girlfriend in Toronto?"

"Yeah, she's an Egyptologist, doctoral student. We met at U of T."

"And she reads Demotic?"

"Demotic, Greek, and other languages. She's very bright, excellent at translation."

"And has Catherine been out to Alberta and the lookout?"

"She was here for a week earlier in the summer. Airfare is expensive for a student, but she made it out. And luckily for me, my ex still lets me fly on her Air Canada comp, but that won't last for much longer."

I had heard about McNeal's former common-law wife. Daniel and Tomas talked admiringly about her, a career flight attendant, slender and attractive with brown, expressive eyes. She could get flight passes for friends and family members, a relationship bonus McNeal was loath to give up.

"I'm not sure how much longer she'll keep my name on file. But that's how I get back and forth from Toronto each season, courtesy Air Canada." McNeal guffawed. "I had to buy a tie, believe it or not. The Air Canada boys make it mandatory for flight pass holders to wear a tie—so I bought a fish tie."

"A fish tie? Get out!" I wasn't sure if McNeal was kidding or not.

"Literally, it's a tie in the shape of a fish. There's nothing they can do; it's a tie. But it's a fish."

Daniel came through the trap door and down the ladder from the cupola.

"A fish tie? I like the sound of that. I don't own a tie either; it's like a noose around a guy's neck."

"Exactly. Now do you wanna eat? Everything's ready. Just grab a plate and serve yourself off the stove."

The three of us crowded around the small kitchen table. McNeal positioned himself by the window next to the deer, so he could look out periodically. The sun was setting, but there was still an hour of daylight and always the possibility of a smoke.

McNeal and I had cracked open the beer; as usual Daniel passed on the alcohol, preferring water. We bantered about politics, the state of the world, and McNeal's travels in India and the Middle East. McNeal had an acute interest in politics and followed current events closely. It was August 16, and the Soviet Union was about to dissolve. In a couple of days, the Ukraine, Uzbekistan, Kyrgyzstan, and the other "stans," places we would not think about again until the post-9/11 world, would declare their independence from the Soviet Union. McNeal had a thorough knowledge of German and Russian war history, even though, on this visit, I had yet to learn that he designed and beta-tested World War II games. Myself, I was always game for a good political debate.

McNeal lit a cigar, blowing smoke rings out the open window. He sat with one leg crossed over the over, European-style, sophisticated, the ruler of his own quiet front. Daniel fidgeted with the fork and knife, restless with all the sitting around. He could tell you anything about fourteenth-century Japanese esthetics, but he was less keen on politics. I searched for a topic other than Soviet politics to include Daniel in the conversation.

From my chair, I could see the foothills rising gently out of the prairie benchlands and the grey peaks of the Rockies, bold on the western horizon. "This is one of the most beautiful places in the whole world." I proclaimed this like a prayer. "I mean, these mountains, the east slope of the Rockies."

McNeal tilted his head back and blew a smoke ring toward the ceiling, nodding. "Yeah, I've been to a lot of different places in the world, and this part of Alberta is certainly in the top ten."

We sat around the table in an awkward silence, the light and warmth of the August day fading.

"Well, Binky, you really made a break from the lookout scene, eh?" McNeal smirked at Daniel. "I thought you might be a lifer."

"Yeah, it's been nice spending summers down in the valley, making pots."

Not only had it never occurred to me Daniel might identify with the depressed rabbit stuck in a dead-end job, but the nickname hinted at the existence of male intimacy I knew nothing about. I wasn't sure whether the Binky label was affectionate, competitive, or homoerotic.

"You know, if you want, I could get you work on an archeology site overseas. You could use your ceramics knowledge in some of these places. Dig up ancient ruins, pottery chards. I could write you into a research grant."

"Hey, what do you think, Daniel? That sounds exciting." I thought the offer generous.

"Oh, you know me, Mr. Bleak. I'm not into travel. Just wanna stay home and make pots."

"Suit yourself, Binky. I thought you'd be jumping all over the chance to dig up pottery from 3000 BC. Learn carbon dating and all that, right?"

"Well, it sounds interesting."

"Interesting is such an interesting word," McNeal jousted. "It would be a numinous experience, Binky, numinous—big time."

"I see you still have the same old cutlery and dishes here." Daniel waved a chipped plate. "What are these, circa 1966?"

McNeal teased. "Oh, come on, admit it! You miss this job and living like a misanthrope, don't you?"

Daniel scratched at the chipped plate. "Kinda, but kinda not. Speaking of misanthropes, have you talked to Tomas this summer? I guess he's still on Mockingbird, eh?"

"We exchange missives now and then. I can't hear him on the radio down here, but I've called him up on channel six a few times."

"Tomas, what a guy! I haven't talked to him in a while." Daniel sighed, pushing back from the table. "I'm going to bring in our gear before it gets dark."

"You guys can sleep upstairs in the cupola, just arrange things to suit yourself." McNeal turned to me, unoffended by Daniel's lack of interest.

"This place has been a real boon for me, you know. I did lookouts all through my undergrad, my master's degree, and now the Ph.D. It's quiet down here; there's hardly ever a smoke to call in, so I can get a lot of work done. I don't know what I'd do without this job."

The metal stairs clanked as Daniel hauled our foam pad and blankets from the car up into the cupola. I was not prepared to call it an early night, craving more intellectual discussion.

"Another beer?" I pulled a can of Rainier off the plastic ring, handing it to McNeal.

"I think I'll switch to wine, thanks." McNeal produced a bottle of red and a corkscrew.

He told me about his forays into English literature before jumping over into religious studies. "I wrote about D.M. Thomas's *The White Hotel* and Conrad's *Heart of Darkness*," he said, as though offering me oysters and champagne.

Damn, I thought. I hadn't read either novel.

"You don't know *The White Hotel*?" he said, incredulous, holding my gaze. "Erotic fantasy. A woman imagines herself confined to a white room with her lover while the violence of the Holocaust is going on outside. A complicated book. You must read it."

As darkness enveloped the lookout, we spoke in hushed voices so Daniel could sleep undisturbed. Our whispers created the illusion we were telling secrets, sharing intimate details of our lives. I told myself: McNeal is just a friend. I am enjoying a warm summer evening with him, that's all. And I resisted the urge to linger there with him.

"I'm going to borrow your flashlight to go to the outhouse and then I'm off to bed."

Out of the blue, he asked, "Do you think men and women can be friends?"

"Of course, don't you?"

"It's impossible. Eros is always present." McNeal half smiled at me. He sat in the dim light, one leg crossed over the other, one elbow resting on the table, an index finger tapping the cigarette lighter.

"I've had male friends and we were truly just friends," I challenged. I hadn't moved from my chair, and McNeal made no move to find the flashlight. "You've never had female friends who were really friends? Come on."

He found my eyes in the low light. "Men are different from women in that way, and it's something women don't want to admit. Especially feminists. Things are never just platonic."

I wanted to stay up, debate, and drink more beer with him. Then I thought of Daniel, sleeping alone upstairs, and I winced with guilt. "It's late. We'll have to continue this debate another time." I stood up to go outside.

"Flashlight's on the counter next to the door."

As I went out the door into the night, I glanced back at the image of an army general who has just realized an infallible military strategy. I'm not doing a Ph.D., I thought to myself, but I can outmanoeuvre him. He's so self-assured, but his thinking is all wrong.

The next morning I slept through the weather sked. Daniel woke early along with McNeal and hung around the lookout, waiting for me to get up. As soon as I'd had coffee, we headed down the road to hunt for clay. Daniel had a spot in mind, across the meadow and down the slope, just off the road near one of the switchbacks. He brought the spade and burlap bags, and dug into the warm clay soil. McNeal and I marvelled at the pink colour.

"Carbondale clay," said Daniel triumphantly. "Carbondale clay!"

"You'll have to send me a bowl made from this stuff," said McNeal.

"First I need to experiment and find out how well it fires." He shovelled lumps of clay into the bag. "Maybe someday."

Daniel could be such a reluctant potter.

After the 1:00 p.m. weather sked, we said our goodbyes to McNeal and drove down the steep mountainside, stopping on the switchback to grab the bags of clay. We drove in silence for a while, and I wondered if Daniel would mention how late I had come to bed. What a strange, unexpected visit. After hearing all the rumours about McNeal, I hadn't expected to hit it off with him so well.

Once we were off the secondary roads and back on the paved highway, Daniel brought up the late-night kitchen party.

"What did you guys talk about for so long last night?" he asked without taking his eyes off the road.

"Oh, just stuff, politics, university, life."

"We call him Captain Midnight, you know."

"Captain Midnight?" I laughed. "What's that about?"

Daniel said McNeal had a reputation for late-night booty calls. Stories circulated about his sexual conquests riding his motorcycle, Big Red, up and down the mountain roads of southern Alberta to romance a lonely woman on a neighbouring lookout enamoured by his radio voice.

"I could care less who the guy sleeps with," he said. "But he did try to get it on with Eileen one year. That kind of ticked me off."

"Kind of! I guess so! What happened?"

One season Eileen worked alone on Carbondale Lookout, Daniel said, and, intrigued by Captain Midnight's advances, she had ended up in a heated embrace but disentangled herself, rebuffing him for his gruffness. There was no sequel.

"We had separated for a bit that summer anyway," said Daniel, "but it bugged me. It doesn't matter now. I let it go a long time ago."

"It doesn't sound like she found him a hunk of burning love." I could see how McNeal would be attracted to Eileen. And I could imagine how Eileen might find him too intense and too opinionated.

"I think she was curious about him, that's all. Listened to his radio voice all summer," he said, impersonating a deep, husky voice. "I told you the story about McNeal and the pack rat, didn't I? Everyone in Forestry knows this story."

"No, do tell!"

"Well, a few years ago, when I did Carbondale and McNeal did Ironstone, the neighbouring lookout, a pack rat took up residence inside the walls of his lookout building."

"Oh God, demolition crew, I know how noisy pack rats are at night."

"That's right." Daniel laughed. "All night the pack rat hauled and heaved debris, gnawing and chewing, while McNeal tossed in bed, banging on the wall and swearing out loud at the rodent."

Each morning, at 7:00 a.m., he cursed the alarm clock, short on sleep. He knew that the pack rat was not going to suddenly move out; he had to outwit the rodent. He reasoned that food would lure the pack rat away from its nest. The generator shed was a few metres from the lookout building, so one night he put out some cheese, peanut butter, and crackers and left the shed door open, knowing the large rat would discover the delicacies. Sure enough, after several hours, McNeal went back with a broom and closed the door, locking himself inside the engine shed with his bushy-tailed enemy. He had a wire travel cage for his cat, and his plan was to sweep the rat into the cage.

McNeal and the rat faced off; around and around the generator they went. He swatted and swiped, but each time he backed the rat into a corner, it ducked under the broom, scooting past him and taking cover under the generator. McNeal poked, prodded, and finally swept the terrified creature into the open cage.

"Rat, you're about to go for the ride of your life," he cheered in triumph.

The next day he called up Chopper John, the helicopter pilot who did fire patrols in the district, and asked him to stop by Ironstone.

When the helicopter landed, Chopper John was on board with Barry, the initial-attack boss, and a few of the firefighting crew in their orange coveralls. McNeal ran out to the helicopter pad, carrying the cage, yelling over the noise of the engine. The rat was doing gymnastic stunts inside the cage, panicked by fear.

"I just need you to drop this off at Carbondale," said McNeal. "It's no big deal, just a joke I got going with Daniel over there."

"You want us to leave it over there?" screamed one of the guys in the back of the helicopter.

"Yeah, just open the door and let him go over there. But bring me back the cage. I need the cage back."

They all laughed. One of the guys in orange reached out and McNeal handed him the cage. The rat's large doe eyes bulged out of its head. The helicopter door slammed shut, and McNeal ran back inside the lookout.

"No doubt he sat by the radio, waiting for Chopper John to call me up. And of course, within minutes, I heard the thwack, thwack and the pilot's voice vibrating from the motion. I wasn't going to sit inside the lookout with those guys on the helipad," said Daniel. "So I went outside and headed toward the commotion."

The initial-attack guys had opened the rear door of the helicopter and put the cage on the ground. Then one of the crew leaned down and opened the latch. The rat dashed toward the outhouse on the edge of the clearing, free to build a nest at his new lookout home.

"They told me they had come from Ironstone, and I told them I don't mind pack rats," said Daniel. "Pack rats are one of my totem animals."

As long as the pack rat took residence in the outhouse and stayed out of the lookout building, they would get along just fine. He would far rather have McNeal ship the creature over for adoption than have it killed.

"I can't believe Alberta Forestry flew a pack rat from Ironstone to Carbondale Lookout because McNeal wanted to play a prank on you," I said.

"I know. It's a guy thing. But that's not the end," said Daniel.

The next year McNeal was posted back to Carbondale Lookout, and the pack rat was still living in the walls of the outhouse. Every time he sat down in the outhouse, he worried that the rat might even the score, biting him in the butt.

"So you kind of got even, then?"

"As far as the rat goes," said Daniel.

That was more than enough talk about McNeal.

"I'm so glad my courses are starting soon," I said, giving Daniel an affectionate squeeze.

As much as I loved our life in the country, I needed more intellectual stimulation. The folks who came to the drum jams and kiln firings were good-hearted people, but I was still dissatisfied. What did I want? When I was in the city, surrounded by mainstream society, I gravitated to the fringe, and now that I was most definitely on the fringe, I desired more sophisticated, intellectual friends who engaged at the centre.

The August sun was like a flame in the sky, lighting our way home. Hours later, as we bumped along the gravel road leading up Silver Star Mountain, I realized we were practically living on a lookout here: the generator and the plastic water barrels; the potholed, winding road leading to our cabin; and, at the top, an exquisite view of the north Okanagan Valley and Swan Lake.

A couple of weeks later, in early September 1991, I booked a seat on a flight to Toronto to visit my family. I had checked my luggage as late as possible and rushed through Calgary International Airport on my way to the gates.

When I strode into the empty departure lounge, I gaped to see Mc-Neal sitting alone on a bench, the fish tie hanging down the front of his shirt.

"Hey, you're a bit last-minute, aren't you?" he said flippantly.

"We've got loads of time—a full five minutes," I replied.

We strolled in the direction of the departure gate, passes in hand, the last ones to board the plane.

"This is a nice bit of synchronicity, don't you think?" he said, smiling. "I mean, what are the odds that you and I would book the same flight to Toronto? Shall we sit together?"

"I don't know if we can swap seats. What do you think?"

"Let me take care of it." He spoke in discreet tones with a flight attendant, and within seconds he was seated next to me.

McNeal was such a big man that he barely fit into the middle seat, so I offered my aisle seat. He folded up his limbs to contain his size, but our arms and thighs pressed lightly together. I sensed his presence in that compressed situation, the way I had at the lookout, except this time we were alone. I couldn't get over the fact that we were on the same flight. There were departures from Calgary to Toronto every hour of every day, but we had chosen the exact same flight.

Throughout the three hours, we talked non-stop about synchronicity, relationships, and the strangeness of life. It was as though we had picked up the thread of the midnight lookout conversation without missing a beat. It was a heady, delirious feeling, a roller-coaster ride at thirty-five thousand feet. I laughed at everything he said, leaning against his arm and thigh, letting my hand linger on the armrest next to his, and stretching out my long slim fingers, marvelling at how small they looked next to his thick hands. The conversation landed on Jung and the unconscious. I said Jung had received no more than ten minutes of lecture time in my whole psychology degree, Freud maybe thirty. He said he'd never been in therapy, too expensive, but in future, when he was earning a good salary, he might explore analysis. I lost all sense of peripheral vision and the world narrowed, occluding everything except me and him, side by side, word by word.

When he excused himself, I wondered if we could both fit inside a Boeing 737 washroom. Should I count to ten and then follow surreptitiously? Maybe he had the same lascivious idea? He would leave the door unlocked, and I would squeeze in, throwing my arms around his neck and shoulders. And why was I thinking about sex with him, on a plane—in the economy cabin? What was wrong with me?

We parted ways at the baggage carousel in the Toronto airport. I waited for an invitation. McNeal was travelling downtown to Spadina Avenue, and I had to go east to the Scarborough suburbs.

"We're going to see Cirque du Soleil this week. You're welcome to come with us." He wrote his phone number on a scrap of paper.

I was positive the spark that ignited inside the Boeing was mutual, but he said "we."

"I'd love to meet your girlfriend," I said. "I'll call."

"Give me a shout and we'll get together while you're here."

Later that week, I met up with McNeal and Catherine, a petite redhead, at the Cirque du Soleil show downtown. A few days later, I rendezvoused with him for afternoon drinks at a pub near his apartment at 666 Spadina Avenue. The address might have been warning enough. He said that he and Catherine had deconstructed the performance and decided it was mediocre spectacle. He was adamant in his opinions. I was attracted to his fiery disposition.

After several beers, McNeal ended the session, saying he had dinner plans. We exchanged hugs and parted ways on the street. I felt a slight roughness as his chin grazed my cheek, and I pulled back, confused. He had almost kissed me. Almost. Perhaps he was testing my loyalty to Daniel. We walked in opposite directions along Spadina Avenue, and halfway down the block, I stopped and looked back. Of course I was loyal.

I watched his back in the distance, and then, sure enough, he turned, yelling over his shoulder, "I'll write."

In November 1991, while Daniel fired the anagama kiln a second time, I dreamt about a big furry rat. It was so vivid I recorded the dream in my journal. In the dream, I watched someone stab the rat over and over again, but it would not die.

Finally, the rat was thrown into the kiln fire and burned to ash.

That winter, McNeal sent personal letters during the holiday season, one to me and another to Daniel, sealed in separate envelopes inside the same package. For me, he also enclosed a book, *The Gnostics*, by Jacques Lacarrière; inside the front cover he had written a dedication in Coptic or Greek that included a reference to "Mapia," the Coptic term for Mary, perhaps a phrase from the mystic Gnostic gospels, the Gospel of Mary Magdalene or the Gospel of Philip, texts dear to McNeal, in which Mary Magdalene was preserved as a companion of Jesus, and in which it is stated: "The Teacher loved her more than all the disciples and often kissed her on the mouth." Underneath the Coptic inscription he wrote, "Best wishes for '92."

I found nothing flirtatious in the letter or gift, but then he telephoned from Toronto on New Year's Eve, his rich baritone voice so close, I squelched a sudden impulse to flirt over the phone. He must be noodling about in the downtown high-rise apartment, unsure how to spend the evening. He made no mention of Catherine, just that he was sipping red wine and listening to Arabic music. You can probably hear the oud, he said. Sitting on the wooden stairs that led to our sleeping loft, I prolonged the phone call, asking about his dissertation, the Toronto winter, and how likely it was he'd return to the lookout next spring.

"Do you want to say hello to McNeal?" I chirped at Daniel, waving the phone like a white flag, aware McNeal and I had been hunkered down in conversation for almost half an hour.

Daniel took the receiver, chatting with him about the coming lookout season. It was the main thing, one of the only things, they had in common.

I yanked open the door of the wood stove, stoking the fire before laying down another log.

"You guys sure had a lot to say." Daniel flipped through the pages of a pottery magazine.

"Yeah, McNeal's a talkative guy, you know him, going on about Egypt and gnosis, and high rents in Toronto."

"Uh-huh."

That was it. Uh-huh. I half expected the need to assure him the call was nothing, but before I could say more, he dropped the whole incident.

"You know what, hon? I think I want to go back to doing fire lookouts next year. I'm going to call up Forestry next week and put in for a lookout in the south, in the Bow-Crow."

I choked on my beer.

"A lookout? Daniel, are you kidding? You just got the kiln built and the pottery studio up and running. You've had two successful firings. Why go back to lookouts now? I think you can make a go of the pottery business here."

"Nope. It's too hard making art and having to sell it. I want to make pots without that pressure. I'm not a production kind of guy. I think I can get Moose Mountain."

"You left on good terms, right?"

"Yeah, of course. The rangers like me. I'm a good lookout man."

"Well, if that's what you want. But I don't really get this plan. We're able to live here for so cheap."

Daniel's mind was already far away. "Moose is outside Bragg Creek, an hour from Calgary. You could hike up whenever you want."

"How long a hike is it?"

"Well, it's almost three hours each way, but you'd be sleeping over so that's not so bad, is it?"

"I don't want to live alone in this cabin for five months every year. If you do a lookout near Calgary, I'd rather move back there and find work in the city. Maybe I could live with Athena for the summer, or at least for a while."

"That's a great idea," said Daniel. "Athena would probably like a roommate. Moose is beautiful; it's at 2,400 metres, way above the treeline, big rock boulders everywhere, really something. You can hike right to the door. The building is small, though, twelve feet by twelve feet, no cupola, not nearly as large as Mockingbird or Carbondale."

"I'll call Athena and see what she thinks about a roommate."

As I spoke the words, I heard the dishonesty in my voice.

McNeal would be back on Carbondale in May, and the lookout was only three hours south of Calgary.

Spadina Avenue

In February, Daniel received confirmation from Alberta Forest Service that he was hired back, assigned to Moose Mountain Lookout, southwest of Calgary.

"They're putting me up May 1," he said, waving the letter like a winning lottery ticket.

"You're awfully excited about leaving."

"It's the paycheque, hon, the regular paycheque I'm excited about. This means when I come home in the fall, we'll have money to do things."

My counselling practice courses wrapped up at the end of April, which meant I could travel with Daniel to Calgary on the thirtieth, and maybe fly up to Moose with him when they opened the lookout.

"Remember, if I get accepted into the program at UVic, I'll be spending most of the summer in Victoria." I expected to get the results of the application process by May.

"We'll be okay, though, right? Maybe you can come out to Alberta in September? Weather's good there in the fall. We'll drive back home to the Okanagan together."

Daniel was right; everything was working out. I would earn a master's degree while he worked on the lookout for the next few summers. Then, in the winter I could do a practicum placement in the Okanagan; he would make pots. Soon, I'd be employed in a new career and we'd have enough money to put a down payment on a small acreage.

So sure were we of our good fortune, and the sense that the last few years of financial strife and thwarted plans were behind us, that we took a drive into the Larch Hills and the countryside north of Vernon, green, rolling farmland, fruit trees and mixed forest, imagining ourselves property owners again. There was a place near the town of Enderby that attracted us, the Grandview Bench, flatland at the top of a low forested mountain, pockets of farms and treed acreages, many with lookout views of the Okanagan Valley spreading to the south, a bit of wildness and a bit of farming.

"Maybe we can find a piece of land on the south side of the bench," murmured Daniel. "It'll be a little cooler up there, but I heard there's a couple who grow ginseng and echinacea."

I nodded, staring out the window at the frozen fields, bare poplar trees, and snowy spruce trees. Like refugees in a new land, we dared to dream again, almost afraid to voice the hope that maybe, with a touch of grace and clear intention, we could plant seeds and they would thrive.

"If we get a long, hot spring, the ranger might want me back in April," he said wishfully. "I'd be on payroll that much sooner."

It was the warmest winter on record in Calgary and southern Alberta. In February 1992, temperatures spiked to twenty-two degrees Celsius, unheard of in that part of the country. Elsewhere in the world that month, Bush and Yeltsin met to formally celebrate the end of the Cold War between the United States and Russia, and inaugurate a new era of friendship and co-operation.

Indeed, the future of the world and our individual destinies looked promising.

In March I made another trip back to Toronto. I must have been bushed after spending winter in the cabin without electricity or running water, because it had been only six months since my last trip. Whatever my purported reason for flying across the country again, after arriving at my parents' house in Scarborough, I telephoned McNeal. To chat.

Without hesitation, he checked his schedule and suggested we meet downtown for lunch in a few days.

I got off the subway at the St. George station and McNeal met me at the corner of Bloor Street. The spring day was crisp and bright, so we walked south on Spadina Avenue in the sunlight, headed toward Queen Street. McNeal talked about his studies in early Egyptian religions, scoffing about the New Age folks who always asked him about the lost civilization of Atlantis. "They're such morons," he jeered. "They assume because I'm studying Egyptian history I'm searching for clues to Atlantis. It's so tiresome."

I winced, inwardly. Those "morons" likely included a number of my friends. I certainly didn't mention how Lance had said that Daniel incarnated in pre-Atlantean times.

Before we got to College Street, he had already acquainted me with some major tenets of Gnostic cosmology. He said Gnostics perceived the material world not only as a dark prison, but also as the mistake of a failed angel or demiurge, a creation that should have never come into being, but which we were now condemned to suffer.

Here was a belief system that should come with a lifetime prescription for Zoloft, or at least a warning about the risks of depression. Even on a sunny spring day, a perpetual optimist like myself felt dragged down by this interpretation of reality, but I could sense that McNeal had shackled himself to the Gnostic world view. I should have pointed out how the polarization of matter as darkness and evil, and spirit as luminous and good, was a theme common to all fundamentalist religions. And inevitably, women got lumped in with the dark matter and evil. But not having comparable academic credentials, I stifled the urge to challenge him.

I aligned with the Hindu yogic view that discriminates between the relative and the absolute, two aspects of one ultimate reality. At the level of relative reality, the world we experience is of course composed of varying degrees of good and evil, which we discern based on our moral and cognitive development. But underlying the diversity of all forms is the eternal, absolute, and unmanifest itself. "The reality of duality is unity," Maharishi wrote in *Science of Being and Art of Living*.

I appreciated that Gnosticism, in its contemplative form, understood subjective experience to be a living laboratory of consciousness, direct perception of the divine our ultimate destiny. But the mythological explanation about demigods and mistaken worlds of creation sounded like a conspiracy theory. I embraced the yogic world view—physical matter as the manifest aspect of the infinite and, therefore, sacred.

"It's a bit depressing, don't you find? I mean, a view of the material world as evil and separate from spiritual reality?" I wasn't ready to frame life on earth as imprisonment in a grand concentration camp.

McNeal was adamant. "Well, sure, it's a bit dark, but look at the amount of suffering in the world. There's a genocide going on in Yugoslavia, there are hundreds of thousands of poor bastards starving to death every year, and we just go on destroying the environment. That's real evil. Don't give me that positive thinking crap."

"I'm not, I'm listening, and I'm a lefty, so take it easy."

"Sorry, I'm passionate about this."

"Clearly."

"I'm also a bit of a contradiction. I want to tell you something, but don't freak out, okay?"

"I promise. Tell me." I half expected him to confess to an affair.

"I spent the winter doing a ton of research for these games I'm designing on contract. War games." He chuckled nervously. "I think I can make a bit of money with it too."

"What kind of war games?"

"They're World War II scenario games based on real-life battles. I had to bone up on the minutiae of various military strategies and their historical outcomes."

"It doesn't freak me out, if that's what you're wondering. I guess it surprises me. Not something I'd be into."

"Good. Some folks practically write me off over this, so I like to be up front with it. I spend a lot of time on the research these days, although I do like to point out that military intelligence is an oxymoron."

I laughed, caught off guard by the juxtaposition. I was enjoying his wit and feverish opinions about the world, but I was tired of walking aimlessly. "Where do you want to eat? How about the Queen Mother Café?"

"Sure. Kind of yuppie for me, but okay."

As we waited in line to be seated, McNeal leaned over and blurted, "You do realize I wear my heart on my sleeve?"

"Uh, if you say so." Surprised, I had no clever response. Why was he telling me this now?

He mulled over the wine list. "I know it's early in the day, but what the heck. Let's have a glass of wine."

While he signalled a waiter, I studied his face, convinced he was wearing mascara or eyeliner. Had he dabbed on makeup before our lunch meeting? I dropped my gaze, not wanting to stare. McNeal had the longest eyelashes I'd ever seen on a man; they curled upwards like dark tendrils reaching toward the light.

He made a wine selection for both of us. I was surprised by his chivalrous behaviour, but as a beer drinker, I didn't care whether we drank Pinot Grigio or Sauvignon. Besides, I was more interested in the metaphysics than the menu. We sipped our way through two glasses before lunch arrived, which was little more than romaine lettuce and croutons.

"We should have ordered a whole bottle," said McNeal. With that regret aired, he flagged our waiter and did.

I was woozy and losing concentration. Failing to solve the problem of world evil, we abandoned that endeavour and replaced it with flirtatious self-disclosure. Each time I drained my glass, McNeal splashed in more wine. He told me how he had met Catherine in a class at the university, how she was younger than him, and closer to finishing up her dissertation.

"She's really into the goth scene," he said.

Now this made sense for a woman fascinated by Egyptian tombs and burial sites. She had moved into his apartment at 666 Spadina after the recent ending of his ten-year common-law relationship. Technically that made her a rebound girlfriend, an observation I kept to myself.

"Maybe she's just after your address," I kidded. "Clearly, she's turned on by the number 666 and the sign of the beast."

"Could be," McNeal laughed. "She's really into vampire culture."

Catherine was by all accounts an edgy woman; however, I shifted the conversation and shared my plans to go back to university and get a master's degree, including the bit about Daniel and I having to live apart for a few lookout seasons.

"Will your relationship survive that arrangement?" he asked mischievously.

"Daniel and I are tight," I said without hesitation. "We don't have to do every last thing together like some couples."

We carried on probing boundaries, exploring our pasts, assessing the stranger on the other side of the café table. By now, the lunch crowd had not only gone back to work, but also gone home for the day. The restaurant was quiet, and servers rotated breaks before the dinner rush.

"I don't think monogamy is natural," said McNeal. "It's an ideal to aspire to, but it takes time and may not happen in every relationship. Let's face it, we all have attractions, and it's better to work through and resolve them—not out, but through."

"I think it's a choice," I answered.

He reached across the table, gently cradling my fingers, toying with the silver rings, as though we were a lovestruck couple. I swallowed the last dregs of wine with my free hand. I let him trace the outline of my fingers without pulling back. Releasing the caress, McNeal fumbled in his wallet for a credit card, while I dug into my purse for some cash.

"I'll get it," said McNeal. He stood up to put on his coat and scarf. I felt small next to him. "Come on, let's go."

The light on Queen Street was fading, the low March sun obscured by Toronto's brick buildings. He put his arm around my shoulders, guiding—or was it pushing?—me toward Spadina Avenue.

"The subway's the other direction." I stopped in the middle of the sidewalk.

"We're going to a hotel now," McNeal leaned down and kissed me on the mouth. "I want you. Come with me, this way."

"A hotel? I don't know."

He grasped my arm, pulling me toward Spadina Avenue. I broke free and walked briskly east on Queen Street away from Spadina, then slowed to a standstill in the next block. What was I doing? I needed to think on my own, to get away from him for a few minutes. My heart raced with anxiety, but my mind circled, slow and dull from the alcohol. I was conflicted and drunk, a notorious combination for regret. He was almost double my weight, yet we had drunk close to the same amount of wine. I stole a look down the block and our eyes locked. He stood, resolute, sure of himself. For a moment I nearly disappeared into the crowd, shaking myself free of the spell and rushing home. McNeal, a head taller than the other pedestrians, stared back like a hypnotist, and I surrendered, a sleepwalker, threading my way back to him.

He did not walk to meet me halfway.

He had a nearby hotel in mind: the Victorian-era Spadina Hotel at the corner of King Street and Spadina Avenue. Sleazy and cheap, the hotel had been part of Toronto's punk music scene and was known for the Cabana Room, a tacky bar on the second floor where the Rolling Stones, Leonard Cohen, the Tragically Hip, and other iconic bands had performed after hours. I had been to the Cabana Room in the eighties, when my musician brothers played the room, and for this reason I had a good feeling about the place.

The front desk clerk handed McNeal the key to room number seventeen, charging forty dollars to his Visa card. Upstairs in the shabby, carpeted hallway, the good feeling evaporated. The room had one double bed with creaky mattress springs, a wooden chair and window curtains that had been fresh during the war years. The bathroom, at the other end of the hall, had one shower and several toilet stalls. There was no preamble, no conversation; we removed our clothes, got in the bed, and performed functional orgasmic sex, missionary-style. There was an urgency, almost desperateness, in his embrace, a goal-oriented maleness that barred any gentleness.

Afterwards, when I got back from the bathroom, McNeal was already half-dressed and ready to go.

"Do you wanna see who's playing downstairs?" I assumed we might hang out together, order food, or see who was onstage in the Cabana Room.

"I have to get home," he said, grabbing the room key, as though he'd turn into a pumpkin after 9:00 p.m.

Thrown off by his unexpected abruptness, I dressed. We were back on the street in less than an hour.

It was damp, cold, and snowing lightly. Picking our way through the wet streets, we stopped to eat at an Italian takeout joint on Spadina near College Street. They sold pizza by the slice on paper plates—thick-crust pizza with yeasty dough and overcooked cheese. McNeal grabbed two stools at the counter facing the large plate-glass window onto Spadina Avenue. I cringed under the brightness of the fluorescent lights. It was dark outside and all I could see was my own shadowy reflection in the glass.

"This is my neighbourhood and more my style," he said. "I'm not crazy about those chi-chi restaurants on Queen Street."

I fixed my hair in the reflection, astonished by my dishevelled appearance.

"It's the just-fucked hairstyle," taunted McNeal.

"Ha." I stuffed the white dough and stringy cheese into my mouth, too famished to reply, starved more by the lack of affection.

The day of wooing was over, and I had made the conquest so easy. Now I had an hour-long subway and bus ride back to Scarborough, not to mention a four-hour flight to British Columbia. McNeal hadn't left his own neighbourhood.

The next day he phoned and I took the call in my father's writing room for privacy.

"Hey, my dear, how are you doing? Quite the day yesterday, wasn't it?" McNeal sounded upbeat.

"I'm fine."

"Well, I just wanted to check in. Don't want you to think I'm some kind of cad."

"No, of course not."

"When do you go back west?"

"I'm here for a couple more days."

"Well, it's only six weeks till the lookout season starts. If Daniel's going up to Moose Mountain maybe we'll cross paths in Calgary? I'll be flying into Cowtown beginning of May and renting a car to get down to Carbondale."

"All right." I was confused, guilt-ridden, and uncomfortable with such a forthright deceit strategy. "I guess we'll just have to see how it all untwirls—as Tomas would say."

"Ha! Tomas! I must call him. But don't mention any of this to him. He wouldn't approve, you know."

"Oh God, no. I haven't seen Tomas since Daniel and I left Calgary. It's been years now."

"Okay, well, I probably won't write before the seasons starts. I have a lot of work to get through before this semester ends. But I enjoyed our tryst, I want you to know that."

Back on Silver Star Mountain, I panicked whenever Daniel looked at me closely, fearful he intuited my betrayal, but he never questioned my activities in Toronto. One day, not long after my return, he wandered around the studio humming an old blues tune under his breath, a song about heartbreak and the ending of a relationship, and for an instant I thought he was mocking me. The melody surfaced regularly for several weeks. Now and then he sang a few verses, absent-mindedly, as he packed art supplies or hauled firewood inside.

Although Daniel was absorbed in figuring out how to jam the Subaru with as much stuff as possible—packing had become an engineering feat—I was sure his unconscious mind trapped thoughts or emotions from the larger field of awareness. Never before had he sang or hummed this song, but he was singing about us. The melody disarmed me.

Then in April, just weeks before we were due to leave for Alberta, we each had salient dreams. Daniel was disturbed by a recurring dream about the lookout. In the dream, he becomes aware that the lookout season is halfway over and he has forgotten to report the weather. He panics with the realization that he's been at the lookout for a couple of months and hasn't done the daily weather even once. *I better call in the weather,* he thinks to himself, picking up the microphone, but he can't remember his call sign. *Okay, maybe I'll just call up the ranger and he'll say my call sign when he hears my voice.* Then he feels sick to his stomach, realizing he can't remember the ranger's call sign either. He can't speak over the radio without a call sign identifying a location, which means he can't use the radio and he can't contact anyone else either. No matter, maybe he'll remember the call sign later. *Oh my goodness, smoke, I should be looking for smoke!* If he can't do the weather at least he can check for smoke, except that now he notices the wooden shutters of the building are closed and he can't see out. He's inside staring at dark window shutters, unable to see the forest or the mountain peaks. *I wonder if I've missed a smoke?* He's alone inside the lookout at the top of a mountain, unable to see or contact anyone, and the forest could be burning. The terror of the dream wakes him up.

My dream was less anxious than Daniel's, but just as odd. I was disturbed by a dream about McNeal, of which I could not speak, so I recorded the dream in my journal.

The Test—Sending Sound

I am with a guide of some sort. I decide to contact McNeal. The guide explains that I must "sound out" his name and if he is the right level of consciousness and "okay" he will be able to pick it up. The sound goes out. I see it travel through black space; it ripples out for a long time. Finally I see it make contact and McNeal acknowledges the sound like a hit on the head. The guide and I are satisfied.

Underneath the dream record, I added a note about how the sound was like the vibration of *om*, reverberating and resounding through space. I interpreted the dream as a sign that McNeal and I were connected on a soul level.

Then why did I not simply cultivate a soulful friendship, enjoy good conversations and debates about spirituality and keep the bedroom door closed tight?

As Daniel prepared for the lookout, cleaning up his work shed and clay studio, I ruminated about the betrayal. I tried to banish the whole thing from my mind, to stop the circular thinking about that day, the nuances in the conversation, intonations, and inferences. Most of all, my thoughts perseverated on Calgary and the lookout start dates. What if Moose and Carbondale really did open within days of each other? Why would McNeal suggest a casual rendezvous when he had known Daniel for years? The questions grew into fantasies, and over the weeks my mind, seemingly of its own volition, obsessed about the May 1 opening and the possibility of another chance encounter.

I steadied myself and completed the application process to the University of Victoria's graduate program in counselling psychology. I desperately wanted admittance. If Daniel insisted on going back to the fire lookout, the regular paycheque would make it easier for me to go back to school. If selling pots caused him stress, I could accept his decision to go back to the lookout lifestyle. This was one of the best things about our relationship: the sense of ease we inhabited, accepting each other's foibles and strengths, adjusting and accommodating. But a part of me was disappointed, as though he had given up too easily. I had hoped he would develop a thriving pottery studio.

For myself, I wanted more than seasonal work. He supported my decision, but in the same way I questioned him about giving up the pottery business so soon, he was skeptical about whether a better job would change my attitude to life.

"I keep telling you," he said, "nothing in the mundane world will satisfy you. After that university degree, it will be something else."

There was already something else, and I could feel it derailing my life in slow motion, an unchecked impulse deep in my unconscious, and unless I rooted it out, and reflected more deeply on its quality and what was driving it, my plans would be snuffed out.

Lovingly, Daniel wrapped the bags of pink Carbondale clay in extra plastic, storing them on his studio shelves. Now we were ready for Alberta. The clay would be there when he came home, moist and waiting to be kneaded.

"If I don't make pots with this clay next fall, my name is mud," he said.

Clay, dense and heavy, the body of the earth itself, was, for Daniel, the most beautiful stuff in the world.

False Spring

It was dark when we crossed over the Continental Divide and the Welcome to Alberta sign flashed by. Herds of elk grazed next to the highway in the Bow Valley corridor, their eyes glowing neon in our headlights. We cruised in silence, the only car on the Trans-Canada Highway, the towering presence of the Rockies on either side of us.

I thought of McNeal packing up his life in Toronto and where he might be in his cross-Canada journey. If we crossed paths by synchronicity, without deliberate planning, then maybe that would be a cosmic sign we were destined to meet up again.

Immediately, I squelched feelings of guilt.

Athena was waiting up when we rolled into the driveway at Sunnyhill Housing Co-op. We sat around the IKEA kitchen table, while Willow, eight years old now, slept upstairs. Athena said she and Tomas had finally signed off on their divorce. Every summer Willow spent several weeks with Tomas on Mockingbird Lookout, father and daughter time, the fire lookout season always a feature of her life. Athena had finished another year in women's studies at the University of Calgary, and worked in the deli at Community Natural Foods. Politically active in the community, she brought up the Rodney King incident. It was the last day of April, and the four white officers who assaulted King, an African-American man, had been acquitted. Los Angeles had erupted into the worst violence and rioting since the 1960s.

"It's outright racism," she said. "I'm so glad I have an analysis of race and gender now. I brought Willow to a Take Back the Night march, and Tomas happened to be watching the local news and saw her waving a placard about ending violence against women!"

"Did he freak out?" I asked. "That's hysterical. What are the odds he would catch that local news story?"

"I know," said Athena wearily. "It certainly didn't help our divorce negotiations. He thinks she's too young for political demonstrations. And I think it's important to educate her about race and gender inequality."

After three years off the grid, Daniel and I needed to catch up on current events and the lives of our friends. But I was distracted. I hid the disoriented feelings brought on by moving and deception, and feigned interest in politics, Athena's studies, and the upcoming lookout season.

Daniel was scheduled to start work on Moose Mountain early the next morning, Friday, May 1. I would drive to Bragg Creek with him and, after he'd emptied the car, take the Subaru back to Calgary for the summer. There was no point in flying in for the opening of the lookout; the radio technician and ranger would be trying to work in the small confined space.

The first weekend in May was so warm I wandered around the city wearing a tank top, short skirt, and flip-flops. After years in small-town BC, it was liberating to hang out in coffee shops, walk for miles along the Bow River pathway, and observe the latest fashion styles and trends. Every time I came back to my room at Athena's, I checked her answering machine for messages. I feared missing a message from McNeal when he passed through town. Emotionally vested in the outcome of my synchronicity experiment, I was falling in deep.

On Sunday evening, I returned to the townhouse and noticed a new vehicle parked in the driveway. I climbed the stairs and hovered in the doorway of the kitchen, watching McNeal and Athena discuss a university course guide. He was giving her advice, applauding her efforts to complete a bachelor's degree while raising a child. For an instant I felt confused; I had expected a grand reception, a howl of surprise and a big hug, but he played a different game, cool and detached. Then I recalled that in the past McNeal had often visited Tomas and Athena and stayed here as their guest. It would be natural for Athena to assume McNeal had stopped by to see her; he let her come to this conclusion.

After a few more minutes of chit-chat, McNeal said, "Hey, do either of you want to go out for a coffee or a beer?"

Willow was too young to be left alone and McNeal knew it.

"I wouldn't mind going out for a beer," I said, looking him in the eyes.

"You two go ahead, I can't leave Willow alone. I don't mind, really."

Mission accomplished.

❋

McNeal and I sped west along Memorial Drive to a motel on Sixteenth Avenue NW, where he had already checked in for the night. He had arrived that afternoon and had a rental car to get down to southern Alberta. He was scheduled to start work at Carbondale Lookout on Monday, the next morning.

McNeal slid open the sun roof, cranked up the radio volume, and floored the gas pedal.

"I got a job, I got a car, and I got a girl, what else does a guy need?" He laughed loudly at his own joke. "Really, that's about it for most men. The schmucks."

Then he turned thoughtful, serious. "Did Daniel get up to Moose all right?"

"Yup, he's there. They flew him in Friday."

"Huh, good for him. I must give him a call. I'm so looking forward to getting up to the lookout myself and just chilling. It's been an apocalyptic winter—oral exams for my dissertation. Really stressful, but I got through them."

He rested his right hand on my thigh, between gear changes. "This psychic subterfuge is too much, don't you think? Illicit affairs. Makes it hard to concentrate and get any work done."

He shoved open the motel door, a standard room, and we lunged across the closer of the two beds, his weight pressing me into the mattress. It was another race to the finish line, an athletic release of pent-up longing. When we rolled onto our backs, satiated, McNeal said, "I caught a glance of us in the dresser mirror, entwined. That is so sexy. I'd love a room with mirrors on the ceiling. What do you think?"

"No!" I exclaimed. "That's so cheesy."

He laughed. "Come on, why don't you sleep here tonight? We'll experiment with the 'mirror,' so to speak, and I'll drop you off tomorrow morning."

"If I don't go back tonight, it's gonna look kind of strange, and Athena might worry."

McNeal threw my skirt and top at me. "Okay, let's go. I'll take you back."

"Do you wanna go for a beer in Sunnyside? It's not like I have a curfew."

"Not really, I'm driving. And I have an early morning tomorrow. I'm going to get up at 5:00 or 6:00 a.m. and get out of Dodge. Calgary is so tedious. If you're gonna be around, maybe you should come down to Carbondale and visit once this summer."

Visit once this summer. I steeled my jaw and stared ahead through the windshield. He made it sound so casual, friends meeting up for a hike. What would it mean?

The thought scared me, purposely travelling to another lookout and cheating on Daniel. "Maybe in June I could drop by." Did those words really come out of my mouth? Who was I kidding? A three-hour drive was no longer in the category of dropping by.

"No pressure," he said. "I'll write. Visiting may not be a good idea anyway. I have a lot of work to get done on my dissertation this season. It can be hard to maintain the right frame of mind on the lookout. A bit of a psychic balancing act."

"Sure, yeah, write when you get a chance."

Sheepish about ending up in the white motel twice now, I needed to get sensible and organize my life. I abhorred affairs and cheating partners; it was time to get my life back on track. First, I had to drive to Silver Star and gather up a few belongings: summer clothes, books, a lamp, and my typewriter. Daniel had crammed the Subaru so full, there had been no room for my stuff. But first, I would scoot up to Moose Mountain, because, fingers crossed, maybe there would be a good letter waiting for me in the Okanagan, and I'd be heading out to school at UVic for the rest of the summer.

Daniel said he'd arrange a helicopter ride so I wouldn't have to hike for three hours with a heavy pack. Flying in, I could bring him more supplies than I could ever carry hiking. I drove out to the Elbow Valley ranger station near Bragg Creek, confident I could fly up to Moose with the district pilot and initial-attack crew on one of their routine fire detection tours.

The first guy I met was the initial-attack leader, short and muscular in his orange coveralls, strutting around the ranger station and eyeing me up and down with lascivious glances.

"So, you wanna go up and see Dan the lookout man, eh?" he said with almost a sneer.

Male competition, I thought. He's jealous because Daniel has an intimate female guest while he, primed and taut, trained to combat a wall of heat and flame, sleeps alone in the bunkhouse with the other guys.

"Yeah, I was hoping you could fit me in on the next tour? I brought groceries for him."

"I guess we can swing by the fire lookout after lunch. Depends on the afternoon weather report though. If the clouds build, we won't be flying."

"It cleared off just now as I drove in from Calgary. Any chance we could go up this morning?" I felt it was risky to wait; the weather could get worse.

"Nope, after lunch, that's when we're scheduled to lift off. Wait here and I'll come back and get you when its time." His eyes flitted at the level of my breasts.

I sat down to wait, relieved the initial-attack guy had more to do than pester me. These guys were certainly a different male species than fire observers. They reminded me of Jack Carter and his *Playboy* wallpaper, unable or unwilling to disentangle sexuality from the personhood of a woman. Funnily, Jack Kerouac had mused about types of men in the forest service when he watched for smoke on Desolation Peak. He pitied tough working-class men, the guys on the front lines of fires.

> I felt sorry for the fellows who had to fight these fires, the smokejumpers who parachuted down on them out of planes and the trail crews who hiked to them, climbing and scrambling over slippery rocks and scree slopes, arriving sweaty and exhausted only to face the wall of heat when they got there.[5]

Kerouac was identifying classes of men, or hierarchies of men within society, but regardless of how low on the ladder a particular type of man might be, as a woman I was relegated even lower.

Around 1:30 p.m., the initial-attack leader barked a command, and I hurried out to the yard with my supplies. I had bags of dry and fresh goods for Daniel: coffee cream, salad fixings, bananas, and chocolate, things he ran short of mid-month, as well as my orange backpack stuffed with a bottle of red wine. I had also dragged along a case of Big Rock beer, in glass bottles, which unfortunately gave the impression I was a party girl.

In self-defence, I was counting on the warm weather to last and imagined Daniel and I outside on the catwalk enjoying a few beers in the afternoon sunshine.

I boarded the government helicopter with four initial-attack guys in orange jumpsuits. As we gained elevation above the Elbow River valley, the pilot pointed at the storm front blowing in from the west.

"I can't land up there if the visibility deteriorates," he said into the headphones.

We flew in a wide arc around the mountain, approaching the lookout from the northeast. From the air the small building could have been a Tibetan meditation hut, desolate on the pinnacle of rock, backed by the Kananaskis Range fanning across the horizon. Ghostly stratus clouds rushed toward us, concealing the vista of peaks, and within minutes, the Moose summit disappeared behind a dripping veil of clouds.

"XMC29, are you by?" The pilot called Daniel over the radio.

"C29 here, I'm totally obscured, zero visibility." Daniel had responded so quickly, I knew he was waiting next to the radio.

"Thanks, C29, yeah, we won't be landing. Looks like a pretty good storm you got there."

Switching channels, the pilot spoke to me. "I'm going to take you back to the station. Maybe we can try tomorrow."

I was intimidated by the radio talk and the initial-attack crew, but I didn't want to go back to the ranger station and drive home with all the groceries, defeated. I could see a grey plateau below the clouds, the Moose dome, a barren, limestone cap of sedimentary rock, streaked with patches of snow.

"Can you drop me on the dome?" I asked. "I'll hike up the rest of the way."

The pilot looked in the mirror and saw I was earnest. "That's a snow-storm coming in. I'm inclined to turn back."

"Can we try, just once?"

He craned his neck, stared down at the mountain, and then decisively changed gears, descending, hovering, and choosing a flat piece of exposed ground. I felt the skids touch the earth, gentle rocking, and then we settled.

The initial-attack leader stood up in the middle of the aircraft, miming a jetliner attendant, both index fingers shooting in the direction of the doors; the others smirked at his pantomime.

"You bail and we'll pass you the gear," he said, yelling above the roar of the engine and rotor blades.

I ducked low, working fast to transfer everything several metres from the helicopter. "Don't forget this," said the initial-attack guy, holding up the case of beer in the wind. "Have one for me," he said, forcing me to pry the box from his hands.

As they lifted off, leaving me in a blast of wind and swirling snow, I heard the pilot's voice crackle over the radio, updating Daniel on my location.

I couldn't hike uphill and carry everything in one trip. I opened the case of beer, stashed a few bottles in my pack, and pushed the rest of the groceries and beer under the shelf of a huge boulder. Digging a scarf out of my pack, I wrapped my head, and faced into the wet snow, plodding up the steep, rocky trail.

I had walked for ten to fifteen minutes, when a dark figure descended out of the fog. "Hi hon, I can't believe you made it!"

Daniel, at ease on the cliff, reminded me of a tribal nomad: dark wool hat pulled low on his brow, a long black raincoat zipped up, and a knit scarf coiled in layers around his neck. We stopped to catch our breath, face to face on the narrow path, the mountain disappearing into the abyss of Canyon Creek down one side.

He shouldered the pack, leading me uphill over loose, snowy rocks, around boulders, deeper inside the cocoon of whiteness. The snow clung to my head and eyelashes, soaking my leather boots, and chilling my whole body.

At the top of the mountain, the one-room lookout building was anchored to the rock with steel cables and grounded to withstand lightning strikes. In the middle of the room, the Osborne fire finder occupied much of the small space.

To warm the lookout, Daniel had fired up the Onan generator. I peeled off my wet clothes, pulled on a dry, oversized T-shirt and sweatpants and sat on a high stool with a cup of coffee. I stared out at the whiteness, wondering if I should come clean and tell Daniel about McNeal. Outside, thick white fog pressed close to the black catwalk railing.

"Watch, it'll be undercast tomorrow," said Daniel. "We'll be higher than the clouds, you'll see."

"I've never been on the lookout when it's undercast. Come to think of it, I've never been on the lookout in a snowstorm either. At least you don't have to look for smoke while I'm here."

"That's for sure, and no hikers today either. It's been a strange season so far. So quiet, sometimes I forget I'm here to work."

"It's only May. Wait till it warms up and those binoculars are glued to your forehead."

Now that we were surrounded by clouds, and fog drifted right up to the door, the lookout cabin was suspended in space, cut off from the rest of the world. My guilty secret, an ugly distraction, intruded into my thoughts, ruining the beauty of the moment. I wished he had to look for smoke—it would take the focus off me.

Daniel flopped into a hammock with Zip. He had suspended the hammock from the ceiling at window level, next to the fire finder, so he could look out while lying down. It was perfect on hot, lazy afternoons, and it was perfect in snowstorms too, when he could relax without worrying about smoke.

"Zip hurt his spine trying to jump up on the bed," Daniel said fondly. "I have to pick him up now, his spine or hind legs seem to have been damaged."

I swore Daniel loved that dog as much as he loved me; the dog had been with him longer. "Oh, poor Zip, that's awful. How old is he now?"

"He's about ten years old, I'd say. Such a good dog. Never barks at hikers or wanders off. I've been carrying him outside to pee on the rocks in the middle of the night. He wakes me up."

"That must be hard in this weather." Zip's poor health made me feel even guiltier.

"Yeah. I think I'll see if Forestry will fly me down to Bragg Creek so I can take him to a vet." Daniel stroked Zip's long blond fur. "He's starting to look like the Maharishi!"

The pale hair around Zip's face had grown long, like a man's straggly beard, and his eyes looked almost human.

"I don't mean it with disrespect. I just mean if you look at Zip and then look at a picture of the Maharishi, it's uncanny."

I laughed. The breed did have a flat face, without a protruding snout like most dogs. Daniel swayed back and forth in the hammock, cradling the injured animal as he would a small child.

"You know what?" he said, perking up. "I'm going to build a miniature lookout building to scale. That's the project I want to work on this season, construct miniature lookout people and mountains too, you know, the whole panorama from Moose based on the actual landscape. Then, I'm going to make a pinhole camera, and I'll photograph it, or maybe make a short movie, a movie without any narrative plot, you know, the lookout man watching the clouds go by, minute by minute."

I listened, glad he was content here, a stream of ideas, puffy cumulus clouds drifting across his mind, more dreams than he could ever make real.

We were like sky and earth, emptiness and form, his airy imagination needing the firm stability of ground. And after six years together, I understood his desire to make quirky art.

I relaxed, breathing in Daniel's creativity, fresh air in a closed room.

It was not the right time to tell him about McNeal.

✸

The next morning at seven thirty, I woke up to the voice of Karen, the Calgary radio operator.

"Good morning, all stations, ready for your morning weather."

I burrowed into the pillow; it was the daily weather sked again, voices I hadn't heard for three years. Daniel had already slipped outside to the Stevenson screen and collected his report data. I watched him as he rhymed off his weather numbers, ending with "obscured and undercast conditions."

"And over to Barrier Lookout." He clicked the microphone shut and the voices carried on, tracing the path of lookout stations along the east slope of the Rockies.

"Are you going back to sleep? Look, it's undercast today! Get up and take a look. It'll burn off by afternoon."

I propped myself up in bed, squinting in the brilliant daylight; sure enough, we were surrounded by blue skies in every direction, and below the lookout, a carpet of white cumulus clouds, a layer of cotton batting, separated us from the world, obscuring the Rockies, foothills, and prairies.

"I'm gonna hike down and get the rest of the groceries before a bear eats that stash. Listen to the radio in case anyone calls, okay? I can't look for smoke, anyway." Daniel disappeared into the clouds, carrying an empty pack, leaving me to wake up on top of the world. He had boiled water on the propane stove for my coffee.

An hour later he reappeared with the groceries.

"Those beer bottles are heavy," he said. "Why did you bring so much beer up here? Sheesh. You had wine. What's going on? You know I'm not keen on alcohol. I guess I can use the bottles for ginger beer. I want to start a fresh batch soon."

"I thought we might enjoy a beer on a hot summer day, that's all—I wasn't expecting a snowstorm."

Daniel circled around the fire finder, now and then surveying the forest, a habit too ingrained to stop even in low fire hazard. "Are you okay? You seem upset."

The corner of my mouth twitched involuntarily.

"I'm fine. Just frustrated looking for work."

✸

That afternoon the clouds dissolved and the skies opened, revealing the vertical folds of the Rockies, grey and purple peaks in stark relief, ancient seabeds that heaved into the sky millions of years ago. At this elevation, there was grey sedimentary rock everywhere, stones and boulders of all shapes and sizes, some mottled with coral, mica, and sulphurous yellow. The marmots emerged from hiding a few metres below the lookout, sunning themselves on the rocks and licking them for salt. To the east, the prairie benchland was greening up, and beyond, ranches, farms, and suburban communities rolled toward Calgary's downtown, sandstone buildings replaced by glass high-rises. Later in the afternoon, when passing clouds cast shadows over the mountains, I poured some wine, contemplating my life as I gazed out the windows, the immensity of the landscape inspiring reflection.

I could look at the Rocky Mountains for hours, their stable presence radiating a kind of peace and expansiveness. "Consciousness is bliss," taught the Maharishi, and at the top of Moose Mountain, the power of the Rockies could unlock the experience of those words; my awareness was the same, one and only, awareness that pervaded the entire universe. The high altitude and vast beauty of the Rockies could help one touch, momentarily, the transcendent.

The next day, the skies clear, I hiked down Moose Mountain with my empty backpack, promising to come back after I got moved from the Okanagan. "Or maybe I'll call with good news about university," I said hopefully.

I told myself all was well, but I had lost the wide transcendent view and once again contracted into the small self.

Invitation to a Fire Lookout

I had never been alone at our cabin in the Okanagan. Daniel had always been there, mucking about in the clay studio, or dragging building materials around the yard. Now that he was at the fire lookout, I operated the generator, split wood, and stoked the fire, dropping into the stillness, adapting to being alone in the woods.

Every day I checked for mail, unlocked the rural post box, and imagined for an instant how my life would change if I received an acceptance letter. Finally, one day there it was—the return UVic address like neon to my searching eyes. I could have torn the envelope open and ended the suspense, but I drove home, put the letter on our pine slab table, and stared at it like a psychic, as though I could intuit the contents. If you feel cold, it's a no; if you feel warmth, it's a yes. Isn't that the number one rule of telepathy? But I couldn't decide whether my hands felt hot or cold. I turned the act of opening mail into a ritual, brewed tea, lit a candle, and sat quietly for a while. What if the letter was another rejection, then what? But surely the letter was an offer of admittance; I was a good candidate for graduate studies.

Grasping the letter opener, I slashed the top edge of the envelope, surgically, a clean cut. Trembling, I unfolded the white piece of paper and forced myself to read the brief paragraph.

My hands turned icy cold.

Earlier that spring, I'd been rehearsing a contemporary dance piece with a group of community dancers. We were scheduled to perform at the end of May on a mixed bill in Armstrong, a town in the Okanagan Valley twenty minutes north of Vernon. Our dance teacher and choreographer had set the work to music by Philip Glass; the pace was fast with long diagonal runs, big leaps, and barrel turns. We galloped like wild horses—four minutes of relentless full-bodied motion.

I would stay to perform in the show and immediately afterwards return to Calgary, hike up Moose Mountain to visit Daniel, and then concentrate on finding a job. I could turn this disappointment around. I have friends in Calgary, I told myself; this is a chance to enjoy the city and escape the constraints of a small town.

One morning I woke suddenly; the loft and bed swayed. I froze under the blankets, listening to the everyday sounds, bird calls, leaves rustling. Was this an earthquake? Then, I heard stomping downstairs, and the building heaved. I leaped out of bed, naked, grabbed a long T-shirt and hopped down the wooden stairs to the main floor of the cabin.

The room appeared exactly as I'd left it the night before.

The cabin swayed again.

I stared through the window of the kitchen door and glimpsed a black hulk scuffling around inside the small porch. The bear stood up on its hind legs, a bag of milk powder hanging from its mouth. The animal shook the plastic bag the way a cat shakes a half-dead mouse. A trail of white powder dusted the floor of the porch. The lid to the food cooler had been pawed open, offering nothing but skim milk for the hungry bear. I grabbed a stainless steel pot, banged it with a wooden spoon, and moved cautiously toward the door.

Spellbound, I could see the individual hairs in the bear's lush, black fur and the folds of skin in the enormous body. If I were crazy enough, I could open the door, reach out and touch the bear's fur coat, stroking the wildness.

The black bear dropped the plastic bag, leaned its massive frame against the wooden door, and stared back at me through the window. The door frame creaked.

I backed away, hands shaking.

Grabbing a whistle I kept handy for hiking alone in the woods, I took a deep breath and blew hard, a long, piercing tone. The high pitch irritated the animal, and it thrashed around in a circle, and then slammed its bulk against the old wood door, threatening to break and enter, literally.

I was out of scare tactics and ran for the loft. As soon as I climbed the ladder, I dismantled the steps, pushing them away from the edge of the upper floor, just in case this bear could mount stairs. Trees, stairs—it seemed possible. I told myself that if the bear kept coming I would squeeze out the loft window onto the roof.

I crouched upstairs listening to the thumping on the porch until finally the cabin became quiet. Half dozing, I huddled in bed for several hours, afraid the bear would return, afraid I'd hear the rumbling again.

The bear encounter changed the rest of my time at the cabin. Before venturing outside, I would stand in the doorway, scanning the yard and nearby forest, half expecting to spot the bear skulking through the trees. Every day I checked the driveway and surrounding area for bear scat, and each time I dashed to the outhouse, the whistle hanging around my neck, fear gripped my body. I removed the food cooler from the porch and stored garbage on the roof of the shed. I no longer enjoyed morning coffee outdoors in the spring sunshine. I stayed inside more and parked the car closer to the cabin, just in case I needed to make a quick getaway.

A few days after the bear encounter, letters and poems from McNeal arrived in the mail. He had addressed the packet to Athena's house in Calgary, assuming I'd be there, and Athena had thoughtfully forwarded the mail to our rural postal box. Again, I refrained from opening the envelope until I was home, composed, sitting in a comfy armchair.

May 12, 1992
Carbondale LO

My Dear Mary—
It has struck me as more than a little tragic-comedic, our trysts in Toronto and Calgary. I was impressed with how "cool" you were after giving yourself to me in the Blue Velvet hotel on Spadina....
And I wonder what is going on in your psyche just now; my certain "coolness" in Cowtown a symmetrical counterpart to your own in TO. Is life such a banal issue of timing: the right mood, the right configuration of people, present, and more importantly absent, the right temperature, the right size and shape, energy, hot and cold: that balance that defines the permutations of the love-act?...
    I sit here looking out upon a snowy landscape—it just keeps coming in daily, around 8 cm or so, and the heat wave has been decisively smothered in wetness....
    My raven is back here and I am leaving snacks. The cats are furry balls of warmth down on the bed—I have to fight my way in, in order to lie and read for a while. Haven't found the rhythm

quite yet, but I am fairly relaxed and enjoying it. I may yet come
to the point.

Say, I'd really like to discuss this book <u>The Metaphysics of
Sex</u> with you…why don't you come up and we'll have a <u>talk</u>?

A couple days later (May 13th):

…Starting to go through my poetry and prime up the right
brain for some creative stuff. I just finished <u>The Sheltering Sky</u>
by Paul Bowles which was brilliant, and rather depressing. Still
going through <u>The Metaphysics of Sex</u>—this you really must
read—and was intrigued to note that he [Evola] indicts Jung for
being fairly shallow on the whole sexual energy thing.…Oh, and
am also browsing through the <u>120 Days of Sodom</u> by de Sade
which is spicy to say the least! Apart from that I am playtesting
this self-designed scenario for this [war] game-system you saw
which is interesting. I did a large amount of historical research
last winter and it is intriguing to see it all come together.…

I've been laughing to myself about some of the stories you
passed on re: Daniel and mongo piles of equipment and artistic
supplies.…He definitely needs a stalwart strong woman like you
huh? I'll be dropping him a line one of these days soon. I tried
calling him on a distance [radio] repeater yesterday without any
success.

What to do?

You mentioned June for a visit which is fine by me; however, you should know that I would love for you to come up sooner.
Don't call or write if the mood grabs you—just come on up.…

love, McNeal, XO
P.S. A few poems. The second one is for you.

There were three typed pages, plus the two poems. The cheery prose sent
for me was titled "Gnostic turpitude (the psychic dilemma)," a term he
borrowed from Vladimir Nabokov's novel *Invitation to a Beheading*, about
a man imprisoned and sentenced to death for the existential inability to
participate in normal society. For context, he employed an epigraph from
Nabokov about being "imprisoned in the fortress in expectation of the unknown but near and inexorable date," which I presume alluded to his own

feelings of being prisoner on the fire lookout. I mulled over the stanzas of the poem, searching for subtext, a hint of McNeal's true feelings, retrieving only dark images such as "black soul, black hole swallowing light in the gravity of dilated excess," or "the occluded lust of libertine Eve curving her lines of light in the dark."

I dismissed the poetry from the abyss, as I dismissed my nightmare, and his congratulatory remarks about my coolness, refusing to see how my emotional detachment had sparked his interest, how the Nabokov-inspired language would never resonate with my experience. He *had* been so cool in Calgary; what had shifted in two weeks? Nothing really, except perhaps his stark realization of a celibate summer on the lookout, but I inserted far more meaning into the correspondence.

I was befuddled by his casual mention of contacting Daniel; given our affair, to me it seemed like a callous move.

On a separate sheet of paper, he had drawn a map, directions for driving to Carbondale from Highway 3 in the Crowsnest Pass. I flushed at his invitation to visit the lookout and then reflected on Daniel alone on Moose Mountain, and guilt gnawed at my conscience like a nesting pack rat.

And then, not long after I received the seductive letter and map, McNeal phoned the cabin one evening in late May. His voice caught me off guard; I hadn't expected him to call from the lookout.

"Hey, it's me. I'm down at the ranger station for a moment and thought I'd call. Did you get my letter?"

"Yeah, I got your letter this week."

"Good. I keep thinking about our time in Calgary. Why don't you come down to the lookout? You want to see me, I can tell. I miss you."

"I was thinking about sometime in June." How easily I relented to the request. To engage deceit, rearrange my life, become his asset.

"Sure, and bring some large festive balloons."

"You're kidding me. 'Festive balloons'?"

"Yes, and wine, be sure to pick up wine." His voice was intimate, persuasive.

"I had a black bear almost break into the cabin last week."

"Ha! Oh yeah, we get bears all the time at the lookout." McNeal made the harrowing experience sound like an everyday event.

"I know, but this is where I live, and I was alone."

"Very Jungian," McNeal teased.

"Jungian?"

"The unconscious, wild animals, affairs, it's pretty obvious, my dear. So, are you coming down or what?" McNeal laughed.

Sometimes his laugh bordered on sinister.

"I was planning on driving back to Calgary in the next few days, soon as my dance performance is over. I really need to find a job."

"Great, take a quick detour and come see me. Here's the Blairmore ranger's number. The rangers are discreet. When you get to Blairmore, call and say you're a friend coming to the lookout for a visit. The ranger will let me know over the radio, and I'll ride Big Red down to the road and get you."

"Big Red? It sounds like a fire drill."

"I know it's a bit corny, but think about wrapping yourself around me on the back of Big Red—that should hold you over till you get here."

"Smartass."

"You know I'm right. So, I'll see you soon, then? You got the map?"

"Yes, got the map, thanks."

I hung up the phone as though in a trance. Part of me wanted to halt the subterfuge now, and part of me wanted to plot how to conceal the detour. If I drove to Carbondale en route to Calgary, this would take an extra day or two. The direct drive from Silver Star Mountain to Calgary was only seven hours. Daniel would call the cabin or Athena's house in Calgary any day now, and if I failed to answer, he would worry. But, if I stayed only one night at Carbondale, I could be back in Calgary by the next evening, leaving only twenty-four hours unaccounted.

Based on this strategy, I had officially joined the ranks of liars and cheaters—and, if I'd been honest with myself at the time, dirty rats. Why was I hanging all this passion on an academic lookout man I barely knew?

From a Jungian perspective, there were no coincidences, and the separation between our inner life and outer life was illusory. Even if the black bear symbolized aspects of my own unconscious coming to light, unfortunately, the Jungian analysis didn't squelch my desire to go to McNeal.

In the next few days I received mail from Daniel. His letter was three pages as well, except it was handwritten, the script so tiny I almost needed a magnifying glass. He had handed off the letter to a group of hikers because my birthday was coming up. But it wasn't his extraordinary handwriting that most affected me; it was his uncanny ability to intuit my double-dealings.

May 19, 1992
Moose Mountain LO

I've been watching lovers on the dome. Heads appear on the horizon, like ants, sure enough, coming up onto the lid of the honey jar and seeing yet another jar stacked above. And here's me like a big beetle peering down through my binoculars. I watch, though I can barely see them, to enjoy the game of piecing together the fuzzy image. So I put my glasses on, and resting my elbows, focus on and between heartbeats (which makes the world bob up and down). I see that which I thought was a guy's knapsack is a woman peeing. The couple walked around a little bit. I sensed they were Asian, Japanese perhaps.

In between viewings I switched to another couple, the first pair had retreated. Again, I saw the woman peeing while the man took in the vista. Maybe he was pissing too, I can't see that detail, but it would have been into the wind, so unlikely. She was shorter than him, long red hair. He in a ball cap, a bit paunchy, striding around this way and that. She put on warmer pants over her purple tights. They hugged and kissed frequently—her head against his chest as she was much shorter. She swung her arms, did spinal twists. And when they sat for lunch I thought I might view some action from a distance. A voyeuristic lookout. The binocular-strained eyes that Tomas laments are not, in my case, caused by looking for fires or burning trees. I want to see passions in flame. But no, they eventually (in the most random pattern I've ever seen of hikers on the dome) wandered away. Hugging and kissing until the moment the horizon ate their bodies up...

Love, Daniel

There was more in the letter, of course; for instance, the "lovely, glossy cocoa brown" he had painted the fire finder, a paragraph about sitar music he recorded on CBC Radio, as well as a short anecdote about a runner who got lost in a spring blizzard training in the foothills. The runner had presented at the door of Moose Lookout, disoriented, and told Daniel he'd been running through sour gas ponds, lost, and afraid of being poisoned.

It was the "passions in flame" and stories about lovers on the dome that unnerved me.

During this time, I also had a nightmare, a warning I could not dislodge. I dreamt I was in a cellar, trapped, behind a brick wall.

I call out for help. Surely someone will hear my screams and rescue me. Exhausted by my efforts to be heard, I suddenly realize the truth. McNeal has betrayed me, and, with Catherine, plotted to wall me in.

The shock of dying wakes me.

At the end of May, after three evening dance performances in a small rural auditorium, I packed my clothes, books, and personal belongings into the Subaru. Closing up the cabin for the summer, I turned off the propane, covered the generator, and carried dry firewood inside. On a clear, sunny morning, I pulled the door shut, put the car in reverse, and backed out of my life as I knew it.

I was still a nervous driver. I drove the Trans-Canada Highway to Revelstoke and then took Highway 93 south to Cranbrook; this was not the shortest route, but Highway 93 was straight, easy driving with little traffic. Somewhere near Cranbrook or Creston I stopped for gas, bought wine and condoms, and changed into a black tight-fitting dress in the gas station washroom. The duplicity was incompatible with my self-image as an ethical woman who stuck to principles—so I repressed those thoughts.

McNeal's driving instructions to Carbondale were accurate and easy to follow. When I turned off the gravel onto the muddy lookout road, he was sitting on the ground, his back against a poplar tree, waiting for me like Adonis in a red bandana.

We embraced awkwardly, the subterfuge and fear of being caught adding to the excitement. I parked the Subaru out of sight from the road and climbed on the motorcycle with my backpack, holding on to McNeal. The lookout road was wet and slick, full of potholes, and in places washed out entirely from spring runoff. McNeal scooted around the puddles and boulders, accelerating and braking like a rodeo cowboy. I clung to his jacket, afraid of being thrown off, until we were out of the trees and on high, dry road.

"The hot tub is ready," McNeal shouted over the engine, pulling up alongside the lookout building. "I've been heating water for hours."

"Hot tub?" I looked at the plastic water barrel outside the lookout door. Steam rose off the water.

"It's hot, so get in. Just let me set the mood with some ambient music."

I wasn't keen on taking a sauna in a barrel, but McNeal had gone to a lot of trouble to heat those fifty-five gallons of water. And after driving all day I needed a bath. This was a hot tub with an unparalleled view: in the distance, the peaks of the Rocky Mountains zigzagged across the western horizon, and in the foreground the green slopes of the foothills, the Castle River, and a patchwork of meadows and forest reached up to the lookout door.

Music blasted from a tape deck through the open door.

McNeal raced around, executing the preplanned lookout seduction.

"Enigma, I love this track," he said. "Listen—the lyrics are so erotic. French and Latin. *Dis-moi.*"

Enigma was a German group, their New Age album, *Sadness*, an international megahit. The musicians had lifted the voices of a Gregorian choir and layered it with an electronic score, a repetitive downbeat, and seductive whisperings of a female vocalist. I had no idea at the time that the Marquis de Sade had inspired the music video and the original release in Germany had been titled *Sadeness*.

I unzipped my black dress, scrutinizing the best way to get inside the barrel. McNeal gave me a foothold with clasped hands to help me over the hard plastic edge. We barely fit inside crouching upright; reclining wasn't an option, because the barrel was only about sixty centimetres wide and ninety centimetres high. After ten or fifteen minutes, we hauled ourselves out of the barrel, wineglasses in hand, and dashed to the bedroom, dripping water across the worn grey carpet. We flopped onto the bed until I remembered the condoms and disentangled myself from McNeal's embrace, fumbling with my pack and dumping the contents to find the package.

"Don't worry about that, I've got a supply right here." He reached for the night table.

Of course he did. McNeal always had a backup strategy.

Our lovemaking was of the athletic variety, fast and furious, concluding more quickly than I'd anticipated. He jumped out of bed, leaving me alone on the wet spot.

"Another glass of wine?" he called out, rummaging in the kitchen.

"Sure, why not."

I surveyed the functional arrangement of the bedroom. He had set up a television on the table at the foot of the bed, stacked a pile of books nearby on the floor, and crammed his shirts and pants into the closet. He hadn't decorated; like most guys, he'd unpacked and moved in. Daniel would have transformed the room with fabric, art, and unique objects.

"Come on, get up," McNeal extended his hand and pulled me out of the bed, holding me close. It was the first intimate moment between us. Despite the fervour driving our "tryst"—McNeal's term for the affair—I felt totally alone.

Once I got back to Calgary, I would contemplate my actions, make sense of things. For now, it was surreal, a blur of adventure, risk, and pleasure.

That evening, as new lovers, we would have cooked dinner, drunk more wine, and talked about our lives for hours, eventually falling into bed again. How mysterious the images that comprise memory. I'm certain we had dinner, and I'm equally certain I did not cook, but I have no recall of the meal we shared. McNeal brought up the war in Bosnia and ranted that mainstream media was remiss in their poor coverage of the genocide taking place.

"I could have been a journalist," he said, wistfully, "if I hadn't gone this academic route."

"You sure have an in-depth understanding of politics and current events. But if you're so concerned about the world, I don't get why you're designing war games."

"I know, it's a giant contradiction. It's hard to explain. I have such a big connection to World War II, as though I was a soldier in a past life. I've studied the battles on the German-Soviet front, vicious, more casualties than any military operation in history. It was brutal, those poor bastards fighting in trenches all winter. So many millions froze and starved to death."

Later, reminiscing, Tomas would remark how McNeal, in specific circumstances, resembled a German officer.

The alarm clock screeched at seven the next morning. Petrified of sleeping through the morning weather sked, McNeal wound his alarm clock every night and put it inside a drawer in the kitchen. With the clock clanging like a fire alarm, he was forced to leap from bed and jog into the kitchen to stop the ringing. I could sleep through the voices on the forestry radio, but I couldn't sleep through McNeal's alarm clock.

After he silenced the alarm, I tracked him as he got dressed and ready for the day. I heard him open the door and go outside to the Stevenson screen. His footsteps reverberated on the metal rungs of the stairs as he bounded into the cupola. I pulled the blankets over my head to block out the crackle of lookout voices passing their weather. The lookouts in the south Bow-Crow Forest were all foreign to me: Ironstone, Junction, Raspberry, and Sugarloaf. At last there was silence again and I drifted back to sleep. When I woke up, McNeal was still upstairs in the cupola, writing, reading, and scanning the district now and then for smoke. I pulled on sweatpants and a T-shirt and wandered into the kitchen.

"Hey, good morning." McNeal's feet and legs appeared on the ladder and he dropped down into the kitchen from the cupola.

"Coffee, I need to make coffee." I was brushing my teeth with a little water I found in a container on the counter.

"Here's the dipper, just grab some from the barrel there." McNeal motioned toward last night's hot tub.

"Yeah, right." I was in no mood for teasing before coffee.

McNeal studied me as I brushed my teeth. "I'm serious—just fill the kettle with water from the barrel."

"Are you kidding me? Is that all the water you have?"

McNeal loved a good prank. Maybe this was his way of testing me.

"Where do you think all that water for the hot tub came from last night?" He was annoyed. "There's drinking water left, but use the water in the barrel for cooking. Boil it, it'll be fine. Besides, we weren't in there all that long."

"That's gross, really gross." I couldn't believe he'd sacrificed most of the water reserves for the hot tub. Peering inside, I submerged the dipper.

I desperately wanted coffee.

Then, I wanted to jump in the Subaru and drive to Calgary as fast as possible. Maybe there I would feel in control of my life again.

It was twilight when I arrived at Athena's townhouse. She assumed I had driven in from Vernon that day.

"Daniel's called a couple times," she said.

"Really? Anything in particular? Everything okay?" I wasn't ready to tell her or anyone else about the affair.

"He seemed to think you'd get here last night."

"Oh, he probably misunderstood. You know how awkward that two-way radio can be. I'll try him soon as I unpack."

My lies sizzled and hissed like embers igniting in the wood stove.

Youthful Folly

I couldn't get back to my life the way it had been.

I felt torn, as though I had crossed over a wide, swift river to a forest fire on the other side, and my old self called out from safety: "Come back, don't go there, it's too dangerous."

I had fallen in love with McNeal, or the parts of myself that he represented. The energy of the attraction simmered inside my being, a ball of fiery potential I could not squelch. I rationalized trips to surreptitiously visit Carbondale Lookout, to satisfy the flicker of pleasure that burned between us.

We were well matched in our physicality, ambling along the ridgetops of the surrounding hills together or hiking around Castle Mountain, one day trudging up the scree to the summit of the Westcastle ski run, and standing in awe at the spectacle of the Rocky Mountains from the top. Another time we scrambled downhill, finding a trail along the banks of the Castle River, and lay naked in the bushes, until McNeal slipped on the grassy incline and thrashed around, grabbing overhead branches to stop a slide into the cold waters, his butt cheeks scraped by rose thorns.

"I'm putting my clothes back on," he said. "This is too risky."

During those visits, he picked wildflowers from the meadows below the lookout and presented me with bouquets of forget-me-nots, larkspur, glacier lily, and white death camas. I had always been involved with unconventional men, and so for me, this traditional romantic act validated the affair and magnified its significance.

We were well matched intellectually, his scholastic drive mirroring my own latent abilities. I was energized by how he tracked current events and voiced world-centric concerns. The UN Conference on Environment and Development, or Earth Summit, had met in Rio, Brazil that June to address environmental degradation and plan a sustainable path for global development. More than one hundred heads of state had negotiated

Agenda 21, a document that included a statement of forest principles, a framework on climate change, and a convention on biological diversity.

"It's so watered down," complained McNeal, his face ruddy with anger. "After two weeks of meetings, there's nothing in that bullshit document that will actually stop the cutting of old-growth forests or slow down oil and gas exploration."

While I cavorted with McNeal in the foothills around Carbondale, Daniel wrestled with art projects at the top of Moose Mountain, and nearly fell over a cliff.

June 2, 1992
Moose Mountain

Well that was nice to talk to you, I do miss you. Ideas on CBC was about "joblessness," I'm looking forward to paycheques.

So, I've been painting the place somewhat. Interior decoration, my hobby at lookouts. As the fumes from the oil paint were a bit much, I took some of the furniture outside. One piece, the wardrobe cabinet, looked real good all painted. On the way in I lost my balance with it (the awkward thing!) and it's down the gully in a zillion pieces now...oops. It was an honest accident, I mean would I have spent 3 days painting it if I intended to chuck it down the cirque. I've told no one, and intend to purchase a better, nicer one from Ikea. So, I need an Ikea catalogue....

I took a tumble on the rocks, after the cabinet went down. I wanted to see where it went, slipped on the snow and somersaulted sorta near the cliff edge. Cabinets can be replaced, I'm a little bruised but okay. Will be more careful.

Then Zip, ole sport, tackled a dog bone and threw his back out. I'm pretty worried, carrying him around so he doesn't wreck it.

Lightning season, some flashes tonight. Some close strikes today, have seen some crows close up on the railing. A big white-headed eagle real close, just missed a photo. Snuck up on a pika for a photo. Some nice little birds, and today a mountain bluebird passed by. It's been very laid back, a nice spring start of a season.

I worry about you driving around out there, do be care-ful—but not nervous (that can make it worse)....I think there's good stuff in store for you. I'm looking for more rocks with coral holes for us, you can have this one. You can probably get a ride up when you want one, they either have a chopper on hand or if they don't they have time on their hands.

See you soon, love you (please bring Ikea catalogue, Athena probably has one).

It was an evening in mid-June when McNeal phoned and pleaded with me to drive to Carbondale. Tired and sweaty, I had just returned from Bragg Creek and a hike up Moose Mountain to deliver the IKEA catalogue. I stretched the beige phone cord from the kitchen into the hallway, gaining a few more inches of privacy as Athena cleaned up the kitchen. Outside, daylight faded above the Crescent Heights bluff; summer solstice was ap-proaching and the longest days of the year.

"Hey, get in the car and come down to see me." It was a command more than a question.

"Very funny. I just got in. Maybe in the next few days I'll try to make it down."

"I'm serious. I want you to come down tonight. Just think, in three short hours you could be here with me. I was going crazy thinking of you up on Moose."

"Oh my God, you are serious! I'm too tired to drive in the dark. It's a bit crazy, don't you think?"

"It's love, sweetheart. And it's a straight road all the way. It won't be dark for a while. Come on, do it for me."

If I pulled out of the driveway now and disappeared for a few days, I would have to explain my behaviour to Athena. Part of me wanted to confide in someone.

As I divulged a few details about the affair, she gaped in disbelief.

"Oh dear, be careful," she said nervously, probably reminded of her breakup with Tomas.

It was after midnight when I arrived at Carbondale Lookout. Mc-Neal met me on Big Red at the bottom of the trail. The cool night air whipped my face as we rode up the mountain on the motorbike. McNeal turned his head, screaming over the engine and the wind. "Someday, years from now, we'll laugh about all this."

He yelled these words on one of the last switchbacks, where the dirt fire road climbs above the treeline, the wind intensifies, and the magnificence of the Rocky Mountains comes into sight.

I didn't share his certainty. Who and where would we be years from now?

Inside, the lookout was warm, the lights low, and McNeal steered me into the bedroom with an amorous embrace. He fused himself to me, a stranger. I clasped my arms around his neck and shoulders, following the intensity of his bodily craving. In several minutes we were spent and lay apart. I wanted to stay up and talk, but he wanted the lights out. He hated to look for smoke without a good night's sleep. By now it was so late, he'd be lucky to log six hours.

"We'll talk tomorrow, I promise. Let's get some sleep now, it's late."

I yielded, but I wanted him to clarify his intentions; after all, I had just driven three hours, removed my clothes, and slithered in bed next to him. I felt like a wilderness escort service, a specialized call girl, answering the call of the wild. And a quick call at that. Surely I deserved a frank conversation.

I ruminated in the dark: it was the deception I abhorred, the dishonest manoeuvring, secret phone calls, illicit meetings. It had become a burden, a weight on my soul, and the only solution was to tell Daniel. McNeal should tell his Toronto girlfriend, Catherine, too, and I would say so tomorrow.

The next day, armed with coffee, I broached the relationship topic, only to learn that McNeal opposed naked truth telling, on moral and philosophical grounds. He said disclosing the truth would be unkind when Daniel faced the rest of the lookout season sitting alone on a mountaintop, and he had no intention of sharing the news flash with his girlfriend over the telephone. How crude that I expected such insensitive action. Well then, I suggested a letter might be in order, but he objected, arguing that a Dear Jane letter would be too cold and abrupt; he wanted to discuss the situation with her face to face in September after he got back to Toronto. I challenged him, asking how their conversations were going in the interim. She must be calling him over the forestry radio.

"Tense," said McNeal. "She suspects something, but I can't tell her while I'm on the lookout. I need to let her down gradually. I can't just end it. That's cruel."

"What do you mean, end it gradually?" That made no sense to me.

"Maybe you're okay with black and white, but that's not how I make decisions. I don't see it that way. I want to let her down easy, talk it through until she understands."

"There's no easy way to end a relationship. You're withholding information. That's controlling and paternalistic."

We argued at the kitchen table, in the same chairs we had occupied the previous August, when Daniel and I hunted for clay. I accused him of dishonesty and a secret agenda, and he accused me of naïveté and reductionist thinking.

"So you're after the white picket fence, after all," he said in an accusatory tone.

He knew the accusation would irk me, but he didn't know the leap in logic would inflame.

"Right, that's why I'm living off the grid in the middle of the woods." I was angry. How many women had bought these weak excuses for avoiding honesty and authenticity, I wondered?

Defusing the argument—to tell or not to tell—McNeal grabbed a deck of tarot cards, the Aleister Crowley Thoth deck, cards I had never seen. Compared to the classic Rider-Waite deck, which I owned, the luminance and colour saturation in the Crowley paintings portrayed a more occult quality. The Rider-Waite cards suggested innocence in their symbolism, perhaps due to the primary yellow and blue hues in the background of each image. He shuffled the cards thoughtfully, turned several cards face up, reflected on the symbols and slid them back into the deck. I wanted him to read the cards but he demurred, suddenly introspective at the sight of the Knight of Cups, Page of Pentacles, and Queen of Pentacles.

On the wall above the kitchen table, there was a framed tarot card, the Tower, a dramatic image depicting a medieval castle in flames, and against a black night sky, people were falling headfirst from the tower to their death.

"Why did you put up that picture of the Tower? Where did it come from?" I had been wondering about the picture ever since my visit at the end of May.

"It's from Catherine. She gave me that as a going-away gift."

"Get out."

"Well, I was leaving for the fire tower, so to speak, and she gave me the Tower."

"But…it's a card of destruction."

"I know. I told you she can be dark. She once joked that we should commit suicide together."

"Oh God, that's romantic. A real *Romeo and Juliet* moment." I was shocked by the disclosure; I had never known anyone who had committed suicide or would have voiced such morbid thoughts.

"I know it's a bit weird." McNeal laughed. "Thanatos and Eros, the two great impulses, according to Freud. Don't worry, I'm not gonna go do something dumb like that."

The radio quiet, McNeal cracked open a bottle of red wine and we sunk into a reverie of pleasure and fantasy, appraising the cards like gamblers at an after-hours casino. He lit a cigar, letting the afternoon winds suck the smoke out the window.

We were circumventing the impasse, avoiding what I perceived to be an inevitable discussion.

"Maybe you could get a job at the kids' camp down below here?" McNeal said. "That way you could visit all the time."

"The kids' summer camp?" I said, incredulous. "Where would I live to work at that camp? In Blairmore, Burmis, Coleman? For one thing, the car I'm driving isn't mine—it also belongs to Daniel. I already feel guilty driving it down here to see you. And I'm paying for gas with money from his lookout salary."

"Take it easy. You said you needed a job, okay? I'll throw in some money for gas, relax. I'm just trying to help."

"Yeah, well it's not helping. I'm applying to graduate programs. Do you really see me singing campfire songs with children?"

"Look, you're complaining about having to drive three hours to get here. I thought it wouldn't be so bad for a summer job."

"Okay, let's follow this through then. What happens after the summer? When you go back to Toronto and I'm left living in a small town in southern Alberta?"

"Listen, I was thinking maybe we could go to India this winter. I can write my dissertation anywhere. What do you think? India in January, you and me in a beach hut, arm in arm on a twenty-mile stretch of sand, fresh fish and rice with Kingfisher beer each night?"

I had always wanted to go to India, and the thatched-hut scenario was seductive, but he wasn't offering to buy my airfare. I had more pressing concerns, like paying rent and buying groceries here in Canada. If I didn't generate some income quickly, I'd be living in a thatched hut on the Bow River in Calgary.

"I'd love to go to India, but I don't get what you and I are doing together. It sounds so vague. After India do you go home to Toronto and I go to Calgary? I want to know your honest feelings. If you're going to carry on with me all summer and then go back to Catherine in September, I won't do that. And why January?"

"Hey, what's with the interrogation? Don't put me on the witness stand." McNeal exhaled a smoke ring forcefully. "You're so black and white, Mary. Do you really think I'm that kind of guy? Committed relationships take time to evolve. You can't *make* them happen. I don't know what's going to happen after India. How can I answer that now?"

I stared at the mess of tarot cards, sullen. He was right, in part; the future would always be uncertain. But I felt he was withholding his true feelings. Why did I feel I was spinning a roulette wheel, pretending it was a normal way to make life-altering decisions?

"I'm going upstairs for a few minutes—make sure nothing's burning." He reached for his binoculars and went outside, bracing the door against the wind.

"Sure, I'll be here when you come back down. Not going anywhere."

The afternoon light poured through the window, exposing the dust and stains on the brown Arborite tabletop. I surveyed McNeal's stuff: a row of books, cigar box, ashtray, pens, Alberta Forestry notepad, and used coffee cups from breakfast. The Marquis de Sade book, *The 120 Days of Sodom*, that he had mentioned in his letter caught my eye. I held the closed volume between my hands, afraid to open the infamous text. Flipping the pages, I let them fall open in the middle of the book.

The marquis, or one of his male characters, takes a woman prostitute captive in a medieval castle, high on a mountain surrounded by forests, fantasizing how he might sexualize and torture her. The perpetrator binds the woman with rope and administers a boiling-hot enema—sadism and cruelty as erotic foreplay.

I slammed the book shut, my hands shaking.

McNeal's footsteps clanged on the stairs. I placed the book on the kitchen table, the cover facing up. He saw it immediately and blushed, hesitating as he chose his words.

"I know it's hard to understand why I have that book; it's depraved, but it shows the darkest side of the human psyche. What Jung called the unconscious shadow."

"Okay, but its graphic cruelty against women? I scanned one paragraph and I feel like throwing up. It's grotesque."

"It's a famous piece of literature. I'm reading it as a scholar."

For me, the presence of the book sullied the natural beauty of Carbondale.

"I don't want violent images in my mind."

"Don't give me that New Age crap. I'm less evolved now, I suppose? You *would* take the moral high ground." McNeal snorted with disgust. "The world is full of evil, and ignoring it does nothing to change things."

I didn't want to argue about a French degenerate from the eighteenth century.

"I'm not calling you evil. I didn't mean that." I softened my voice in a gesture of feminine consolation.

"We're both degenerates. Look at this place, wine bottles, ashtrays— you're a bad influence," McNeal teased. "I don't normally drink like this in the afternoon."

"Well, neither do I."

"Let's keep going then. Why stop now?" He yanked open a trap door in the kitchen floor leading to a small underground cellar. "I've got some beer staying cool down here." McNeal stocked good beer in glass bottles, Guinness and other quality brews. He passed me a Guinness.

"It was Daniel who framed up this little storage room years ago, you know." He laughed. "The guy is so creative. I think he sublimates emotion into all his projects though."

"Let's not analyze Daniel, Hector projector."

"Fine, I won't then." He held up a copy of *Love in the Time of Cholera*. "This is what I'm actually reading right now. Gabriel García Márquez, very good, you must read it."

Giving me the Coles Notes synopsis, he explained the story of Florentino Ariza, a man who lost his true love when young and, heartbroken, waited his entire life for her, over fifty years, his passion never subsiding, until finally, when the woman's husband died in late life, they reunited, spending their elder years and the rest of their lives together.

I listened, surprised by the romantic narrative.

McNeal continued on with the punchline. "But during those fifty years, he sleeps with over six hundred other women."

"Oh brother! There's Latin machismo for you."

"Hold on, it's a great novel. What you and most women don't realize is that every man wants to sleep with as many women as possible. It's the male fantasy. We're hard-wired. And we can still be in love with one woman."

"I don't think you can speak for all men. It sounds like it's true for you though?"

"Sex isn't the point; it's about the complicated nature of the human heart."

"Right. Let's focus on the man's complicated heart."

I was irritated, by Sade, by Márquez, and by McNeal.

"Don't look so disapproving," he said, grinning. "I'll make us some nachos to go with the beer." He put away the book, went to the kitchen, and sliced open a bag of tortilla chips, spreading the chips across a flat tray.

I banished the Sade passage from my mind and watched McNeal cook. Methodically, he positioned each tortilla chip, ensuring all the corn rounds were evenly spaced on the pan. Then he grated cheese, sprinkling each chip with precisely the same amount. I was surprised by this side of him, careful and structured, in contrast to the loquacious, seemingly impulsive and passionate man I was entranced by. He mashed an avocado until the pulp was thoroughly smooth, mixed in some pressed garlic, and produced a jar of salsa from the fridge.

"Why don't you stay a few days, or stay the whole week? Come on."

"I can't stay a week. What if Daniel phones when I'm up here? It's too complicated. I'm going back to Calgary tomorrow—and I want to hike up to Moose and tell him."

"Whoa! Wait a minute. We haven't resolved things yet. Not out but through, remember?"

McNeal adored the pithy saying "not out but through." I assumed he'd borrowed it from Jung, which would have bestowed the phrase with some degree of credibility. Years later I would learn it was Robert Frost who said, "The best way out is always through."

In terms of his moral stance on relationships, Kerouac would have provided a better defence than Robert Frost. In *On the Road*, the lookout bible, Kerouac rebelled against convention.

> ...the only people for me are the mad ones, the ones who are mad to live, mad to talk, mad to be saved, desirous of everything at the same time, the ones who never yawn or say a commonplace thing, but burn, burn, burn like fabulous yellow roman candles exploding like spiders across the stars...[6]

I was mad to talk, except that no amount of talking would convince McNeal the way forward had to be through honesty. We were more like a

Redbird matchstick than a yellow Roman candle, snubbed and extinguished after a quick burst of flame, leaving behind the smell of sulphur and a tiny wisp of smoke.

McNeal would sooner stand on Carbondale Hill in a lightning storm than agree with my plan to tell Daniel. I had harboured the lie for three months, and I couldn't bear to carry on the duplicity any longer—definitely not for the rest of the summer.

"I wish you wouldn't do this. It's not a good idea."

"I have to, I can't keep lying."

"Then call me as soon as you get back down from Moose," he sighed.

I searched his narrow brown eyes for a sign of trust, and all I could see was anxiety.

Later that summer Tomas would write to me from his lookout, defending McNeal:

> Mary, you are indeed one of the deep rooted members of our little social web, especially now with the McN link, you have obviously graduated into the inner world of the madcaps....I know McN relatively well, you can be assured after so many years of intense missive exchanges, the soul of the other is bound to be exposed; we have come to know each other's most intimate thoughts. There is a speck of genius in the man, all which goes to say that I value your masculine taste. He is a radical, in fact he swims against the current of status quo mentality, a subversive with a powerful impact. To have become involved with him is not a mistake Mary— and I really want to emphasize that; he is a poet, a musician, with a refined understanding of love in relationship with a woman.... His view on sexual love and relationship are antithesis to John's i.e. the left hand path instead of the right; he has the psychic poise to give freedom and not own a woman....
>
> Tomas
> Mockingbird Lookout

I had never aspired to the Kerouac school of madcaps, but I had been deemed worthy of honorary membership. By virtue of an affair with McNeal, my value, from Tomas's perspective, had catapulted me into a special category of madwoman. If I spent the summer travelling back and forth between Moose Mountain and Carbondale Lookout, like a migratory sparrow, I would definitely be deserving of a madcap badge. So far, that's all I had done—I had no job, no income, and no future plans now that my application to grad school had failed. And the more time I spent visiting men on fire lookouts, the less time I had for my job search.

I opened my tiny pocket copy of the *I Ching: The Book of Change*, translated by Thomas Cleary, which I have kept to this day. I had learned to perform a divination by tossing three coins, usually pennies, as an alternative to the traditional Chinese method of assembling and disassembling fifty yarrow stalks. I closed the door of my bedroom, lit a candle and a stick of Padmini incense, and prayed for guidance.

I cupped the coins, shaking them in the palm of my hands, and let them spill across the bedspread. Heads were worth three, tails worth two; as such, each toss of the three coins could add up to a value of six, seven, eight, or nine, depending on the combination of the falling coins. I tossed the coins six times, recording the results of each toss with a prescribed line marking. My double trigram complete, I consulted the *I Ching* to learn the outcome.

-- --
-- --

There are sixty-four possible trigram combinations in the *I Ching*, and I had landed the one and only trigram referred to as Fidelity. The trigram is composed of Sky over Thunder or strength/creativity over action/nature. Shaken by the synchronicity, I stared at the prose accompanying the trigram. A passage in the text read:

> Fidelity is very successful, beneficial if correct. If you deny what is right, you are mistaken and will not benefit from going anywhere....Thunder travels under the sky, things go along with fidelity....You should be true, then you will be blameless.[7]

Sky, or the Creative Spirit, was over Thunder, the Arousing—the trigram was instructing me to ensure my actions were in accord with a higher purpose, and my own creativity, rather than desires of the personality. I stared at the reading, awestruck, and told myself a story about fidelity—about how I would be true to my own heart. My unfaithful heart.

How much hubris was there in requesting divine guidance and then bargaining with the answer?

I dragged out the orange JanSport backpack Daniel had given me, throwing in a change of clothes and some personal items. Tomorrow was summer solstice, June 21, the longest day of the year, a good day for truth telling. The trail would be swarming with hikers on a Sunday, but if I started walking later in the afternoon, I would arrive at the summit after folks had headed back to the city.

The first few kilometres of the hike were gentle, a pleasant walk through mixed aspen, spruce, and pine forest. I stole glimpses of the fire lookout, romantic in its isolation, through openings in the trees. The trail steadily gained elevation, but before leaving the treeline, I encountered a steep section of the trail where boulders protruded from the earth, obstructing the old fire road. The grade here was steep and the direction of the trail due west. I scrabbled around the big rocks, and the sun, diamond bright, almost blinded me. I heard voices on the trail ahead, and a couple of hikers came around the bend, bracing their feet on the gravelly descent.

"You must be Mary," said one of the hikers.

"Hey, how do you know that?"

"We walked all the way to the lookout, and the guy working up there said we'd probably pass you coming down. He's waiting for you. We left some chicken and salad for your dinner."

Fidelity, constancy of heart. My resolve softened for a moment. I had no desire to split up with Daniel; perhaps telling the truth was a dreadful mistake.

After thanking them, I hiked on, ascending a high, barren ridge, where tiny, blood-red flowers poked out of the shale. The sunlight, radiant that day, permeated the mountain with golden light. Puffy cumulus clouds floated across a vast, spacious sky, and as I trudged higher, closing the gap between me and the rocky summit, I deliberated what to tell.

Staying on the old fire road, I followed the switchbacks up a steep wall of scree to the Moose dome, and reached the top, panting for breath. I saw the big boulder where I had stashed the groceries in the May snowstorm. Now, Daniel would spot me in the binoculars.

I could see a figure on the catwalk. Then I heard Daniel blow into a conch. The echo reverberated across the mountain peaks, calling me higher. I quickened my pace, driven by the trumpet-like call, which pulled me up the final pinnacle of rock.

He had swung open the heavy metal door, and the crackle of radio voices drifted over the side of the mountain. For me, the intrusive quality of the forestry radio had become a signal of home, strangely familiar and comforting. On warm, dry weekends like this, when thousands of Albertans headed to the foothills to go camping and hiking, rangers monitored the recreation areas closely, and the lookout was bombarded by radio voices. But by Sunday evening most hikers had gone back to Calgary and the forest was calm, a temporary respite before the next onslaught of fire-suppression activity.

"Hey, you must have passed those last hikers. They brought up fried chicken and gave us the leftovers." Daniel hugged me tight.

I disengaged, stepping back. "I know, they told me. I met them right as they came down off the high ridge."

He circled the fire finder, breezy and carefree, his eyes tracking the landscape as he chattered about the chicken, hikers, Gore-Tex, and his latest observation that most hikers wore clothing branded with the Mountain Equipment Co-op logo. I listened, unable to concentrate.

"I have something to tell you." I had to unburden myself.

Daniel halted, sensing my tone, and leaned against the fire finder.

"I don't know how to say this, so I'll just say it: I got involved with McNeal."

"McNeal—really?" Daniel was motionless, staring out the windows.

"I didn't want to keep lying. It hasn't been going on for that long."

"How long is 'not that long'?"

"Well, since that trip to Toronto in March." I cringed with the admission.

"Really, that's what, three months now. And you're telling me because it's ended?"

"Well, not exactly. I haven't ended it."

Hearing the words aloud, I felt mean, punishing. Here I was hiking to a fire lookout, announcing my betrayal, and then leaving the next day.

I sat on the high stool where I always sat at Moose, and where Daniel sat when he was alone. He leaned his back against the fire finder, facing me. I swivelled sideways, half-turned toward him, half-turned toward the windows. We gazed east, toward the prairies, the direction we always looked at Moose. Looking east was natural and restful, open and inviting, low undulating hills, stands of aspen, spruce, and farmland stretched into a long distant vista; whereas to the west, toward the wilderness, the Rockies' massive presence was so close it occluded a long gaze. The finger-like folds of the mountains turned purple and then steely grey, as the sun set lower and lower in the northwest. Twilight would last until almost eleven o'clock that night.

"*Not exactly* over?" Daniel trained his gaze on me, as though spotting a smoke.

"It's still going on. I'm still going down to Carbondale."

"I guess we're splitting up then," he said. "That's what you're telling me, right? Everybody's just trying to be happy. You're just trying to be happy, I guess."

I had expected anger, a show of pleading or bargaining, but Daniel's resignation caught me off guard. I wasn't prepared for such rational finality, for no resistance. He put on music, the theme to *Twin Peaks*, Angelo Badalamenti's grand, solemn composition. We sat for a long time, watching the light fade, the light of the longest day of the year, falling away tone by tone.

"Do you really think you're going to be happy with that guy? I can't believe it, sheesh. I thought he was planning to go to Egypt or Sudan or somewhere far away and exotic. How's that gonna work for you?"

There was a wide space between us. It felt surreal. Daniel circled the fire finder, careful to avoid physical contact. He tidied his work desk, shuffled papers, gathered dirty cups, and folded up leather for his drums. Zip stirred, stretching at his feet, and Daniel scooped up the dog and slid into the hammock, cradling the animal on his lap, picking at the knotted blond fur. Maybe I had made a mistake and confused the airy height of the lookout with my real life in the valley? Maybe the perspective up here was warped? Could I be dizzy, altitude sick, seduced by the panorama? Instead of expressing doubt and moving closer, I forged ahead with the visionary plot.

"Maybe I'll go to Egypt too."

Daniel looked as if I'd said I was converting to Islam.

"What? It's possible. Maybe I could go to university in Cairo, if McNeal gets that director's job at the Canadian Institute of Egyptology."

"Really." He stroked Zip's fur, swaying in the hammock, and said, "Well, I'll keep the door open. In case things don't work out."

"Do you mean that?"

"Yeah, I do. You were the best partner I ever had. The door's always open."

If I was hoping for absolution, surely this was it.

The next day, sadly, I hiked off Moose, picking my way downhill along the rocky path, feeling like a character in someone else's life. There was no animosity or harsh words. If I had doubts or had dissociated from what was happening, the implications of my actions were made clear—and public.

As soon as I was gone, Daniel made a stack of sepia postcards depicting Moose Lookout on the barren rocks, and in the coming weeks he proceeded to write all his friends and family with the news of our breakup. He must have had over a hundred contacts in his address book, and by announcing the news over and over again, *Mary and I have split up, she's seeing McNeal,* he adjusted to being single. Not that he didn't miss me, or feel sadness, but he didn't indulge in self-pity. I suppose the postcard project was therapeutic, an expressive way of coming to terms with our sudden breakup.

In keeping with the history of our relationship, even the breakup was harmonious, but Daniel had kept a secret about his past while we were together—a secret he would eventually tell.

More than ten years earlier, in the spring of 1981, Daniel had also been posted to Moose Mountain Lookout, his first season on a southern lookout in the Bow-Crow Forest. After surviving two mosquito-filled summers on bush towers in northern Alberta, Cowpar and Birch Mountain Lookout, he was elated to be assigned a location where he could have visitors.

That first year Daniel worked on Moose Mountain, a young woman named Faith was hired as a radio operator at the Elbow Valley ranger station. Faith wore cowboy boots to the office, real cowboy boots that had known saddle stirrups and manure. She had grown up on a nearby horse and cattle ranch in the Bragg Creek area, and her father and brother rustled cattle and mended fences for a living—men's work.

"Good morning everyone, this is XMC26 for your morning weather."

Faith had the softest voice in the world. Dreamy soft. Daniel wanted to lie down on the bed and let his body soak up Faith's voice. Her voice was soothing, like balm of Gilead oil, but waiting his turn to pass the weather to her gave him the jitters. Daniel positioned the microphone with care, striving to modulate his voice more perfectly. Should he speak more softly, like Faith, or should he let the natural enthusiasm in his voice resonate over the forestry airwaves?

One evening, preoccupied with Faith's voice and her unknown appearance, Daniel took a risk and called her up on channel six, the "off-camera" channel, hoping she might chat. The radio had been quiet for hours. They talked for a while, but afterwards, he worried he had blathered for too long, hardly giving her a chance to speak, to bless him with her silky speech. He plotted a reason to fly down to the ranger office with Jim, the district helicopter pilot, one day when it was low hazard and she was on shift in the radio room.

Faith was tiny, petite, with a pale complexion and long, dark hair, a woman so delicate Daniel instinctively wanted to protect her. She had strange eyes, like the eyes of a cat, and they were sanpaku, the white sclera visible above the iris. He invited her to dinner on the fire lookout, and she accepted, saying she could hike up Moose on her next day off. Jim, the pilot, got wind of the whole flirtation and flew Faith up by chopper, delivering her to the top of Moose Mountain like an exotic gift from one man to another. Then, he lifted off the helipad without making arrangements to fly Faith back down.

They talked easily for hours, about growing up in Alberta, about their jobs and the rangers and initial-attack guys, the other fire lookouts and guessing what people were like by listening to their radio voices. Faith was unlike any woman Daniel had ever known. She was a true country person, a self-taught naturalist who knew all kinds of things about the local Alberta landscape and history. Daniel was unlike any man she had ever met, a vegetarian who meditated and listened to strange Indian sitar music. Faith had brought along an art book about Michelangelo and she showed Daniel her favourite paintings, all of which had religious themes of salvation and suffering. Daniel suppressed his disappointment in her Christian beliefs, feigning interest in Michelangelo and European painting.

They lingered in each other's company until almost 2:00 a.m., and then Faith gathered up her things, saying she had better get home. She had parked her Bronco at the trailhead.

"I'll go with you, it's so dark." Daniel couldn't bear to imagine her walking alone on the trail. There were cougars and black bears on this mountain.

"But then you'll have to hike all the way back up. I'll be all right on my own."

"I have all night and I don't have to pass weather until seven thirty tomorrow morning," Daniel insisted.

"Well, okay, it is kind of late to be hiking alone."

They set off, stumbling in the dark on the rocky trail, stopping to catch their breath when they reached the dome.

"We've been walking for half an hour and we haven't gotten very far." Faith's voice was even softer than usual. "This is ridiculous, let's go back. I can hike down on my own early in the morning."

"Okay, I can give you my bed and I'll sleep on the floor tonight." Daniel was elated.

Inside the lookout, Daniel kept his promise without complaint, making himself a bed on the floor with spare blankets. He felt peaceful: this beautiful creature was only an arm's length away for the entire night. They whispered in the dark, Faith's tender voice so close Daniel was too excited to sleep.

"Why don't you come up here with me? This isn't right, you down there on the floor."

"Really?" Daniel couldn't believe his luck.

"Yeah, you should sleep up here." Faith's voice was like a feather, teasing.

Daniel stripped off the sweatpants and shirt he had put on for protection against the cold floor. He dived into the narrow bed, and the cowgirl moulded herself perfectly inside his limbs. Faith's Christian faith no longer mattered—for Daniel, her body and her presence were a revelation.

It was mid-season, just past solstice or early July, when Faith slept over, and for the rest of the summer, Daniel encouraged her to hike up on her days off. It was different hearing her speak his call sign on the radio now. The fantasy evoked by her soft voice had been partially diminished, but now he was falling in love. He accepted that she couldn't visit every weekend, and he never pressured, but he missed her all the time. No sooner had she left than he longed for her next visit.

Every time a female hiker popped into the frame of his binoculars, his pulse quickened, his mood surged, and his mind began the endless loop. *Was that her coming over the crest of the dome? Surely she'll be back soon?* He wondered whether she thought about him. The intrusive thoughts overtook him to such a degree, he told himself to forget about her until fall. Once he was off the lookout in September, or maybe October if it was a dry year, he'd find her in town. The fall was coming, a few months, weeks really.

They had shared many details of their lives. Daniel had disclosed his complicated, on-again, off-again relationship with Eileen, his years of teaching meditation, assigning mantras, and the commitment to his current guru. He had told Faith he had no interest in a regular career, only the desire to make beautiful pots and become spiritually enlightened.

He worried he had said too much.

The news of their affair leaked out to other Forestry employees, and Daniel heard that one of the initial-attack guys had posted a sign at the office: "Who is going to win the competition for Faith?" Later the sign was replaced with another message: "Daniel won the competition over Faith." The whole thing creeped him out, but there was nothing he could do from the top of Moose Mountain.

Daniel imagined spending the next winter in Bragg Creek. He and Faith would buy their own farmhouse. In the spring, he could go back to the lookout job and Faith could keep the farm running. He would marry her and keep Moose Mountain as his lookout, and when he went to work, his wife would always be nearby. Maybe they could find a property with a view of Moose Lookout from the backyard. He would build a studio in the farmhouse and make pots during the winters.

Daniel and Faith.

The day the ranger closed Moose Mountain fire lookout for the season, Daniel headed straight to Faith's house in Bragg Creek. When lookouts close up for the season, the announcement goes out over the radio, so surely she knew he was coming down. In forest circles, they'd say, "Dan, we're taking you down next week." Taking you down. And the lookout would tell everyone, "I'm coming down next week," not "I'm going home." It was always about *coming down*. Down to the ground, to the regular world, to reality.

Daniel knocked on Faith's door, the ranch house where she lived with her parents. He had met her mother briefly that summer, during a quick trip to town for groceries during a rainy spell. Surely her mother would help him find her.

She wasn't home. He phoned her repeatedly, and checked for her at the ranger station. He looked for her in town. Maybe she was shopping or having coffee. Any minute he would find her and she would throw her arms around him. All day he waited, hoping she would call him back at the ranger station.

He obtained permission to sleep in the bunkhouse at the ranger station, which was empty at the end of the firefighting season. He lay alone in one of the bunks, unable to sleep, confused and deflated. He tried to calm his mind, to arrest the feeling of dread; after all, he was the student of a major American guru, and he should be able to calm his mind and find equanimity, despite what was happening. Except that he didn't know what was happening, or why Faith was avoiding him. Would a woman named Faith really betray him?

The next day he started the search again. He found her car and left a note under the windshield wiper. He left another note. And another. He drove around Bragg Creek hunched over like depressed Binky, unable to stop looking. The sight of Moose Mountain on the horizon crushed him with memories of their intimacy, and sent him reeling into a fresh cycle of anxiety. Nothing made sense. He had to talk to her. He had to know why things had changed.

The bunkhouse became home, a prison cell he occupied voluntarily. After several weeks of waiting, the ranger offered him temporary work on the Forestry Christmas tree farm, thinning young spruce trees. Daniel accepted the job, determined to stick around until he found her and they spoke. Every morning the workers crowded into a shuttle van and drove from Bragg Creek to the tree farm, and every evening they drove back together. Then, one morning Faith boarded the van, a co-worker, one of the Christmas tree thinners. They worked together daily for several weeks.

But Faith refused to speak to him about their wordless breakup. Obviously she had no intention of being with him, but Daniel persisted, living in the bunkhouse until December, perhaps one of the most committed acts of his twenty-seven years.

One day at work she broke the silence. "It'll never work between you and me, Daniel. We're from two different worlds. You should marry Eileen. Go. I want you to be with Eileen. Things are right that way."

At last Faith had spoken. She was a Christian cowgirl and her life path was incompatible with a lookout man and artist like Daniel. For her, their differences were irreconcilable; for Daniel, their differences were simply mysterious, a curiosity, grist for the mill of life.

Exhausted by the disappointment and months of waiting, Daniel instructed Forestry staff that he would not be returning to Moose Mountain. He was done working on fire lookouts and would launch a pottery studio in British Columbia. He packed up his belongings, drove over the Rocky Mountain Great Divide, and descended into the Okanagan Valley.

That winter he constructed a beautiful pottery studio with clay drying racks, a kiln, and wooden birdcages housing exotic quail.

The next spring, in April 1982, with no income from his pottery, he contacted Alberta Forestry and requested any fire lookout other than Moose Mountain for the coming season. He could not bear to return there and listen to Faith's voice over the radio. To protect himself, he accepted a lonely post in northern Alberta, Birch Mountain, a fire tower he had done in 1979. Packing up a few boxes of belongings, he boarded the Greyhound bus in Vernon and travelled to northern Alberta near Fort McKay, where he was flown in to the lookout. The only visitors he had for the entire season were the ranger and helicopter pilot who delivered his groceries and water once a month.

Later he learned that Faith was pregnant when she sent him away; he was not the father.

How was it that Moose Mountain could be so unkind, so unlucky? Two women had left him on the rocky pinnacle, as though his destiny were inscribed in this place; he had become the Beloved of the mountain Herself.

As the weeks of summer passed and Daniel contemplated his unexpected freedom, the formations of the surrounding mountains assumed the curves and features of a woman's body: the gorge reminded him of the fold of a thigh; the bulge of a rock outcropping, a breast; the moss-covered clearing above Canyon Creek, a pubic bone. For hours at a time, he gazed at the contours of his beloved, his binoculars sweeping over the natural rock surfaces. Their femaleness circled and enveloped him, an enduring presence that offered comfort.

Zip

At the end of June, the summer days cooled off abruptly and a low-pressure system with rain and grey clouds ushered in July. If it was this overcast in town, I knew Daniel would be sitting up on Moose in heavy fog conditions. The cloud and fog could make it impossible to see anything except the black catwalk railing. Because Zip's back had never fully healed from the bad jump, in the middle of the night, Daniel still had to carry the dog outside to pee on the rocks below the catwalk.

It was during this rainy spell in early July that he called me over the forestry radio, his voice flat, serious. At first I figured his depressed tone was due to our breakup and he needed to talk.

"Something terrible happened today, and I want to tell you about it."

"Of course, what is it?" I imagined a hiker had an accident on the mountain or ran into an aggressive bear.

"Zip was attacked by a cougar."

"No! A cougar? Oh God, what happened?"

"I'm still in shock, but basically a cougar came right up to the door of the lookout."

He told me how the white fog had drifted up against the building, and he had left the lookout door open because it was a calm day, and the small space felt larger and less claustrophobic in the fog when he propped open the door. But then it got chilly, and he had turned on the propane heater to stay warm.

The foggy weather never deterred hikers; he couldn't see them coming in the fog, but he could hear them approach, boots crunching on the shale rock, voices calling out in exclamation on the final section of the trail. A young couple emerged out of the fog, and eagerly accepted the invitation to come inside and warm up. He said the couple looked like novice hikers, too urban for the outdoors, almost out of place on the mountain.

After entertaining a few questions about the loneliness of lookout life, he carried on with his daily tasks as they talked, and grabbed a can of Pedigree dog food to feed Zip.

"The smell of canned meat is so overpowering, I always feed Zip outside, right?"

That was true; I was used to watching him open the can of meat and dash outside with the dog bowl to prevent the odour from fouling the lookout.

Outside, he spooned half the can into a bowl and placed it on a wooden platform, the remains of the old cabin floor, a few metres from the lookout. He went back inside to rejoin the hikers, pacing in front of the fire finder, and glancing out the window now and then, but Zip's white fur blended into the fog.

Then, there were sounds of growling and scuffling outside. "I told the couple it must be more hikers arriving with big dogs."

He stepped outside onto the catwalk in his socks and looked toward the platform where he had left Zip.

A flash of brown fur, the back of another dog—or some other animal. He peered into the fog. What kind of animal was down there?

The flick of a long curled tail. The head of a large cat. He was watching the body of a tan-coloured cougar glide through the fog, mouth half-open.

The cougar gripped Zip by the neck and the dog's body hung upside down, helpless.

Daniel grabbed a nearby wooden plank, about sixty centimetres long, and ran onto the jagged rocks, lunging at the huge cat. The cat gracefully moved aside, purring loudly. Missed. There was only two metres between him and the cougar, but without shoes, he couldn't move as nimbly as usual on the sharp rocks. He chased the cougar and swung the board at the cat again; the animal effortlessly jumped aside. Daniel stopped to assess the situation and stared into the yellowish eyes of the cougar. The animal crouched and purred from the back of its throat, holding Daniel's gaze.

"I couldn't chase the cougar, it was futile, so I picked up a few heavy rocks and threw them at the animal's head."

The cougar dodged the ammunition, moving aside with ease, as though flaunting its strength and superior reflexes.

The city-slicker hikers had come outside after seeing Daniel sprint across the rocks, and witnessed the gory events from the safety of the catwalk.

"Be careful," they yelled. "Don't get too close."

Ignoring the hikers and the cougar, Daniel focussed on Zip and spoke gently, "You're a good dog, Zip, such a good dog."

Distressed, he hobbled back to the lookout, plucked his Nikon camera off the counter, slipped on boots, and ran back to the resting cougar. He snapped three photographs, speaking to Zip softly the whole time.

"I love you, buddy. You've been the best dog, Zip. You've been a really good dog. It's all right. It's okay."

Zip wagged his tail, his round, human-like eyes pleading at Daniel.

The cougar clenched its jaw tight, and Daniel said the life force exited Zip's shaggy body. Then the big cat skulked over the rocks, Zip hanging limp from his mouth, crossed the hiking trail, and vanished over the south side of the mountain in the clouds.

In shock, Daniel went back inside the lookout and sat down.

"I had Zip for ten years," he told the couple. "I got him when I lived in a spiritual community in California in the eighties. He was such an unusual dog, my best buddy."

"We're so sorry this happened. Do you think it's safe for us to hike down? That is, if you're okay." The young man and woman looked terrified.

Daniel said they wanted nothing more than to get back to Calgary. "I think you'll be fine walking down."

After they were gone, he radioed the Forestry office and reported that the cougar had killed his dog. A few minutes later, a neighbouring fire observer, Milt McGee, called him.

"C29, go over to channel six."

Daniel switched to the private radio channel.

"Daniel, sorry to hear about the cougar attack. Listen, man, that's a huge shock. At five o'clock this afternoon, I'm going to do a reiki healing for you, send you some positive energy. Okay?"

"Thanks, Milt, sure."

At five, he lay down on the bed and tried to relax, the last images of Zip flashing across his mind.

"Poor Zip," I gasped. "I'm sorry you're alone up there. Do you want me to come up?" I could not believe this had happened two weeks after we separated. The timing was uncanny.

"I'll be all right, that's okay. I just wanted to talk. You know, I don't think the nerves in his back were ever going to heal. I knew he might be at the end, but I never dreamed a cougar would come so close to the building."

"Yeah, does it make you nervous?"

"Not really, I don't think a cougar is going to jump a six-foot-tall man."

"Now, don't take this the wrong way, but I'm surprised you were able to take photographs."

"I know, it's just me. I had to document it. I had done everything I could to save him, and when I realized he was going to die, I wanted a record of what happened. I don't intend to show the photos to anyone, not you or anyone. They're for me."

"I'd rather not see them anyway."

"Well, I better get off the radio. Talk to you later. Good luck finding work."

Daniel's encounters with wild animals did not end with the cougar.

The next day after the morning weather sked, he hiked over the rocks in the direction the cougar had walked, searching for signs of Zip's remains. He discovered a drop of blood on the rocks near the lookout, a small piece of fur, and dog excrement. He kept walking, slid down the side of the mountain in the scree, toward Canyon Creek, and scanned the grey rocky slope, expecting to see more blood, red stains on grey, snatches of Zip's white and blond fur, or even body fragments.

Nothing.

Feeling he was being watched, Daniel turned and looked up at the ridge south of the lookout. A lone grey wolf stood in silhouette. Daniel stiffened on the incline; the back of his neck tingled. For a second, he and the wolf locked gazes, and then Daniel scrambled back up the cliff, heading for the safety of the lookout.

He had never before experienced or heard about a wolf sighting on Moose Mountain.

Wolves represent monogamy and loyalty; they also symbolize freedom.

All Is Fair in Love and War—or Is It?

"Binky, oh man, when I hear how he reacted, I think maybe he was kind of relieved, you know what I mean?"

"Relieved? Uh, I don't know about that."

"Yes, relieved." McNeal challenged me like a psychoanalyst voicing an uncomfortable perspective. "Think about it—most men would be pretty angry to get that news."

"Daniel isn't like most men. He's not reactive, he's reflective."

We sat in the kitchen at Carbondale and rehashed my trip to Moose, speculating about Daniel's response to my disclosure.

"Sure, Binky's a sensitive guy, but his partner just told him she was sleeping with another guy and he calmly says, 'Everyone just wants to be happy'? Come on. On some level he's partially relieved."

McNeal and I were both analytical, but somehow we always reached opposing conclusions. His interpretation hurt: if Daniel was relieved to have his freedom back, then that was a harsh review of our relationship.

"He doesn't believe in convincing anyone to do anything."

"That's a ridiculous position. Didn't he get upset or angry at all?"

"Not in front of me. We slept in the same bed too. He stayed way over on his side, though, as if I had a contagious disease." I studied McNeal for a reaction but he gave nothing.

"Oh man, I've been on the lookout in circumstances like that—*in extremis*. Big time. It sucks. I should send him a letter when I get serviced."

"What do you mean—an apology?"

"An apology? No, we're all consenting adults here. But I've known the guy for years, I like him, and I want him to know as far as I'm concerned, he and I are still friends. Maybe I'll send him over a box of Oreos." McNeal laughed. "He'll binge his way through the whole box in one day!"

Under the circumstances, fraternity humour seemed inappropriate. I was certain Daniel would be baffled if a chopper pilot landed at Moose with a box of Oreos from Captain Midnight.

Why was McNeal compelled to reach out to Daniel in the guise of the Sugar Prankster? Maybe I had it all wrong. Was McNeal asserting his "sugar" territory, awarding Daniel a compensation prize for placing second in a boys' competition?

"I don't think Daniel will find Oreos all that funny," I said, keeping my analysis to myself.

"Sure he will—it's hilarious. It's a lookout thing. I used to hang my ex's panties from the radio antenna when she came to visit!"

"Like a waving flag?" I said.

McNeal nodded in agreement, snickering as though it had just happened.

I had trouble connecting the masculine dots. How did the panty raider and sugar prankster map onto the religious studies scholar? To me, the panty flag was adolescent; it was also a symbolic announcement to other men that he had a woman at the lookout. After all, raising flags is about territory. As for the Oreos, perhaps I was wrong and Daniel would find the sugar prank gut-wrenchingly funny, rather than a replacement for sexual appetite.

If so, I'd have to reassess my understanding of men and masculinity.

It had been overcast and drizzling at Carbondale for days, the damp weather confining us indoors. A shroud of cloud and fog surrounded the lookout, and the ennui of cabin fever set in, a hint of boredom and the realization we could become tired of the company that had once brought such excitement. We had arrived at the doorstep of a familiar daily routine interspersed with predictable sex. One night McNeal complained that because we watched the news at 11:00 p.m. and then had sex, he was always shortchanged on sleep.

"Well, that's easy to solve," I said. "As soon as the news is over, we'll go right to sleep. I prefer a relaxed afternoon session anyway."

"That's not what I mean," he said, laughing self-consciously. "I'm just saying."

"I know what you're saying, I'm the Queen of Sleep. But I can't change the CBC broadcast schedule."

"And we can't really reverse things," he said, as though thinking out loud. "It wouldn't work so well to have sex earlier and wrap things up by 10:55 to get ready for the news."

"We could," I countered, playing along. "It's not like either of us has any problems in the libido department. But it's a bit structured, don't you think?"

"Yeah, I'm not suggesting it or anything," he said.

"Anyway, it's not like there's hours of lovemaking going on into the night."

"Is that a complaint of some kind?" He bristled.

"No, I'm talking about the time issue, that's all."

"Good, because I want to know all your fantasies. I want to get inside your head. Tell me everything." He pulled me toward him, cradling my head in his hands.

In the flash of bodily resistance, I had to admit that I didn't trust him with my fantasies or feelings. And definitely not with my underwear.

The fire hazard had been rated low for over a week and the forecast predicted more rain, so McNeal radioed the Blairmore ranger station, and, with his rare gift for doublespeak, obtained permission to be away from the radio without divulging his exact plans. He implied, in a roundabout way, that he might be doing a long hike in the area and unavailable to answer his call sign for the rest of the day.

We locked up, scooted down the hill on the motorcycle, jumped into the Subaru, and drove out of the bush, cruising north on Highway 2, straight road all the way to Calgary. It felt wrong to be sitting in the passenger seat of the Subaru with McNeal driving.

"Where'd you get this vehicle—from *The Flintstones*?" He pointed at the holes in the floorboard; the pavement flashed by under our feet.

"I know, I know. It's rust. The dampness in BC corroded the metal."

"I feel like Fred Flintstone driving a prehistoric car, you know, the ones you pedal with your feet!" He jabbed me in the ribs, delighted with his own joke.

"This is the last trip this car's making to Carbondale," I said. "Daniel needs it to get back home in the fall. And it has to last through the next winter in the country."

"Okay, okay, lighten up. Let's not argue. We're going to Cowtown."

McNeal turned forty years old in a few days, and he was keen to throw a birthday party on the lookout. I couldn't figure out who would come to this party, but he was confident he could solicit party guests from the forest district. He wanted to shop for snacks, beer, and champagne in Calgary, because the selection would be better than in Pincher Creek. I think he also wanted a break from the lookout and the incessant rain and fog.

The traffic was heavy and congested in the city, especially on Crowchild Trail and Memorial Drive. Impatient with other drivers, McNeal darted in and out of lanes, changing gears constantly, his hand on the stick shift as though in a car race.

"Do you always drive like this?" I asked.

"What?" he said. "Look at that idiot trying to make a left turn. Stupid asshole. Where'd he get his fucking licence?"

I felt like a hostage, the only person who could hear his angry outbursts.

We shopped in Sunnyside, making quick stops at the liquor store, Earth Harvest, and Safeway.

"Let's go back to Athena's and take a break," I suggested.

"Sure, I got everything I need for the party. Let's go relax."

After the drive with Evel Knievel, I definitely needed to relax. Athena had gone to the Vancouver Folk Music Festival, leaving us alone in the townhouse. We lounged on the futon couch, the steady percussion of rain in the background.

There was news I had not shared with anyone yet, and I had waited for the right moment to tell McNeal. Earlier in the month, I had received an offer from the University of Victoria to join the master's program in counselling psychology. This was the program that had rejected my application earlier in the spring. Unexpectedly, a space had opened up in the two-year, summer-based program, and the director had offered the place to me, making it clear I would have to move to Victoria immediately. The program had already started on July 2, which meant there was no time for deliberation. The Victoria cohort included students from the preparatory courses I had completed in Kelowna the previous winter. I felt comfortable with those folks; they were mature individuals and would be a positive and encouraging group for learning and practising counselling skills.

When the department secretary phoned, she said she needed my decision as soon as possible. "This offer cannot be postponed. If you turn it down, you will be given no advantage in the future. This is an exceptional situation; it's not an offer you can negotiate for a future placement."

I reflected on what it would take to move to Victoria, financially and emotionally. I had no savings, but if this is what I wanted, surely I could find the resources? The program ran until the end of August, after which I would need to move to Kelowna or Vernon to complete the part-time winter components. It was doable, but I certainly wouldn't be spending time with McNeal on Carbondale this summer. In September he would return to Toronto to complete his dissertation, curtailing the chance of developing a relationship.

There was a part of myself, an idealistic, relational, and feminine self that clung to the notion I could combine my life with McNeal's beyond the lookout. I just needed more time—or so I believed. To the degree that traditional masculinity defaults to autonomy, independence, and stoicism, traditional femininity defaults to relatedness, dependence, and emotional-ity. As such, the next day I phoned the university and declined the offer. They were annoyed; not only had the department made an exceptional offer, my peers had lobbied on my behalf and I had let them down.

Here was proof I could make poor decisions with or without tarot cards.

I told McNeal the short version, hoping he would support my deci-sion and encourage my studies at a more opportune time.

He looked incredulous. "Why did you say no? I thought that's what you wanted?"

"When I applied this spring, I had no idea all this was going to hap-pen." By "all this" I meant getting involved with him. "I couldn't see how everything would fit together. If I move to Victoria now, you might be headed back east by the time the eight-week program ends."

McNeal was silent, obviously disappointed by my decision. I stared through the glass sliding doors to the outside world; the city was obscured by low grey clouds.

"Plus, I'd have to do a counselling practicum all winter," I continued, "and I wouldn't be able to go to India. I thought we had a plan for the winter?"

Raindrops pinged on the balcony railing.

I fidgeted, waiting for reassurance.

"You should have taken it," he said firmly. "You should have put your career first."

Over the next few days, the skies cleared and a high-pressure system blew over the Rockies, bringing warm, summer temperatures back to southern

Alberta. In keeping with my über-feminine decision, I put aside career issues and focussed on my audition for the role of Super Girlfriend. I baked
a chocolate birthday cake for McNeal, prepared finger foods, vacuumed
the worn, grey carpet, and helped him tidy up the kitchen.

While I rehearsed my supporting role, McNeal lined up a playlist,
going through his music compilations and stacking his best Middle Eastern music next to the tape deck. On the day of the party, he opened the
lookout doors and windows and strains of Araby blasted down the sides
of Carbondale Mountain. Before any guests arrived, I reticently presented him with a gift: *Iron John: A Book about Men*, a mythopoetic blend of
Jungian psychology, fairy tales, and Robert Bly's verse. I was going for
scholarly, literary, and masculine in one small package. I was afraid he
might scoff and declare the choice New Age, but he accepted the book
with grace, impressed perhaps because Bly had translated the great mystic
poets, Rumi and Hafez. He inspected the table of contents, turning the
pages with interest.

"Thank you," he said in earnest, planted a light kiss on my lips, and
then reached for a smoke, as though a book about men sanctioned a cigar.

By early evening, vehicle engines chugged up the hill, and folks
crowded into the lookout. I knew none of them. As host, McNeal didn't
bother with introductions; I was on my own. There was a young, pretty
Forestry employee whom I had met at Carbondale on another occasion.
McNeal guided her upstairs into the cupola, under the auspices of showing
her something of import related to the fire finder, and spotting smokes.
She giggled, climbing the ladder in front of him, as he teased her about
leaving her husband at home. There was a blond woman everyone called
Laurie, a lookout observer from Porcupine Lookout, north of Carbondale.
She insisted McNeal light her cigarette with a pink Bic lighter, leaning
into him when the breeze extinguished his first attempt. I thought any
moment they would go mouth to mouth exchanging smoke. Then McNeal
dug out a box of cigars to celebrate and all the smokers were delighted to
be smoking indoors.

As usual, I drank American beer in a can, weaving a path around
guests, chatting with strangers at times, trying to catch the backstory of
people's lives and their position in the forest. I hoped no one would ask
me what I did, because I had no clue anymore. I was the only guest staying
overnight at the lookout, but I felt uncertain of my identity, intimate with
the host, an outsider at his party. There was never a moment when McNeal

and I held a conversation side by side, when he touched my arm, or indicated in even a subtle way that we were together.

When twilight came, McNeal herded everyone outside to a campfire in the meadow north of the lookout. The alcohol overrode his introverted tendencies, and he entertained the circle with witty stories about his travels in Sudan and Egypt, spicing the tales with the language of religious studies: the numinous, personal epiphanies, the light of the pleroma, demiurges and misanthropes. The women, enthralled, asked questions about his dissertation, could he explain Gnosticism, briefly, without using such mysterious words, yes, yes, he could oblige. It was like the Sermon on the Mount.

The next morning, the first thing I noticed was the pink lighter, an irritant, in the middle of the table.

"Geez, look at that," I said. "Laurie left her lighter behind, maybe it's a sign. I guess she'll need to come by for that sometime."

McNeal was on the offensive, his liver processing the alcohol excess. "So, she forgot her lighter. Big fucking deal. You're not gonna turn this into the Inquisition, it's nothing."

"You two flirted all night. And—you never introduced me. She had no idea we're involved."

"That's private, why should she know? I figured you knew Laurie."

"How would I know Laurie?"

"Through Daniel. She's been doing lookouts for years."

"Well, I don't know Laurie and she didn't speak to me all night."

Angry, I flicked the lighter open and the flame burned, blue and yellow. I was certain Laurie knew Captain Midnight.

"I'm going for a hike." McNeal put on his beige Tilley hat, which made him look like he was going on safari with the royals. He drew the string tight under his chin to prevent the blustery winds from snatching the hat.

"I'm going too," I said, grabbing a sweatshirt, and wrapping it around the waist of my cotton dress.

McNeal walked fast with long strides, putting as much distance as he could between us, but I scrambled down the ravine, keeping his backpack in sight, and managed to keep up. I had no idea where we were headed; we thrashed through the brush, scrambling downward into the shady ravine, and then climbed up, out of the ravine, onto high, dry ground. Northwest of the lookout, there were narrow trails etched into the ridges, undulating pathways that snaked a course across the foothills. We walked steadily

along these ridges and after forty-five minutes at the military pace, Mc-
Neal stopped to rest, letting me catch up. There was a boulder, shaped like
a large, smooth saddle, and he motioned for me to sit. Unzipping his pack,
he yanked out a bottle of champagne.

"Shall we?" He smiled.

I groaned at the sight of more alcohol.

"Hair of the dog, come on, let's toast my fortieth, you and me." He
popped the cork with his army knife and passed me the bubbly wine.

I took a swig.

"Don't be so downcast," he admonished, recalibrated by the vigor-
ous walk.

"I'm upset," I said.

"I know—but remember, all is fair in love and war," he guffawed.

I flinched, his words like a warning. "You think so? Actually, all is *not*
fair in love and war, which is why we have divorce courts and the Hague
Criminal Court."

Handing him my camera, I said, "Take my picture."

In the photo, I rest on the polished surface of the giant boulder, my
arms bare, streaky brown hair tousled by the wind, the bottle of champagne
clasped in my lap. Behind me, the long spiny ridge leads into the distant hills, green at the height of summer, and on the horizon, Carbondale
Lookout is a small, dark bulge against the hazy sky.

The next day, troubled, I left Carbondale and drove to the Kootenays
near Nelson, BC, to take a summer dance workshop. I danced for days,
until the sheer pleasure of movement and physical exhaustion transcended
the repetitive thoughts about my chaotic life.

When I returned to Calgary, there was a letter from Daniel, who
summed up the situation.

August 1, 1992
Moose Mountain

Mary Theresa Kelly, my dear, a nice snappy lightning display
chased the hikers off the abdomen of the dome (ab-dome-an).
I call that swollen protuberance such, because it seems to me
that I'm watching an embryonic creation unfold before me, as
hikers first appear as sexless specks, go on to develop arms, legs,
sex parts, hands, noses, fingers and Tilley hats. Sometimes they

abort the hike even before the final push, and then they disappear, specks into specks.

Jerome [technician] has done something to my antenna, which may make it difficult for me to use good ole channel 6. I'm still creatively experimenting. I wrote McNeal, a few pages, but don't feel I've much to say. Of course some would think I'd have lots to say, but I don't really. (I liked hearing all your stories, but I don't really want to hear all his for some reason.) It's one thing to have fallen in love with my partner, but I don't want to be requested to solve the problems that may have been created (Catherine etc....). I was kind of miffed to hear the general gist of your discussions. Sounds like he has his life (& money) all planned out and if you can pay your way it'd be nice to have you along—in Egypt, India, Carbondale. Does he share gas, insurance, & mufflers when you visit him? Perhaps he does but (as you say) it's a different kind of intimacy he seems to want than we may be used to....

I feel sorry for you, to tell you honestly, that it seems so difficult. But there's something there you wanted to check out and get into! That part is a bit mysterious to me, which is why I still tend to imagine it has as much to do with you wanting a change from the (perhaps stifling) harmony we enjoyed. We did enjoy that, but we knew big changes were coming to adapt to.

Most of all, I hope you find some work! A pay-cheque is a big pick-me-up! Stop worrying about boyfriend problemos and get a job! (Oops, I wasn't going to persuade anyone of anything—strike that last sentence.) I bet you had fun dancing (that's what I want to do more and more, weird). You and your gossamer jammies, wow! Good stuff.

I ordered "Solitude," "Yellow Silk" and "Eros and the Mysteries of Love: The Metaphysics of Sex"...see what friends we still are....

I got the Oreos. Why? He's looking after you, for when you visit here! He sounded peeved I wasn't writing & sharing, a few sly jabs well placed. Means no harm I'm sure but I tire of demands sometimes, to write & discuss & etc. etc. etc. You know the story with me. Distance makes the heart grow absent.

I'm glad you got an assignment! Yahoo. That's what I say, good, good, good. I wish you the best, whatever that might be? For you to find out!

Love,
Daniel

We had enjoyed harmony, a rarefied mutuality, but instead of opening the door to reinvigorate the space of relationship with more oxygen, I had lit a fire—and burned down the house. Now I was forced to rebuild my life from the ground up.

Cline Lookout

After the summer dance workshop, I drove back to Calgary, taking Highway 93 north to Banff National Park and linking up to the Trans-Canada Highway: this route ensured a detour to Carbondale Lookout would be impossible. As I coasted along the highway and stared at the world through the bug-splattered windshield, my own problems occupied my awareness, as though, myopically, I was at the centre of existence. We perceive in this egocentric and habitual fashion, despite knowing that all of manifestation, all pleasure and pain, is arising simultaneously, interconnected in a vast unified field.

Given how the summer had gone, what more could go wrong? That depended on how large a perspective and how much of the world I was ready to embrace.

I ran up the flight of stairs into the kitchen and put on the kettle for tea. Athena heard me rummaging around and came downstairs.

"Hey, you're back," she said. "Boil enough water for me. I'll have tea with you." She reached into the cupboard for a couple of Daniel's tea bowls.

"Sure," I answered, feeling an edge in her voice. Maybe Athena needed to raise my rent, or worse, maybe she wanted to reclaim her space and I would have to move out next month.

It was neither.

"John attacked Dinah at the lookout." She stirred milk and honey into the tea, the metal spoon scraping the sides of the ceramic bowl.

"What do you mean, he attacked her? They got into a fight up at Cline?"

"No, I mean literally, he *attacked* her, the asshole. Her face is black and blue."

I was bewildered. I had never heard about John and Dinah embroiled in conflict. She was no doubt tired of parenting alone half the year, but overall, to me, they seemed committed to each other.

"So, what happened? This is so weird, Athena!"

"I know. He's convinced she's having an affair with one of the Waldorf School parents."

"Oh God. This is awful. You've talked to her?"

"Yeah, she phoned while you were away."

"Should we go out to Bearspaw and see her?"

"No, she vacated the farmhouse and took the boys to her mom's place in Ontario for a while."

"So, what happened at Cline? She went up to the lookout in July, right?"

"Right. John had been freaking out for months, writing letters, phoning. Asking when she'd get to the lookout. He started to worry, and assumed she delayed the trip because she was having an affair. I think he may have accused her of cheating. But you know Dinah—she's busy and doesn't spend a lot of time crafting letters, the way Tomas does. If she was at home when John called, they spoke over the radio, but you know what that's like. It's not private."

What strange logic, I thought. A woman couldn't possibly be unavailable because she was engaged in her own life—she must be having an affair! How ridiculous. I felt smug in my judgment, momentarily, until I realized that's exactly what it *had* meant in my case.

"Yeah, the forestry radio is so frustrating," I said. "I hate it. It's good for grocery lists, but that's about all. It feels like everyone in the whole forest is listening."

"That's because they are, Mary." Athena grimaced and poured more tea. "Anyway, in the middle of July she finally packed up the car with kids and groceries, and made the four-hour drive into the mountains."

"Cline is west of Rocky Mountain House, isn't it?"

"Yeah, remote. Leave it to John to choose a lookout that's hard to get to."

"Hmm, I wonder why he never put in for a lookout closer to Calgary?"

"You wonder? Because he's John, that's why. Because he romanticizes the whole isolation shtick. Dinah's been doing this lookout scene for twelve years now, maybe more. The boys are nine and eleven, so their whole life has revolved around John going to the lookout. It's so male-focussed."

Athena was steadfast in viewing the world with a feminist lens. She had empathy for Dinah's situation, knowing first-hand what it was like to have a family with a seasonal dad on a fire lookout. "The whole thing is horrifying," she said. "Listen to what happened."

It was a sunny afternoon when Dinah boarded the forestry helicopter to fly into Cline with the two boys. They were eager to see their dad, squirming to catch first sight of the lookout building and the adventurous father they had not seen since April. The forestry pilot radioed the lookout, as usual, when they lifted off from the ranger station, and when the chopper landed, John came outside, approaching the helipad. The boys knew helicopter protocol; they waited for the pilot's nod and jumped out, ducking low and carrying bags into the lookout. Without delay, the pilot lifted off, giving the all-clear over the radio.

John yanked Dinah by the arm. "Don't go inside the lookout," he hissed. "You're not welcome here. Stay away! Do not go inside."

"You mean, as soon as she stepped off the helicopter, it started?" I couldn't help but interrupt. It sounded so extreme. Surely John wanted to have a conversation?

"No, he didn't want to talk," Athena said firmly. "He had already made up his mind. Dinah said his behaviour was strange right from the beginning. He was totally cold and aloof, which was so odd given he'd been pleading with her to come and visit."

Then, before disappearing inside, he scowled in her direction. "An unfaithful woman will not come in this lookout," he said.

"That's the phrase he used, 'unfaithful woman'?" I asked.

"Yes, archaic isn't it? Just wait." Athena continued.

Feeling exposed in the centre of the sunny meadow, Dinah walked toward the shelter of pine trees and shade at the edge of the forest. She needed to collect her thoughts. *An unfaithful woman? He must be convinced I'm having an affair. Because I didn't get here sooner. Or write more. Oh geez, this is just like John to make it all about himself.*

Leaving the boys inside the lookout, John strode across the meadow with unswerving purpose, robotically, as though he had Dinah in the crosshairs of the fire finder, a target in degrees and minutes. She detected his disturbed mental state from a distance.

His fury boiled, nourished by months of solitude and rumination.

He grabbed her with one hand and, with the other, slapped her hard across the face. Dinah fell backwards a few steps, shielding herself. "Stop and we'll talk," she said, but the blows kept coming. Feeling the enormity of his rage, she ran scenarios through her mind. *What to do next? How best to protect herself?* Then he punched her in the face with a closed fist, crouched over her, gripping her by the shoulder, and pressed her into the ground.

John reached into his pocket and pulled out a box cutter. He slid his thumb down the handle of the blade, flashing steel close to her face, and screamed. "I'm gonna cut off your nose, you bitch. If you come anywhere near this lookout, I'll cut it right off. Don't you know that's the punishment for an unfaithful wife?"

The immense space of the sky and mountains condensed, crystallizing into one small point on her face.

Hearing the threat, Dinah stopped her efforts to resist. She lowered her eyes in deference, avoiding his glare, and yielded to the ground, limp and lifeless. Focussing inward, she slowed her breath and played dead, the way she had mentally rehearsed in case she ever encountered a grizzly bear.

The voices of the children pierced their locked hold. John turned his head toward the lookout, and, feeling his grip lessen a notch, Dinah half opened her eyes and saw the boys in the doorway, calling out. The intensity of John's anger interrupted, she gathered herself into a ball and sprung out of the ground.

John knew he was being watched by his own children. "Get outa here, bitch," he said, standing between her and the boys, "or I'll cut off your nose."

Dinah seized her moment of freedom. As much as she feared leaving the boys, she wasn't running away from them, she was running toward help. She ran straight into the bush, into the protection of the forest, listening for any sign John might chase. Numb from the attack, she instinctively slowed for a few minutes; then adrenaline flooded her body, and she broke into a run, bushwhacking through the undergrowth, searching for a trail, afraid John would track her.

She ran as fast as she could without tripping over logs or rocks, blood trickling down her face, one eye swelled partially shut. But it wasn't her injuries that concerned her now; it was getting off this mountain and getting her boys. The mental picture of their innocent faces staring back impelled her escape. She had never hiked in or out of Cline and had no idea whether a hiking trail existed, but she knew hikers rarely, if ever, walked to the lookout. She didn't want to spend the night alone wandering around in the dark. If she kept walking downhill she would eventually come out on Abraham Lake. She had no water, food, or extra clothing.

Breathless, she pushed on for hours, unable to find a trail, picking her way through the aspen and pine forest, steadily descending. The spruce and pine trees became taller, their trunks wider, as she made her way down the side of the mountain. She had a mental map of the area. She was on the wilderness side, the east side, of the thirty-two-kilometre lake, and the highway and recreation areas were on the west side. To cross over to the civilized side of Abraham Lake, she had to find the bridge at Siffleur Falls and the confluence of the North Saskatchewan River.

Dinah thrashed her way downhill, eventually finding herself at the edge of a deep ravine, a roaring stream in the bottom. The sides of the ravine were rocky, and the banks of the stream high with steep drop-offs. She couldn't figure out how to safely cross over, so she followed the high banks of the stream, knowing it would flow into the North Saskatchewan River. If she ended up walking parallel to Abraham Lake by mistake, and came out of the bush on the North Saskatchewan River, at least she could find the highway from there. Inside the ravine, surrounded by the crash of water tumbling over rocks, now she was more scared of being tracked by a grizzly bear than John; the Siffleur Wilderness Area and east slope of the foothills here were known grizzly habitat.

She stayed with the stream and at last the ravine widened, the terrain levelled, and the forest opened into natural grasslands. Now she could cross over, so she searched for a long branch to use as a pole and forded the rushing water, wedging the pole for balance and stepping on half-submerged rocks.

Across the stream, Dinah felt safer; John was far behind.

She touched her face, feeling the cuts and bruising. I must look like shit, she thought. At least when I find someone and tell my story, they'll see my face and believe me.

She had made it to the Kootenay Plains; there were scrubby aspen trees and tall wild grasses growing among the white spruce. She hiked awhile in the open grass and then, in the distance, the colour of pale turquoise glimmered through the trees. She scrambled toward the gravelly shores of Abraham Lake, ecstatic to spot several people fishing on the opposite shore.

"Help!" she yelled as loudly as she could. "Help, I've been attacked. Call the police, help me!"

The fishermen looked up and saw a young woman waving frantically, screaming on the far side of the lake. There were no recreation areas on the east side of the lake, and they could probably sense her panic.

The fishermen waved back at Dinah and yelled a response, which she couldn't hear across the expanse of water. Then one man put down his fishing rod and walked away from the others. *Good, he was going for help.*

"Stay right there," they seemed to be shouting. "Wait there."

The lake was too wide to attempt a swim; she would have to wait. She must be so close to the bridge at Siffleur Falls, but it was better to wait here, in view of people and the safety of the other shore.

She sat down on a rock to rest, the limestone cliffs at her back. She stared into the turquoise water; she was so thirsty, but her thirst didn't matter, all she could think about were her boys. She knew she had done the right thing under the circumstances and that John would not hurt them.

After about an hour, the thwack-thwack of a helicopter echoed across the lake. She stood up, waving her arms overhead to make sure the pilot could see her. The aircraft landed nearby, and when she climbed inside, her face bruised and bleeding, the RCMP officer whisked her away for questioning.

Dinah wanted to go back to the lookout immediately and pick up the boys, but the officer insisted he needed to take an official statement before he could authorize any action. They landed at a recreation campground just off the highway, a few minutes away by air, and a female RCMP officer led Dinah into a trailer to conduct an interview. They let her get cleaned up in a campground bathroom first, and brought her juice and water.

Dinah told the story, while the officer recorded it longhand. Then, the officer gave her a notebook and asked her to write down everything in her own words.

"I need to get my kids," Dinah said. "Can't we fly in tonight?"

"I don't know if that's the best course of action. It's getting late, the sun is going down, and by the time we get the okay, it's going to be too late for the pilot to lift off. These pilots can't legally fly after dusk. We don't know how long we would need to get your children out safely after we land up there. We can't risk making a bad situation worse by getting stuck on the mountain after nightfall."

The RCMP officer was firm, and Dinah had to admit, given John's mental state, she didn't know how he would react to a police helicopter showing up that evening. He might refuse to co-operate, forcing a standoff with the police.

The woman officer convened with her colleagues and returned with a plan she explained to Dinah.

"Here's what we can do," said the officer. "It's a bit of a mission. We'll let your husband cool down overnight. First thing tomorrow morning, we'll fly in with a crew—a judge and a few RCMP officers. We won't radio ahead, we'll ensure Alberta Forest Service is in the loop, and we'll surprise him. We'll bring your children out."

Dinah thought the boys would be okay overnight. "All right then. Do I stay here tonight?"

"Yes, we'll make arrangements with the campground manager. And just to clarify, tomorrow, you won't be flying in with the police helicopter. We'll have you wait here."

The next morning at sunrise, the RCMP helicopter put down at Cline. The judge and two RCMP officers apprehended John and he pleaded guilty to attacking Dinah the day before. The police issued a restraining order and instructed him not to go near Dinah. John released his children into RCMP custody without resistance, and the boys were reunited with their mother that morning.

Dinah and the boys drove home to Calgary that afternoon.

Athena finished off the tea. "So, that's what happened. Unreal, eh? I always felt John was a bit of a patriarch, you know. His attitudes to women are so traditional."

I'd never had a private conversation with John; we didn't have that kind of friendship, so I wasn't aware of his attitudes to women. The first thing that occurred to me, as I imagined Dinah hiking off the mountain alone, was the Greek Artemis, or the Roman goddess Diana. In this crisis she had been guided by her namesake, the goddess of feminine independence who roamed the forest alone.

"Did Forestry leave John up there on the lookout?" I asked.

"Yup. He's going to finish the season there."

"Really? He attacked his wife, and they leave him up there? Seems strange to me. Wouldn't most organizations suspend the person for misconduct? It happened on Forestry property."

"I don't know, that's the deal. He's on Cline until the end of the season. Christos and Alice flew up to check on him."

"Holy smokes, really? I wonder how that went?"

"No idea," said Athena. "I haven't seen them, but Dinah sure is pissed off. She didn't want them to go and they insisted. She's not speaking to them now. From her perspective, they took John's side by going up there to support him. They may have been the first people she phoned too."

"What a mess."

"Well, it looks pretty clear to me," said Athena. "The men are hedging, waffling on naming this for what it is. Tomas and Christos worship John."

"Daniel won't defend him," I said with conviction. "He must know about it by now."

Athena smiled with affection. "True, Daniel will be shocked."

Within days I received a letter from Daniel about the attack. As mercurial messenger, he had written postcards and letters to friends inside and outside the forest service denouncing John's actions and defending Dinah's decision to sever communication with her husband. The news spread like wildfire, and Daniel feared that John might come to Moose Mountain for retribution.

August 9, 1992
Moose Mountain

...I want to get some cayenne spray and will be locking my door at nights, I have visions of calling the Elbow [ranger station] and saying 'John, 5 foot, 11 inches, is at the [lookout] door and I feel threatened, won't let him in.'...

Ingrid and Tomas should hear in a day or two about the knife-man. El disgusto. I don't know how he can live with himself....Whaddya do with a guy like that? I have told people when I write and stuff. What if the courts hardly do anything? Tomas's comments in a letter were curious, like "why do men always get the blame and take the heat, when women can turn psychological knives in [men's] guts to compensate for [lack of physical] strength" or some such. Of course he realizes it's much more complex—but he has that slant on the male/female thingie. I disagree, myself. J threatened Dinah lots, men do that just as well as women I'd say. He doesn't know the whole story yet. I wonder what John will concoct...."Tell it to the judge, John."

...I am more and more revulsed by these old male cronies who warp the *shakti* and strip her of grace in an attempt to subdue her to their male precepts. They need to go dancing! To make music! Set her free!

[I'm] slowly rising out of the ashes of debt....

Take care in the big city and country. Take $50 for the phone bill, take a break, take an aspirin,

Love, Daniel

It would take a lot more than an Aspirin to alleviate the distress.

There was a crossfire of letters and telephone calls, as we all struggled to make sense of what had happened. John's actions were like a lightning strike, a direct hit on Dinah, and the repercussions knocked out connections among the entire Lookout Supper Club. For me, Athena, and Dinah's women friends, the condemnation of John was categorical and swift. Whether Dinah had had an affair was not the issue, we exclaimed—and even if she had betrayed John, in Canada, we don't condone assault or cut off women's noses for infidelity. There was no middle ground for the women or for Daniel; John was guilty and should make reparations. If he did not, he would be eternally banished. By everyone's accounts, John was sticking to the irrational and shocking claim that Dinah deserved punishment.

I wanted to hear Christos and Alice's account. After all, they had talked first-hand with John and presumably understood what was going through his mind. I contacted them and they agreed to tell me their version of events.

Christos said that when Dinah called and told her story, he and Alice felt the need to check on John, because he was isolated and they were concerned for his mental health. They expected when they showed up at Cline and listened to his version of the attack, he would admit he had lost control, needed help, and would seek to make amends with Dinah.

Christos insisted that they weren't taking John's side, but that Dinah had interpreted it that way. He and Alice had been friends with Dinah and John for over ten years, and they could not comprehend John's actions. "We were appalled and upset, but we wanted to speak with him first-hand," said Christos.

"Of course he's in a terrible mental state," Dinah had retorted. "He attacked me—violently. So why do you want to go see him? Christos. I don't understand why you guys want to go up there."

Christos said he had tried to explain their decision. "I'm not defending him, Dinah. I just think someone, a friend, should talk to him. Surely, he realizes what he's done and wants to make amends. I think I can talk him through it."

Frustrated, Dinah had hung up the phone.

"So, I called up the Forestry office and they said they'd fly us in," said Christos.

They requested time off from their jobs at the forest research station in Vernon and headed east on the Trans-Canada Highway in their old

Volvo, first to Banff, then north toward Jasper on Highway 93, until they reached the junction of Highway 11, the David Thompson Highway.

Highway 11 runs through a wide plateau between the White Goat Wilderness Area and the Siffleur Wilderness Area, parallel to the North Saskatchewan River, which flows out of the Rocky Mountains into the Kootenay Plains, filling Abraham Lake. An artificial body of water, blocked by the Bighorn dam at its northern tip, the aquamarine lake is finger-like in shape, thirty-two kilometres long and bounded by grey limestone mountains rising abruptly above its waters. Cline Lookout, high above the eastern shores of Abraham Lake, is accessible by helicopter, or five-hour hike, one-way, from a trailhead near the southern tip of the lake at Siffleur Falls.

Their destination was the district ranger station near Nordegg on Highway 11. From there Christos and Alice had made arrangements to fly up to the lookout with a forestry pilot. They wanted to spend three days and three nights with John, hopeful this amount of time would soften any defensive reactions. On the long mountain drive to Nordegg, Christos and Alice reflected on the history of their friendship with John and Dinah. They were like family—dharma bums, as Kerouac said—the same spiritual principles guiding their lives.

"He just needs to seriously look at his own psyche," Christos said to Alice as they drove through the Rockies. "I mean, this is a guy who became a meditation teacher twenty years ago. He must get what he's done."

Cline Lookout was built in the traditional mountain lookout design: one room, twelve feet by fifteen feet, windows on all sides, fire finder in the centre. Like Daniel, John had installed wooden shelving around the entire room, above the windows, to display his paintings and artwork, creating the effect of an art gallery in the clouds.

John stayed inside while the helicopter landed and answered his call sign, *That's copied XMA571 clear,* acknowledging the pilot over the radio. At two thousand metres altitude, the summit of Cline was wide and flat. Christos walked across the grassy alpine meadow to the lookout building, hugged John, and stared into his eyes, searching for signs of remorse.

For three days, the friends talked; at times they sat in silence. Christos encouraged John to tell his side of the story, striving to comprehend his perspective. He could sense John was hurt and disappointed by his own undoing, but he was disturbed by the cavalier rationale.

"She deserved it," said John. "She was having an affair. She betrayed me. It's a tradition in some cultures to cut off the nose of an adulterous woman."

Alice and Christos left a long, spacious silence after that provocative comment, gazing at the clear, aqua lake below. From the wooden deck around the lookout, they could see for miles, north and south, up and down the length of Abraham Lake. Right below the building, wild mountain goats leaped onto the helipad, kicking and butting playfully.

"Don't you think you need to make amends, starting with an apology of some kind?" Christos said.

"No," answered John slowly and deliberately. "For me, saying I'm sorry is like crawling on glass."

"You attacked your wife with a knife, John," Christos replied, his voice steady.

"I know, man, I know. And I'll take the consequences."

Later in the month I received a letter from Tomas, implying, in the most oblique manner, that he and Daniel had reached an impasse due to the John-Dinah "incident." In referring to the attack as an "incident," I felt he had minimized the violence.

August 22, 1992
Mockingbird Lookout

…The John-Dinah incident really opened up a can of worms for many of us. As you know, in the once upon a time ago Daniel and I exposed to each other our shadows, and it seems the John scene assisted in reopening some old wounds. Right now I feel that with John being the scum of the earth by the collective, by having been his good friend, it seems I am absorbing some of the residual projections. In Daniel's letter, his words were interwoven by affect that John and I sit in the same boat. And in retrospect, I am glad that he wrote me that letter, for it seems we have mysteriously transcended this summer's superficial attempt to mitigate our friendship; at least now, the worms are open to the light, and we are forced to directly deal with integration. The bottom line is I like Daniel and his creative disposition, his artistic subjectivity, and free flowing orientation on life; yes, another madcap…

Tomas

For the men, John confirmed troubling aspects of traditional masculinity: fear of emotional vulnerability, the inability to express strong emotion other than anger, and the use of spirituality to bypass their feelings.

McNeal weighed in when I told him what happened, calling John "the dark shaman with a knife."

The dark shaman with a knife! I whipped around to find him laughing nervously, pleased with the clever turn of phrase.

"It's not funny," I said. "He beat her up and held a box cutter to her face."

"Well, the guy's obviously a jerk," McNeal replied. "I'm not condoning him."

That was true, but we never discussed the violence seriously; we talked around it, jousting with the idea, baffled by the reality.

Myself, I was terribly disturbed by the news of the attack, the image of the box cutter etched in my mind. What if John had pushed the knife an inch closer, slicing flesh? Hearing the account of what had happened evoked the image of uncontrollable rage, a smouldering underground forest fire exploding into flames, treetops crowning in a tornado of fireballs. But surely, the fire would burn out quickly? Like Christos and Alice, I assumed with time John would emerge from the ashes, contrite, begging for forgiveness, willing to man up to his own jealousy and violent actions. When I thought about the act, clearly planned in advance, I could not make the connection in my mind's eye to John, mild-mannered artist. What had gone so horribly wrong and why did no one spot a problem sooner?

Later I would learn that after the attack Dinah was anxious in her own home, concerned John might abandon Cline and enter their house at night while she slept. The first night, despite her exhaustion, she had been afraid to fall asleep, dreading the sound of a key turning in the lock. It would be just like him to prowl around at 3:00 or 4:00 a.m. The next day she stared at the walls of their home, incredulous; John's mark was everywhere, his art hanging in every room. Methodically, she removed all his paintings and art pieces from sight.

She spent several weeks at her mother's home in Ontario and then in August returned to her job at the Waldorf School to prepare for the next academic year. Soon after school started, she moved with the boys to a house in southwest Calgary, purposely leaving behind the farmhouse and the memories it evoked. Ironically, I also learned that Dinah never had an affair that summer. Although she was a highly attractive woman and spent half the year alone, affairs and betrayal were not her style. There was one man, a good-looking parent who participated in school outings—he had sparked her interest. The past winter, on a school ski trip, she had shared a glass of wine and a conversation around a campfire with this man, not alone, but surrounded by children. They had lingered around the fire that evening and, as a result, Dinah arrived home later than expected. John intuited the attraction, his psychic radar scanning his wife's demeanour, the smell of woodsmoke on her clothes like tangible evidence of a rival. This was her transgression.

For Daniel and me, the magnitude of our own breakup was dwarfed in comparison to John and Dinah's schism. Not long after Cline Lookout closed for the season, Daniel reflected in a letter how he struggled to comprehend what his long-time friend had done.

Sept 11, 1992
Moose Mountain

By now, J. [John] "the punitive" (reminds me of David Franz in the TV series "The Fugitive") is at large. He saw Tomas & Tomas reports how repentant he feels, signing up for counselling, will sort out the financial muck of what he hasn't contributed all summer (makes me wonder when he began to realize he was a bit off). At least, for me, the visions of him torching my place have receded from the fore. (He may MOVE TO VERNON.)...I suppose now John is so penitent I'll get to play the bad guy again, for writing people and telling them about it etc. Can't believe Alice & Christos telling Dinah how "it takes two to tango." It takes 2 to commit murder too. (A dead person and a killer.)

It takes one to be deluded.

Unreal.

Here come some touristas in blue anoraks, walking billboards for Mountain Equipment Co-op....

Glad you've some more work.

Here they come—specks grown whole, so I'll say goodbye now and keep writing till they take it away. I've only 4 stamps left. What a summer scribe.

Anyway, I'll send this along, "they" are here now & I've some things to do.

I'm making a final ginger beer batch, as I figure I'll be here another 10 days or so, if not more. Who knows!

To Vernon ASAP...to Vancouver as well. Firewood, clay, truck tires & repair, visiting, drumming, dancing, be-friending, shopping (frugal).

Love, Daniel

There was no contact between Daniel and John that fall. Their friendship of more than fifteen years simply ended. I think they each intuited, accurately, the perspective of the other and on the inner planes cut ties.

I respected Daniel's decision; in fact, it kindled doubt. Why had I left a creative man with such clear thinking and values similar to my own?

August Snow

Almost all summer long, I searched for work. Finally, in August, a non-profit agency that advocated for persons with developmental disabilities hired me as a part-time support worker. The agency placed individuals in paid jobs that matched their capacity, and by providing a support worker on the job site, they could guarantee the work would meet a specified standard. The expectation was that I would model job skills and over time the individual would learn to execute the job tasks on their own. The program was framed as a win-win situation: the individual earned a real paycheque, and the employer received minimum-wage labour while demonstrating community goodwill.

I was unsure if it was a win for me.

My first client, Troy, a young man in his twenties, was developmentally delayed and diagnosed with epilepsy. My official job title was something akin to "employment coach," which was a bit sketchy, given I'd been searching for suitable employment for years now. I encouraged Troy to think about the kinds of jobs he might want to do. "Towel boy," he said unequivocally. "Towel boy for the Calgary Stampeders." I didn't know whether football teams really had towel boys or not, but accepting that sports was one area Troy's knowledge probably exceeded my own, I typed up a resumé for him, and we hopped on the bus, delivering his one-pager to the Stampeders' head office. I followed up the towel-boy possibilities by telephone with no results, not even a rejection letter.

I explained to Troy that while towel boy was a good first choice, he needed to expand his job search. "Sports, I want to work in sports," he insisted, seemingly oblivious to his own chubby stature and lack of muscle tone. It was remarkable that despite his cognitive handicaps, Troy had internalized the image of the ideal male athlete, the longing for perfect manliness, strength, and toughness. I wanted to tell Troy that he stood a better chance of winning the lottery than he did of finding a sports-related job, but I restrained the impulse. After all, Troy and I were in a similar dilemma. We were underemployed with high aspirations.

"Let's see what's listed under 'sports' in the yellow pages," I said, handing him the heavyweight directory. "You read out the numbers and I'll dial." Of course, the odds of landing a job interview by cold-calling managers was also like winning a lottery, but I persevered.

Fortunately, the agency sent Troy and me to a potential employer, a small woodworking operation that needed a person to feed lumber through a mechanized planer. Troy watched another worker carry a six-foot piece of lumber to the machine and guide it through safely. Then it was his turn. He wobbled as he lifted the plank and struggled to swing the length of lumber into position and hold it steady. After a few practice attempts, we agreed the risks were too great: Troy could put a dent in someone's head swinging six-foot boards around the workplace. Spatial awareness was not high on his skill list, and the setting too dangerous for his abilities.

Then an opportunity stocking shelves at a Safeway grocery store came up. This seemed like a more realistic goal, and a task I could teach Troy to do on his own. I swallowed my organic pride and set out for the grocery aisles with Troy. Facing, as we call it in the grocery business, is a mundane but essential task. To face a shelf you simply pull the items forward and rotate the cans, ensuring the labels face front. Troy resisted facing shelves, and the importance of facing the English, rather than the French, label eluded him. I could face up an aisle in minutes flat, but Troy was the one who needed to master the task. The minutes and hours dragged by, as he handled each box or can numerous times. Sometimes he rebelled and in-sisted on pushing the inventory to the back of the shelf.

Exasperated, I pulled it forward. "How will shoppers find what they want to buy, Troy?" I explained the scenario: you're shopping, you need to read the label, you read English, not French. But Troy had never gone shopping on his own, and I suspected he lumped shopping with "feminine" chores his mother performed. This confounded me because most of the stocking clerks at Safeway were men.

I persevered; maybe slicing open boxes with a knife and stocking the shelf would have more manly appeal. I demonstrated clean technique: slice the cardboard case open with a box cutter and slide the cans of soup into neat rows. Troy, apparently, despised straight rows; he improvised a clus-ter method and shoved the cans together in crowd formation, one flavour merging into another in random order.

"What are we going to do about these rows, Troy? You know they're not right."

"I'd rather collect shopping carts." He stared out the store windows at the parking lot.

We put on our coats and walked outside, ready for action. Troy scanned the asphalt lot, searching for carts. He strolled off, retrieved several loose carts, wheeled them back, and hooked them to the train in the middle of the lot. Once the roundup was complete, he stood next to me, poised to intercept customers as they left the store.

Troy crept toward a shopper, snatching his target as the woman's last grocery bag cleared the cart.

"Wait until they've unloaded their groceries," I shouted. "You can't just seize the cart, it's not a holdup."

It was all about timing with Troy. His timing needed work, but he had found his groove. Troy was a parking-lot superhero, rescuing stray carts, one by one, from the perils of abandonment and theft.

I reflected on the timing and order of things in my own life: the affair with McNeal had been such poor timing, and now my whole world was out of order. Perhaps there was a cosmic pulse to our lives, and when we lost the beat, we drummed ourselves into chaos.

Then the inevitable happened. Troy and I were hooking up a train of shopping carts one morning, and abruptly his stance locked next to me.

"It's a seizure," he said under his breath, bracing to fall. Then he lost consciousness.

"I got you," I said, guiding his stocky body to the ground, ensuring his head did not hit the pavement.

He convulsed, his limbs jerking in rigid spasms, his head and neck thrown back. A crowd of shoppers gathered with their carts, a wagon train in circle formation with Troy at the centre.

"Give him sugar," cried one shopper. "Anybody got sugar in their groceries?"

"He's not diabetic," I yelled back. "He has epilepsy, it's a seizure."

"Put something in his mouth so he won't bite his tongue," cried another helpful bystander, moving toward Troy's head.

"No, do *not* touch him, leave him alone," I said, guarding Troy.

The shoppers stared in fear, well-intentioned but ignorant.

"If you want to help, go call an ambulance. He needs professional help. We have to wait it out and make sure he doesn't hurt himself."

In a couple of minutes, Troy's body quieted and consciousness returned; he fluttered his eyelids. A paramedic assisted him to stand and
checked his vitals. His parents arrived and took him home for the rest of
the day.

During every subsequent shift, I worried about the possibility of another seizure. But Troy lived with the condition and adapted without complaint, returning to work in a couple of days, eager to stalk forsaken carts.

In mid-August, I rode the Greyhound bus to Pincher Creek, hopeful
that a final visit to Carbondale Lookout might end in harmony. The town
of Pincher Creek was about thirty minutes from the ranger station, and
McNeal said he could borrow a Forestry truck and swing by if I arrived
in the evening.

When the bus rolled in at 9:30 p.m., McNeal was parked outside the
depot, waiting in the ranger's green pickup truck. I climbed into the passenger seat and he thrust a long-stemmed red rose toward me.

"For you, my dear," he said with a half smile, "one red rose."

"Thank you." I accepted the gift, holding the long stem with both
hands, examining the dark-red, velvety bloom. I wanted to receive it as a
simple love offering, the sign of a truce after weeks of arguing, but I was
distracted by a scintilla of doubt.

"Where did you get a rose so late at night in Pincher Creek?"

Baffled, I truly wondered how a man on a fire lookout could procure a
rose at 9:30 p.m. in small-town Alberta. The streets of Pincher Creek were
dark and empty, the shops closed since six o'clock.

"Oh, come on. Can't you be more gracious than that? What does it
matter where I got the rose? I'm presenting it to you."

"It matters, because I'm wondering if someone gave *you* this rose, and
you're regifting it."

McNeal turned the key in the ignition. "Sure, ruin a nice moment. I
can't win with you."

"I'm just asking you where you got the rose, that's all."

"Where the hell do you think I got it?"

"Well, you certainly didn't get a rose in Pincher Creek, unless it was a
wild rose growing at the side of the road! This rose came from a florist shop."

"Perhaps you underestimate me."

"You know what I think? I think the junior forest rangers hiked up to the lookout to say goodbye for the season, and some teenage girl gave you this rose. That's what I think."

"Oh, fuck, here we go. You're jealous of a seventeen-year-old girl."

"No, I'm not jealous of a seventeen-year-old girl. But if the rose didn't come from one of the junior rangers, then where did you get it? Hikers don't carry long-stemmed roses." I didn't dare raise Laurie's name, but she did come to mind as a suspect.

"It's not your business where I got it."

I dropped the interrogation, convinced McNeal was hiding something. If he'd been resourceful enough to get a forest ranger to buy the rose, why wouldn't he just say so?

We sped toward the foothills, twisted our way through the hills of the Castle River valley, past the general store at Beaver Mines, and bumped across the cattle gate onto the gravel road in darkness. I brooded in silence the whole way.

The thorns of the rose stem between my fingers, I felt more anxious than loved, more suspicious than open-hearted.

Outside the lookout, the wind blustered with such force McNeal struggled to hold the door open. Relieved to escape the ferocity of the elements, I plunked down in a chair, laying the rose on the table.

McNeal glared. "Are you going to sulk?"

Ignoring the comment, I stood up and found a vase. I put the rose in the centre of the table. I looked him in the eye. "Can I ask you something?"

"What? I'm tired. It's late."

"Well, I was wondering, how would you describe us? I mean, if you were telling a friend about me, would you say we're a couple, or, like, what would you call us?"

McNeal reflected. "I'd say we're intensely involved, that's what I'd say."

"Intensely involved?" What the hell was that supposed to mean? I searched his face for a sign of authenticity.

"What? That's a big deal," he said. "Intensely involved, what's wrong with that?"

"I don't know what that means in this situation. I get intensely involved watching a movie. I get intensely involved in a political conversation. It sounds vague."

"Listen, I'm doing the best I can under the circumstances. I have Catherine on my case, disappointed and begging for answers; I have you demanding we seal the deal, like some 1950s couple, and I have a dissertation to write. And—newsflash—I have to go to Egypt in September. I applied for a research travel grant in the spring and the project has been approved. It's a huge opportunity and critical to my research. Although I have to admit, the whole thing feels ruined now."

He had trumped my play. "Egypt! You're going for sure? I thought you hadn't decided yet."

"The grant is approved. It would be foolish not to go. It's important for my career and only a three-month trip. Not that long."

"Is Catherine going with you? She's part of the Egypt trip, isn't she?"

"Well, she was written into the grant because she's an Egyptologist. She can help me decipher inscriptions on the temple walls. It's not like she and I would have to be a couple to do the trip. It doesn't change what you and I have or how I feel about you."

"It just seems like everything revolves around your life and your plans. You've got Egypt with Catherine in the fall, and possibly India with me in the winter. Then Toronto and Catherine for the spring, and back to me next summer for the next lookout season."

"You're determined to frame me as the bad guy in this, aren't you?"

We argued like this for two days, until I threatened to end things completely if he went to Egypt with Catherine. McNeal spat back that ultimatums were futile. From the Egypt trip, we launched a debate about monogamy, the validity of marriage, and the ethics of bringing children into the world.

"Well, I don't see the point of monogamy if children aren't involved." McNeal always circled back to this idea. "Do you want children?"

"Do you?" I flipped the question because it seemed surreal discussing children given our deadlock.

"I'd like to be a father someday," said McNeal.

My heart softened. "Really? That surprises me, I had no idea."

"What about you? Don't you want children?"

"I've never had a desire to have children," I said. "You know how some women desperately want a baby? I'm not one of those women."

"Well, if you had children, I would not have gotten involved with you."

"What kind of moral compass is that? You don't have sex with mothers? What are you saying?" That just pissed me off. I wanted to throw something at him.

"I'm just saying I don't think people with children should have affairs. I would never have an affair with a married woman who had children."

"So, as long as a woman is child-free, she's a possible sexual partner. Isn't that criterion unfair to a huge number of women?"

"Knock off the sarcasm."

"I can't believe you're serious."

"It messes a kid up, big time. A kid's parents are like the god and goddess of the universe, and if that reality is shattered, it fractures their psyche for life."

"Fifty percent of marriages end in divorce. It's better for children to be raised in a household without conflict and unhappiness than to grow up with adults pretending they have a good marriage." I couldn't believe a man who studied philosophy and religion at the graduate level had such murky logic and prehistoric values.

McNeal was putting everything on the table, next to the red rose, so to speak. Now that we were arguing family values, he proceeded to tell me how he would discipline a teenage girl.

"If I was the father of a girl who joined some weird spiritual cult, say, a spiritual group like the one Daniel belonged to, I'd have her deprogrammed."

"What? Are you insane? What do you mean you'd have her deprogrammed?"

"As her father, it would be the ethical thing to do. Gurus are bullshit. In fact, I'd deprogram her myself. I'd lock her in a room and I'd sit there and talk to her until she gave up the crazy beliefs."

"Come on, isn't your hypothetical daughter entitled to her own beliefs?"

"Not if she's been brainwashed by a religious cult."

"That is wrong on so many levels."

"Mary, there's genuine evil in the world, and it's up to us to combat it. It doesn't go away by reading some New Age self-help book."

The more we talked, the more we argued, and the larger the gap between us grew. It felt as though our words reignited centuries of acrimony and bitterness between men and women; a violent history unfurled inside our bodies and spurted from our mouths in judgment.

Periodically that weekend, McNeal would retreat upstairs to the cupola and look for smoke, and I would read downstairs in the kitchen or take a short walk when the winds subsided.

On the afternoon of the second day, I started making a chicken soup with wilted vegetables and a leftover chicken carcass he had in the fridge.

After the 1:00 p.m. weather schedule, McNeal disappeared into the bedroom to take a nap, and soon he was calling out for painkillers. He had drawn the curtains tight to screen out any light and propped his head up with pillows.

"It's a migraine attack," he muttered from the darkness.

I offered a bowl of homemade soup; he groaned in misery.

"No, no, I'm going to throw up. Get something quick."

I ran to the kitchen, grabbed the enamel wash basin, and sprinted back to the bedroom, thrusting it under his chin. He hurled the contents of his stomach, liquid and partially digested food from the night before. I headed outdoors with the basin.

"You don't have to deal with that, just leave it," said McNeal, embarrassed.

"No big deal, I've seen people throw up before." Like a nurse in training, I strode outside, emptied the basin on a patch of grassy hillside, and then rinsed it clean at the kitchen sink. I placed the basin on the floor next to the bed. McNeal writhed under the blankets with pain and nausea.

"My head feels like it's going to burst," he cried out.

"Do you want another painkiller?"

"God, no, I'll just throw it up again."

"Well, I'm right here if you need anything. How about some water?"

"Okay, bring water."

I held the glass to his lips and he sipped an inch of water before falling back on the pillows.

"Just leave me alone. There's nothing you can do."

I sat down at the kitchen table, positioning myself with a view of the bedroom, trying to be as quiet as possible. By early evening, McNeal's distress had heightened, and the headache and nausea had not subsided.

"I need to go to the hospital," he yelled from the bedroom. "I can't go on all night like this. They have drugs for migraine."

"The hospital? How will we get there?"

"Get on the radio and call up the Blairmore ranger station. Just say it's XMC33 and tell them I need to go to the hospital."

I balked. "I'm not sure when to click the mic open and when to click it shut. I've never spoken on a two-way radio."

"Oh, for Christ's sake!" McNeal heaved himself out of bed, staggered from the bedroom and squinted, shielding his eyes from the light. He fumbled with the microphone, unsteady on his feet. "XMC33 here, do you copy, Blairmore?"

"Go ahead, Carbondale."

"Yeah, I need to get to the Pincher hospital. Can someone drive up and take me in to emerg? No, it's not an accident, I'm sick, migraine, big time, and I need to go now. Thanks, C33 out."

Within forty minutes, we heard the truck engine whining on the switchbacks. The female ranger jumped out of the vehicle, took one look at McNeal, and helped me guide him to the truck. Wobbly, McNeal clung to my arm, moaning as we crossed the gravel. The three of us squeezed onto the bench seat, me in the middle, and we bounced down the mountain road.

"Hurry," commanded McNeal, eyes half-shut, swaying in the cab like a drunk.

As soon as we hit the pavement, the ranger stepped on the accelerator and warned McNeal to let her know if he was going to throw up.

His face contorted. He braced himself, one hand on the dashboard, the other on the passenger door, as we sped toward relief. The hospital in sight, he leaned over my thighs, bowed his head and grunted, throaty, guttural sounds like an animal in distress.

"Hang on, almost there," shouted the ranger.

I cringed and bowed my head, preparing for the shower of vomit.

A gasp of laughter erupted in the cab.

"Just kidding! Ha ha, got ya, didn't I!" roared McNeal.

I twisted around in disbelief.

"Good one, eh? Couldn't let an opportunity like that pass by," he said, delighted with the prank, briefly forgetting his misery.

We were the only people in the emergency room and the clerk admitted McNeal without delay. A doctor met us in the patient waiting area and told me and the ranger to sit down.

"I want to go with him," I said, assuming I could accompany McNeal behind the white curtain into the treatment room.

The doctor looked at McNeal. "Is she a family member? Your wife? What relation is she?"

"She's a friend," said McNeal. "A friend."

"Only family members and significant others are allowed in the treatment room. Have a seat and we'll bring him back after we're done."

I slumped into one of the plastic chairs. A friend. He had told a total stranger, a person he would never meet again, that I was merely a friend.

"I am so more than a friend," I said to the ranger, wondering if she might entertain a woman-to-woman chat about McNeal, but it became clear gender would not win over Forestry stripes.

"It's just a formality," she answered cheerily. "He sure is sick, isn't he?"

Like all rangers, I knew she monitored the radio. I wanted to ask her about the rose, and when the junior forest rangers had visited, and whether McNeal had other friends at the lookout this summer. It was the perfect opportunity for investigative work, but I controlled the impulse, respecting her privacy. And his.

In half an hour, McNeal reappeared with the doctor, who explained how the drug they administered stopped the blood vessels from dilating in his head.

"Wow, miracle drugs. I feel human again." McNeal grinned sheepishly, the colour back in his cheeks, his stance grounded.

"Stress often precipitates a migraine attack," said the doctor. "Go on back to work, you should be fine now."

The next day, I asked McNeal to toss in for half my bus fare, which he did, as well as arrange for the ranger to drive me to the Pincher Creek bus depot.

Nothing had been resolved.

Given the cool weather, in a few weeks the fire season would be over.

"I'll take you down to the road on the bike," he said, avoiding eye contact.

Outside the lookout, he veered away from me and climbed the stairs onto the catwalk. Then he reached into his pocket and hurled a raw egg across the driveway onto the flat roof of the engine shed. *Splat!*

"What the hell are you doing?" I yelled.

"That's for Poe, my raven," he said. "Edgar Allan, that is. He loves the yolk."

In Calgary, it snowed on August 23, a thin sprinkle of icing sugar, coating the sidewalks, car roofs, and poplar trees along Memorial Drive, stealing the remnants of summer. The daytime high barely reached five degrees Celsius, a dismal situation, which, in the face of the inevitable Alberta winter, felt cruel and unfair. I perceived the unseasonal cold weather as an allegory for my love life, dampened by forces beyond my control.

The week of the August snowfall, I received a letter from Daniel.

August 18, 1992
Moose Mountain

I am troubled that you are troubled, that things are so crazy for you with this…"new fellow." His radio call was to inquire about technical clay details.…I'm rather tired of all the drama even though I'm isolated from it up here, it all seems so needless at times, something to distract ourselves.

But no, folks 'r' just trying to be happy and getting pretty damn frustrated at times. (I'm such a reductionist!) I've decided not to say "I have trouble with men" again. I feel this isn't true really. I have trouble with some people, yep. Perhaps all this Men/Women "processing" only keeps the dilemma in place, secure as long as the definitions are there to divide "into two," the sense of dilemma itself (it/self).…That's what I've been feeling today, there is a sense of dilemma, ego/soul's feel and search for relief from, concepts of power, sexes…and thereby continue endlessly. I've promised not to persuade anyone of anything anymore.

Solitude: A Return to Self, Anthony Storr. I've ordered a copy. In a book I got yesterday (*The Joy of Not Working*) it is quoted: "If we did not look to marriage as the principal source of happiness, fewer marriages would end in tears." Substitute "marriage" with "committed couples." I think there's something interesting here. According to studies, singles have more friends & "well-adjusted" ones have less headaches, anger, and irritability. Perhaps the torch-hunt for the twin-flame is the main cause of burnout?

Ah (next day), I'm not supposed to be persuading (was I?). Nah. I feel a bit wiped, hikers, windy night, not eating enough, time to shampoo and gobble up something. I'll send this note although I know it falls short of a real consideration of anything, but I've a few tasks to do here, shelves, bills to pay, cooking, vacuuming, cleaning up the fly specks. Talk to you again soon. Wish the radio/phone worked better, you didn't sound too buoyant the other night, don't sink Mary! I'll send you energy in my gravitations, my anti-gravitations. I'll send another cheque, too, $300, Sept 1st-ish? Sorry I haven't said much, I'm getting verbal constipation.

Love, Daniel

Daniel sounded worn down by all the endings: the end of our relationship, the death of Zip, and now the end of his friendship with John, and possibly Tomas, depending on how Tomas rolled with John's violence. Then, within a few days, I received a letter from Tomas, who also weighed in on my situation—and women in general.

August 22, 1992
Mockingbird Lookout

Dear Mary,

After our brief telephone conversation yesterday, I have decided to sketch a follow-up letter; something does not feel right, especially after hearing about your renewed tension with my dear friend McNeal, who no doubt might be pissed off at me for some reason....

...Life can be merciless Mary, in all its deception and disguise. In these last months I had to swallow some bitter raw waters of truth, with the agony of "this hour has seven days" in which there was nowhere to run and hide. And no doubt, by the sounds of things, you are also in a most unique life constellation; in fact it seems you wandered right into the heart of the dragon. But right on! At least you took the risk, which means at least you are living, at least you are alive. At least you are polishing the stone in terms of maturation of personality, as in understanding the mysterious subtleties of the syzygy.

I would suspect that with McN you have found your match....Sometimes I feel I have not completely understood McN, his vision of women and relationship, and so any judgment passed would be folly....

You are different Mary, a mature lady who is not a mother, and thus your relationship to a man is not just focused toward the mere fulfillment of your instinctual need of mothering. In this light do I see McN's attraction to you, a psychic alluring.... Only now am I awakening to this significant difference between a woman as a lover versus a woman as a mother, the voltage is entirely different in terms of a woman's need for a man.

And come to think of it, he [McNeal] did warn me about the "dark shaman," in his words, the one with the knife....

Of course we were intimate friends at the time, bubbling in the enthusiasm of our relationship....

Life goes on. I don't know your plans, but I hope we have another chance for a discussion one of these days.

Tomas

Well, Tomas may have been having a sexual awakening of some kind, but to me his letter revealed confusion about women. But he was right about my lack of reproductive drive. On the occasions we had discussed children, he was awestruck when I declared having a child was not a desire or goal. I was never sure if the intensity of his response was admiration or the assumption of mutant chromosomes.

It wasn't clear how he weighed in on John. His letter implied he and McNeal had acknowledged the attack as inexcusable. Despite the admission, I was uncomfortable with Tomas's reluctance to speak more explicitly about John's rage and violent behaviour. His quest to understand the power of intimate relationships between men and women was authentic, but sometimes, from my perspective, he mirrored ancient fears about women's sexuality.

In some future scenario, I had imagined Daniel and I might have children, but it had never been a compelling desire in the day-to-day present—for either of us. That summer, however, I briefly fantasized about McNeal and me having a child, then scrubbed the idea and chastised myself for indulging in such a clichéd form of snagging a man. The idea embarrassed me; a barely discernible voice, imprinted by generations of biological necessity, insisted that if I became pregnant, McNeal and I would be hooked for life, and then, maybe, things could work out. Moments later I would recoil at my naive sentimentality and remind myself this old trick would leave me vulnerable, attached to an overeducated lookout man who deplored commitment.

I never let McNeal know my feelings, always insisting I had no interest in children. If all was fair in love and war, then that was classified information.

By the beginning of September, my contract as a support worker expanded to include a second client, Darlene, a woman who performed cleaning duties at the Waldorf School where Dinah worked. Darlene was energetic and well suited to her job; she had been placed in the position months earlier with a coach, and I was told she needed some backup support now.

The first thing I noticed about Darlene was, despite her enthusiasm, she raced through the tasks and more often swirled the grime around with a dirty rag as opposed to removing it. She had managed to emulate the physical movements inherent to cleaning a window or door, but she did not seem to understand the concept of hygiene. I asked Darlene to take me through her daily routine and show me how she used the trolley, which was equipped with cleaning fluids, mops, and rags.

She led me to the front doors of the school, floor-to-ceiling glass, which needed a squeegee washer to clean the streaks and fingerprints. Darlene splashed the squeegee into a pail of water and dragged the sponge every which way, expending enormous energy, and then triumphantly packed up the trolley.

Gently, I motioned at the streaks. "We want the front doors to sparkle, Darlene. Watch." I grabbed the squeegee and pulled the vinyl edge down the length of the glass, leaving more streaks. Darlene giggled.

"Wait, we need newsprint," I said. "I can do a better job with newsprint. Didn't anyone show you that trick?"

I marched into Dinah's office. She was engrossed with budgets, financial planning, and spreadsheets—professional work. I stood in the doorway and interrupted her, the front of my T-shirt wet from the squeegee spray.

"Darlene and I need newsprint," I said, "to polish the glass in the front doors."

Dinah turned from her paperwork. "The front doors? Right, I don't think there's any newsprint around. Just use a clean rag, it doesn't have to be perfect."

"Well, there's no worry about that, believe me." I backed away.

"I think I've met someone," she said.

"What—really? That's great. Who?" I was surprised. It had been only two or three months since the lookout attack and she was already dating.

"He's an actor. We met at a dinner party a few weeks ago. I told him I didn't date smokers, so he quit smoking—the same day."

"Just like that, he quit smoking so you'd go out with him?"

"That's right. Done."

"Wow, that's incredible."

"I know, I can hardly believe it. I'm in a program at the YWCA. It's for women who have experienced domestic violence. I didn't understand the extent of the problems in my marriage until I entered this program. It's helped me make the decision to end things and move on with my life. In fact, psychologically, I think I already had."

"What's the new guy's name?"

"Paul. He's not into meditation or any New Age stuff. Totally different circle of friends. You'll meet him soon."

Dinah appeared genuinely happy. This was not a woman resentful as a single parent, or wallowing in victimhood. She beamed optimism, almost contentment.

"And what about you? I heard you were going to Egypt or somewhere?"

"Oh that, no—it fell through. Looks like I'm not going anywhere." Speaking it out loud, the disappointment and sadness welled up inside me. I held back tears. "I should get back to Darlene. Who knows what she's up to."

I hurried down the hall, forcing myself to concentrate on the cleaning task. If Dinah could pull her life together so quickly, surely I could. Things would get better, I told myself. They always do.

I inspected the glass doors from several angles before calling it good enough. Then Darlene snatched the trolley and I loped down the hallway behind her. She wheeled into the boys' washroom, springing toward the urinal.

"I clean this every day." She grabbed a bottle of liquid soap, aimed, and sprayed.

The urinal received a robust cleaning, after which Darlene proceeded to wipe down the sink basins and faucets—with the same rag. I gasped and instructed her to stop, but Darlene worked as though she'd just snorted a few lines of cocaine.

I hated to criticize her work, but there were basic hygiene issues at stake here. I explained to Darlene there was a correct order to everything, and in the boys' bathroom the urinal should be cleaned last. She waved her cleaning rag at me and zoomed out into the hall.

"Okay, put that rag away now. Put it down." I had to get tough. "Darlene, get rid of that rag. It belongs in the laundry."

She darted into the girls' bathroom and I dashed behind.

The same pattern was evident here. Darlene had chosen to wipe down the toilets first. Next she tackled the sinks with the same rag, and then to finish off she deposited the filth on the door handle of the bathroom.

It was a miracle the Waldorf School had not suffered an *E. coli* outbreak.

Darlene's enthusiasm and commitment were admirable, but I would have to retrain her work habits. Ideally, I might have formed a relationship before introducing change, but the image of Darlene swiping the sides of the urinal and then swooshing the same cloth around the faucets disgusted me.

When I modelled the new order of tasks, she shook her head no, vigorously, and looked away. To her, my requests were interference, a criticism of her personhood. How could I explain the notion of invisible bacteria and germs to an individual who would never have the capacity to complete elementary school?

Maybe I was the one who needed to change.

"You're an excellent worker, Darlene," I said, offering praise, "but from now on we're going to clean the doors and sinks first. Okay? We'll save the toilets to the end. Not a big deal. And remember, don't skimp on those clean rags. You have a whole stack of them on your trolley, right there."

She frowned and eyed me suspiciously.

"You're doing a fantastic job, Darlene. I'm not criticizing you. You're the best cleaner the school ever had."

She softened for an instant, then scooped up her supplies and pushed the trolley out the door, speeding into the hallway.

Before giving chase, I allowed her a moment without me.

Here I was, standing in an elementary school washroom, inspecting the cleanliness of toilets and urinals. I could not fathom how I had ended up here. Who or what, exactly, was directing my life?

As much as I recognized the equality of all human beings and had empathy for Troy and Darlene, I was not suited to the front lines, supporting clients with disabilities. Bored and frustrated, I felt the prime of my life slipping away as I watched, unable to stop or change the flow. I felt trapped, and blamed my external circumstances; but I was also trapped inside the confines of my own choices. I had more opportunity than ninety percent of women around the world, but I was unable to galvanize that advantage, mysteriously seduced and captivated by attractive, troubled men.

On the Banks of the Bow River

On the banks of the Bow, I slumped against a cottonwood tree and watched the river flow around Prince's Island. Tears streamed down my face and blurred my vision, coursing around the edges of my face. My relationship with Daniel was destroyed; the summer with McNeal dried up. And the camaraderie of the Supper Club had chilled, the warmth of friendship dissipated. I was forced to accept that I couldn't make things happen by trying harder. I couldn't will circumstances to happen, any more than I could change the current of the river or force McNeal to choose me.

As a young, educated, postmodern woman, I expected good endings—endings that merged into exciting beginnings. When endings persisted, I had become more demanding. I remembered my father cautioning me as a child, "Don't force it, Mary Theresa, don't force it." That was my natural bent in the face of obstacles, to muscle up and push forward. I wanted to author my own life and evolve into a successful creative person, but I didn't yet know how to simply be with what was unfolding—to flow. I had been frustrated and irritated for so long that instead of reflecting more deeply on my own actions, and cultivating a centre of strength before acting in concert with reality, I pushed harder on the external world.

Things as they are.

I recoiled inside, unwilling to accept things as they were in my life.

One evening in mid-September, I arrived home from work and discovered McNeal in the house. A déjà vu moment in Athena's kitchen, minus the excitement of the spring rendezvous. It was too late in the season now; things had ripened and spoiled.

"Hey, I'm done for the season. They closed Carbondale today and I drove straight here. Picked up a couple bottles of Chilean red, good vintage, decent price."

He and Athena had already poured themselves a celebratory glass and transformed the family kitchen into an intimate wine bar. They sat adjacent to each other, attentive, arms resting closely on the IKEA pine table. What were they discussing, I wondered, Athena's bachelor's degree, or McNeal's genius doctoral thesis? Whatever the topic, it was all-consuming.

"Grab a wineglass, Mary, and join us." Athena was flushed from the wine and the male scholar. She turned to McNeal. "You'll be staying the night, I suppose?"

"If that's no trouble, yes, thank you. I planned to spend a day or so in Calgary before heading back to Toronto."

McNeal had donned the noble Heathcliff persona, mysterious rogue from the English highlands. It wouldn't be trouble for Athena—he planned to squeeze his big frame into my futon bed.

"I'm going to take a quick shower, and I'll be right back." I dashed up the stairs, hiding my surprise. If Carbondale had closed, then Moose would be right behind.

When I returned to the kitchen party, Athena held up a photocopy of *The Thunder: Perfect Mind*. "Do you know this text, Mary? It's so beautiful."

"I thought you might want to use it for a term paper," explained McNeal.

"Shall I cite your doctoral thesis too?" Athena laughed self-consciously at her own compliment.

"Not quite yet. Maybe next year I'll defend. But look, I'll send you a feminist-friendly citation for *The Thunder: Perfect Mind*. De rigueur for academia these days."

I felt excluded from the conversation. Granted, McNeal had stayed here many times during his trips to visit Tomas and, therefore, was comfortable socializing with Athena, but I smelled smoke, even though I couldn't pinpoint it. *The Thunder: Perfect Mind*, a sacred Gnostic poem, was one of his favourite texts. He often spoke of it, although he had never presented me with a copy. The manuscript, translated from Coptic, was part of the Gnostic writings unearthed at Nag Hammadi, Egypt, in 1945. For scholars like McNeal, the historical texts were key to understanding various religious sects around the second century AD.

The many stanzas in *The Thunder: Perfect Mind* had been written in a female, first-person voice, as though the speaker herself transmitted the divinity of Isis or Gnostic Sophia.

For I am the first and the last.
I am the honored and the scorned,
I am the harlot and the holy one.
I am the wife and the virgin.[8]

After *The Thunder: Perfect Mind*, the rest of the evening was a sacramental blur. The three of us knocked back the Chilean red; Athena produced a third bottle of Portuguese red, donated to the house by her newest love interest. We sat at the kitchen table until the bottle was empty and then climbed the stairs to bed. I slept poorly and woke in the middle of the night with a thundering head, not a perfect mind. Clutching the edge of the futon, I squirmed to defend my half of the bed, while McNeal sprawled next to me in deep sleep.

When he woke up and scrambled over me at 8:30 a.m., I burrowed into the blankets. "I'm sick!" I moaned. "I should never drink red, just white!"

"Come on, get up, you'll be okay. I've only got a day here." McNeal nudged me.

"No, I have to sleep. Leave me alone. I have a wicked headache."

It was noon before I got out of bed, swallowed a couple Aspirin, and stumbled into the shower. My eyelids were puffy, my face pale.

I pulled on an oversized T-shirt and jeans and went downstairs. The house was empty. I checked for phone messages. Daniel had left a chirpy greeting. Moose Mountain was closing today and he planned to drop by this evening.

Perfect. My head throbbed.

I spent the afternoon scooting around Calgary with McNeal. He insisted on taking me to the war games store in east Calgary, a dark retail space, jammed with tiny miniatures, soldiers, weapons, maps, and war paraphernalia.

"I'm not into war," he clarified—again. "I'm intrigued by the *history*, understanding the strategies and battle decisions that changed the direction of the world."

Who was this man? I had fallen for a military strategist. What was the endgame?

We walked along the Bow River pathway and stopped at Heartland Café for a latte. I asked about Egypt. He said Catherine was so angry with him that she had backed out of the trip. She had called him a whore when he finally owned up to his affair with me. I didn't fully grasp the career significance of the travel grant, but I no longer cared about it either. I didn't trust him; if they went to Egypt together, that was the end for us. McNeal said I was manipulating him with ultimatums. I said he approached love as though it were a game of war.

There had to be an ending for him, too, I thought. He wanted everything, sex, romance, travel, a career, and advanced credentials without any loss or responsibility.

That evening Daniel dropped by Athena's house. McNeal and I were hanging out in the living room drinking tea.

"Hey, big guy," said McNeal, throwing his arms around Daniel.

"Just thought I'd say hello, can't stay long." Daniel crossed the floor and took a chair on the other side of the living room.

"What do you mean, you can't stay long? What are you doing tonight?" McNeal appeared to believe their friendship was unchanged.

"I'm having dinner with a friend—Laura. She lives a few blocks from here."

I pierced Daniel. "Let me guess, she's a hiker you met on Moose in the last couple weeks?"

"That's right." Daniel smiled, pleased to share this news. "She hiked up on her own and we kinda hit it off. Laura's a vet; she does chiropractic adjustments on horses."

"On horses! Can't she be a regular vet or a regular chiropractor? She has to be both?" Veterinary school and chiropractic college were both competitive, well-paid professions. I couldn't hold back the interrogation. "How old is Laura?"

"Oh, I dunno, maybe twenty-nine or thirty."

McNeal smiled and I pierced him with a glare too.

Daniel was unperturbed, as usual. "Like I said, I can't stay. I'm heading out tomorrow, so I guess I'll say goodbye now."

Pitifully, I couldn't help myself. "Is Laura going with you?"

"No, she has to work, full-time job, right? But she's gonna plan some time off and drive out to BC in a few weeks."

I composed myself. A vet. It would be over within weeks, I told myself. Wait until she saw the old cabin in the woods without electricity or running water.

"Well, buddy, good to see ya." McNeal was far too cheery. They both irritated me. "Have a good winter, eh." He slapped Daniel on the back.

"You're going to Egypt or somewhere overseas, I hear?" Daniel inched toward the door. I knew he didn't give a hoot about Egypt.

"It's complicated," said McNeal. "We do what we can, right?"

I hadn't pictured the evening unfolding like this. I wanted a chance to speak to Daniel privately before he drove off for the winter.

"Give me a call from the Okanagan when you get settled," I said. We embraced lightly, conforming to our new social roles. It felt weird to hug Daniel like any other friend, to ignore the familiarity of his body, to let go of his presence.

McNeal and I sat together awkwardly in the vacuum of Daniel's exit. For the first time, we had absolutely nothing to say to each other.

"We might as well go to bed," he said. "It's my last night."

"I know it's your last night, but it's kinda early to be going to bed." I wasn't ready to end the evening. There were too many things unsaid and uncertain.

"Come on, I have to get up early, let's go." McNeal put his arm around my shoulders.

I followed him upstairs without a word. We brushed teeth, undressed, and slid under the blankets. I turned over, away from him, and folded myself into a sleeping position. He leaned over and kissed my neck, pulling me toward him.

"Come on, it's our last night," he whispered.

"Well, things haven't exactly worked out. What difference does one more night make? Let me go to sleep."

He bristled. "You're upset about Daniel," he said.

"I'm not. I just want to go to sleep."

I was angry and disappointed about everything, the lack of authenticity, the false appearances of friendship, and the endless fire lookout affairs, my own included. Mostly I was angry with McNeal for his inability to be with me. I should have been angrier with myself, since every choice had been my own, but I blamed McNeal for his lack of commitment and Daniel for his hyper-acceptance. I had freedom, youth, good health, and intelligence, but I let the quicksand of resentment suck me into a downward vortex.

I clenched the side of the futon, my back to him. He firmly yanked on my shoulder, rolling me toward him. "I'm not doing this," I said, my own rage welling up.

"Yes you are, and you want to, you know it." McNeal pressed the weight of his body into me.

I lay still, commanding my body to go limp, submitting in revenge, a wordless statement of disinterest, a stance that, to me, was more powerful than a diatribe about "no" or another futile argument. He could go through the machinations of desire and I would give back only contempt.

This was one possible ending.

A few days later, McNeal phoned from Toronto. He was leaving for Egypt with Catherine in a week. He said he'd been humiliated, called a chump *and* a whore, but after screaming at him for days, she had decided to go. Her father advised her it was best for her career.

"I knew you'd convince her," I sneered.

He told me to calm down; they were travelling together as colleagues and scholars, and hoped to publish their research findings in the future.

"Congratulations on your winning strategy," I jeered. "Fuck you!" I slammed down the receiver of my pink phone.

A firestorm of rage engulfed my body. I had never experienced this much anger. It burned from an unknown source, seething waves of indignity, self-righteousness, and hurt pride.

On October 12, 1992, CBC Radio reported an earthquake had rocked northern Egypt, killing hundreds and injuring over six thousand people. The journalist said the epicentre was in the Cairo area. I panicked, fumbling with the handset of my pink phone, my rage dissolved by the news report.

"Can you get me the phone number for the Canadian embassy in Cairo?"

"One moment, madam."

I dialled the country code and the embassy phone number. A woman's voice greeted me in English and Arabic.

"I'm trying to find out if any Canadians were injured in the earthquake."

"Let me check, please hold."

I imagined McNeal, unconscious, trapped in a pile of rubble, unable to move or yell for help.

"Madam, we have no reports of Canadians injured in Cairo."

"You're sure?"

"Yes."

"All right, thank you." What was I doing? McNeal was somewhere in Egypt with another woman; why should I care whether he was buried alive? Maybe he was inside a pyramid when the earthquake struck, and debris had blocked him inside without food or water. If he died in the next few days, no one would tell me. I'd hear about his death from Tomas, or a total stranger, long after the funeral was over. Then again, maybe it was cosmic justice if he was buried alive in ancient temple ruins.

I vacillated between revenge and despair, waiting for a letter or phone call from Egypt; none arrived. Instead, I received a letter from Daniel, alone at the cabin on Silver Star Mountain. He sounded defeated, maybe depressed.

Thursday mornin',
Oct 15, 1992

It was hard coming back here the first time, with all your things here. Now with them gone, I'm feeling even more sad. It seems quite empty, and I wonder what has happened. Given all that has occurred, I don't know how else it could go. Lovers & interests & choices & economics & culture & etc. etc. Passionate Dreams.

I'm feeling horrible about hurting you. When I know more about November (and when I'll be in Calgary) we could see Lance. That could be useful...? I think.

Drummed with David & Willy today @ lunch @ the college. Tomorrow @ Salmon Arm college, before going to Vancouver.

Came home for tape for this package, throw a log on [the wood stove], catch my breath...

I had a puff of stuff, and can't think straight.

Should I bring the couch in? Paint rooms white? Knock out the counter? Hmmm.

No time right now, going to Kelowna...mail this...load a laundry.

Will talk to you next week.

Take care.
Love,
Daniel

This letter was the first admission that he'd been truly affected by our breakup. It was as though he had to descend to a lower altitude before he perceived his own feelings.

The month of October passed with no word from McNeal. One day at Safeway, stocking the soup aisle with Troy, I broke into tears and rushed outside to the parking lot to conceal my grief. Afraid Troy would follow, I detoured into the women's washroom to compose myself. Staring at my reflection in the mirror, I summoned false strength. I would send a letter overseas and patch things up.

After work, I sequestered myself in the bedroom and tapped out my longing and regret on a small portable typewriter. Maybe I had spoken too hastily in our last conversation, I mused, especially the part about "fuck off." I aimed for a sexy, airy voice, making light of our fights and infidelities, hinting I had taken a lover in despair but only as a temporary consolation. I cloaked myself in an ardent, easygoing tone. I rained down compliments and praise on McNeal, boosting his ego, avoiding any blame. After dabbing at the typos with a bottle of whiteout, I indulged one last melodramatic strategy. Applying fresh burgundy lipstick, I folded the pages and pressed my lips to the blank page, sealing the letter with a kiss.

Why could I not see it? This was simply a battle of wills, a play to win at the competition of love and remedy my own bruised ego. Operation Kiss.

By November, with not a word of Coptic or Demotic from my man of letters, I took up smoking. I smoked bidis, tiny, hand-rolled cigarettes from India packaged in a delicate cone of pink paper. The Indians wrapped their tobacco in a brown, bark-like leaf, and although I had never smoked, now I relished the texture of a slender bidi between my fingers. The nicotine lifted my mood, and for a time I would feel optimistic and make light of the affair.

I embraced cynicism and took solace in black. Black T-shirts, black pants, and black boots. I bought a darker shade of lipstick and streaked my hair with mahogany-red highlights. I tried to wash that man right outa my hair, but my hair turned brassy like my mood. When I tired of the defiant colour, it would, unfortunately, take the rest of the nineties to eradicate the scarlet tones.

✺

During November, while I pretended to send the McNeal affair up in smoke, Dinah agreed to a telephone conversation with John. In the intervening months, her feelings had softened, and she was willing to speak with him and hear what he had to say. She said that after finishing the domestic-violence program at the YWCA, she felt empowered to hold her own in a dialogue.

She expected and wanted a heartfelt expression of regret, a thorough examination of what had transpired; instead, she recalled that John wanted to immediately restore intimacy. She heard the regret in his voice, a fleeting apology, and then he circled back to pinning some responsibility on her for what had happened at Cline Lookout. Dismayed by the tone of his appeals, she rebuffed insinuations they should, or could, get back together. After that disappointing conversation, she stopped hoping for John to make amends and focussed on rebuilding her own life.

He had been mandated to appear in court that fall on assault charges. Christos had promised that he and Alice would come to Alberta to attend court with him. They were certain that by the time the court date arrived, John would be ready to express remorse. The night before the court hearing, Christos and Alice slept on the floor of John's small apartment, a basement suite in the Mission neighbourhood south of downtown.

The next day, in the bitter Alberta cold, the three friends huddled in the car on the way to the hearing, the tension bristling, their conversations strained. Christos began to wonder if John would ever take off the armour and drop his stubborn facade.

Aside from John and legal staff, Christos and Alice were the only people in the courtroom. The judge charged John with assault causing bodily harm and sentenced him to sixty days in a provincial correctional centre, ruling that John could serve the sentence on weekends.

John complied with the sentence and every weekend presented to the guards at the correctional institution—he didn't mess with those rules. During the week he was free to hang out with friends and drop by the pub or pool hall, but he must have longed for the farmhouse on Bearspaw Road, the rambling walks in the hills, and the outdoor fire by the Dragon on the back forty with friends.

Over the winter John participated in anger management therapy. There was a rumour in the Supper Club that he faked his way through the program, intelligent enough to know what view to express in a therapeutic setting, obtaining a get-out-of-jail-free card. I doubt he asserted to therapists that his actions were deserved—that Dinah, "the adulteress," had brought the attack on herself—but in reality, it seems he clung to this position, and never expressed remorse or regret to us for his actions.

The correctional institute John attended was located on the northwest edge of the city, a facility Calgarians referred to as Spy Hill. Strangely, John had done time there in 1970–71, after being charged with marijuana possession, along with many others, in what came to be known as the "Nanton bust" (Nanton is a town south of Calgary).

On a blustery winter day at the end of December, I came home from work and Athena said McNeal had called—from Ontario. "He just got back from Egypt," she said pleasantly. I felt cheated, missing the call.

"Did he leave a number?" I asked.

"I wrote it down and put it in your room. He's staying at his mother's in Kingston."

I ran upstairs and called the number. McNeal answered, voice subdued.

"You didn't write or call for three months," I exclaimed.

"Actually, I did, but the mail system in Egypt isn't exactly efficient." McNeal sighed.

"What's wrong?"

"I'm exhausted. Kind of down. Feeling blue these days. Not depressed, just low."

"Maybe we should get together? Why don't you fly out here? Fares are low in January."

"Fly to Alberta? That's out of the question. I'm broke, with no place to live and I have this dissertation on my back."

"When will I see you?" Like a girl spy, I was determined to attract him back to my camp and regain influence over the covert operation. He had turned, a double agent, but I needed him, and if I forgave the past, surely he would come back to my cause, where he had once pledged true allegiance.

"I don't know, Mary. I'm working things out. Don't make demands on me, please. I can't take it right now. I'll be back at the lookout in a few months."

"Right, and we'll pick up where we left off. How convenient for you." My resentment surfaced and immediately we were thrust onto the battlefield.

"Let's not do this right now. I'll call you another time, okay?" McNeal retreated, his quick wit obliterated by the dark mood.

Not long after the depressed phone call, a stray letter sent from Luxor, Egypt, reached Calgary. The airmail letter was handwritten, a loopy, slanted cursive, composed of tall, thin letters curling back on themselves. Small, exotic paintings of Egypt were embossed on the other side of the page: a view of Cairo, the Philae temple, Ramses III temple, a sandstorm near the great Sphinx, and a depiction of the Giza pyramids on the Nile. McNeal's flip, vibrant self spoke from far away in the Middle East.

December 15, 1992
Luxor, Egypt

Dear Mary Magdalene,
Well, a couple of your <u>special delivery</u> letters just caught up to me here & I am responding forthwith. You managed to strike a plangent chord my dear as I gather the headstrong Taurus is more into amorous felicitations (as opposed to seeing red and goring, that is). Well I am glad, and sorry that you have been downcast at not hearing from me—I gather an early postcard did not make it? (Those things happen.) What about the card from the Sudan? No, no, you are not out of my life, dearest, I want to feel those strong, slim legs wrapped around me again, but ahem, for now a newsy brief so you will know what is going on. We will be returning to Toronto around the 27th of Dec if the tickets can be confirmed (an on-going process). The "research" has gone fairly well although C is disappointed with her findings. The Sudan was a good experience but I am afraid it is over at this point. Egypt is alternatingly wonderful and terrible on a daily basis—I'll save all the lurid details 'til I see you. But I don't have the money to carry on—I <u>would</u> certainly have taken you up on India <u>even</u> at this late date & even tho' you treated me so shamefully earlier on—but the trip has been far more expensive than anticipated for various mundane reasons. More than this I just want to get back & work on my computer. I'm worried

about C in Toronto as she is a financial disaster & I want to get a place <u>on my own</u>. I'll be living on my visa when I get back until my next scholarship & then back to the tower—of course.

We went through the area where the tourists were shot w/ a police escort: 10 heavily armed soldiers escorting us here & there. Fun in a perverse sort of way. But enough "tourist" news…I may be buying some lapis for you on the way back & you better damn well like it. You didn't think getting involved w/ the Ultimate Guy would be easy did you? You damn wench. I do miss you. I'm sitting—now—on the terrace of the Old Winter Palace Hotel overlooking the Nile drinking a Stella beer (C is sick back at the house) & I wish you were here—good enough for you? Are you still stamping Taurus mad, or loving & horny? <u>Lots</u> of poems in the can, which I'd love to show you. <u>Yours</u> was damn fine stuff sweetheart. You must be in love or something. The job in Cairo is still a distinct likelihood as I have heard through the grapevine that the man is petitioning his termination—this year, next year? I'm not sure. Very few letters or information received at this end. Onwards we go.…I love the idea and feel of bathing in your innermost reaches.…I hope you're squirming in your seat. I will call you when I'm back. Miss me—it's good for you. I love you. xoxoxo

Mary Magdalene and the Ultimate Guy. Did that make him Jesus Christ?

I couldn't make sense of McNeal's flirtatious letter in light of the recent miserable phone call. What had happened in the intervening weeks? I could go mad speculating. Unable to tolerate his mood swings, I couldn't keep waiting for him to show up unconditionally. There was always an exotic obstacle to overcome, an emotional crisis to endure, or a once-in-a-lifetime opportunity to chase.

Over the holiday season, the whole world had paired up. Athena had a new boyfriend, Paulo, a Portuguese-Canadian poet, who first came to the house to help her with conversational Spanish, a required course in her degree program. They had started out practising Spanish verbs in the kitchen, and now they were speaking in tongues in her bedroom. I had spoken to Daniel on the phone at Christmas, and he and Laura, the vet, were cocooned at the cabin, basking in their own electrical voltage. Dinah's date with Paul, the new smoke-free actor, had blossomed into a committed relationship, and they were living together, entertaining actors, writers, and directors in their home, fire lookout culture relegated to the past. Ingrid and Jim were still happy together in their big Calgary house, and there were rumours that Ingrid, like Tomas and Christos, had maintained a tenuous dialogue with John.

I was the only single woman among us.

Around about this time, Daniel kept insisting that a woman without a man is like a fish without a bicycle, a feminist aphorism he extolled; however, this bit of comfort did not stick.

When my friend Doug, another fire lookout observer and TM member, observed my brooding attitude to the way things had blistered after McNeal, he handed me one of his favourite books, *Fuck, YES!: A Guide to the Happy Acceptance of Everything.* A *Fuck, YES!* devotee, Doug could see I needed to change my outlook. Not that my bad attitude was well hidden, or that Doug possessed superior insight, but he was willing to call me out.

Fuck, YES! was about the practice of transcending complaining and resentment into joyful acceptance. When I told him about the Ultimate Guy letter, without missing a beat, he said, "Mary, I think he's the Penultimate Guy."

"Penultimate?" I asked. Being a competitive Scrabble player, Doug had an excellent vocabulary.

"Yes, penultimate," he said confidently. "Next to last."

Doug was the guy with the van, a brown GM panel van, and he drove around as though he were in the middle of a move. His van was a permanent storage space for his stuff, his friends' stuff, finds from the alley, and bulky objects that someone inevitably needed to move. On one occasion, we parked at the community centre, across the road from the Bow River, and flailed around in the van. Suddenly, Doug released his embrace, a green toque pulled tight over his forehead and ears.

"If I was a poet I'd write you a love poem," he said. "But I'm not, Mary, it's just not in me. I'm sorry." He gripped the steering wheel, despite the vehicle being in park, ignition off.

"That's okay," I said, the tangle of used tools, Rubbermaid storage tubs, and long-forgotten garage-sale deals in twisted glory at my back.

Despite the mayhem, he had a sweet honesty that was refreshing after months of war strategy with McNeal. "Not everyone can be a poet. You have other skills." I leaned sideways in the dark to kiss him. My front teeth rammed against his.

"Ouch, sorry, but that hurt," I touched my front tooth to make sure it wasn't chipped.

"You need to be careful with those teeth," exclaimed Doug. "Maybe it's time you got your teeth straightened?"

In lieu of love poetry, Doug persuaded me to attend a free orthodontic assessment to consider the possibility of dental surgery and braces to straighten my teeth and improve my bite. There was no room for wabi-sabi imperfection in his approach to dental health.

By the end of the consult, I was demoralized, forced to confront large images of my weak jaw profile and uneven toothy bite. I was diagnosed with TMJ, which could be remedied, said the orthodontist, if I agreed to let him break my temporomandibular joint with a hammer and reset it. Then, I would have to wear braces on the upper teeth for two years, along with a mouth guard every night. Doug was delighted when the technician displayed a model of my future, perfect bite.

"But I'll turn forty with braces," I protested. "What am I supposed to do for two years, stop dating altogether?"

The price tag ended the intervention: it would take thousands of dollars to upgrade my jaw, and I had no dental insurance.

"But it's an investment in yourself," argued Doug. "Once you straighten your teeth, your life will straighten out too. You'll be more confident, attract better situations, you know how it works. Say yes!"

I pushed my tongue against the back of my crooked front teeth and mused. I was not prepared to bite. As friends, Doug and I could rescue each other from loneliness, and his *Fuck, YES!* philosophy may have been the perfect antidote to McNeal's Gnostic hell, but getting straighter teeth and bypassing my negative emotional state was not a skilful solution.

On my bookshelf, I had a hardcover copy of *Blood Memory*, the autobiography of the great modern dancer and choreographer Martha Graham. Daniel had given me the book as a gift last year at winter solstice. He had signed the fly-leaf: "To my dancing partner, with love and respect, Daniel, December 1991."

There was one passage, in particular, that I treasured, marking it with a sticky note. Graham described how many women appeared at her studio expressing the desire to dance in her company. They came to her "with conventional notions of prettiness and graceful posturing." She advised the young women: "I wanted them to admire strength. If I could give them only one thing, that would be it. Ugliness, I told them, if given a powerful voice, can be beautiful."[9]

Not that I was ugly, but I was grasping at conventional ways of being a woman. When Graham said "strength," I believe she meant inner strength, the ability to cultivate and radiate power, a quality we, as a society, continue to resent in women. Throughout history we have celebrated beautiful women; more recently we have honoured intelligent and creative women. But do we respect, value, or encourage powerful and strong women?

It was ugly to deny my own strength. By staying involved with men who were not right for me, especially McNeal, I had undermined myself.

Mired in chaos, I was letting emotional entanglements dictate the direction of my life and drain my strength.

Sometimes it was important to say *Fuck, no!* I had been saying yes for far too long.

Ash

The next spring I rented a small furnished bungalow, up the Crescent Heights hill not far from Athena's townhouse in Sunnyside. Another look-out observer, a friend of a friend, had agreed to the sublet, and the luxury of my own living space, temporary as it was, lifted my spirits. Sunlight poured through the windows of the front porch where I sat with coffee every morning, dreaming about possibilities.

Good things would come.

It was during this time of transition, when the deciduous buds uncurl, delicate, ever-so-pale green, that McNeal tracked me down on his way back to Carbondale, to present a gift, a jade necklace he had bought in Cairo—"green jade because it's the same colour as your eyes," he said. The necklace was strung with eighty round stones, which later a jeweller told me were imitation jade. "This is aventurine quartz," the jeweller said with conviction, a common, less valuable stone.

Nevertheless, on the day, I treasured the gift, accepting it as symbolic of new beginnings in springtime.

I should have galvanized a stronger defence and arranged to meet him in public to receive the gift, but I allowed him to cross the threshold, and sleep overnight in the small house.

The next morning, on the way to Heartland Café, McNeal said I shouldn't read too much into the romantic stopover, because after all, he needed space to work on the dissertation and sort through the chaotic events of the past year. He adjusted his designer sunglasses. "But if you need to talk, call me any time," he said, his eyes two dark shields.

My throat constricted. I squinted in the sunlight, mute.

Months later, the first time I ever wore the necklace, it snapped, the eighty stones spilling onto the sidewalk, rolling in all directions. The string had not been knotted between stones, a simple technique that would have secured the necklace, averting the cascade. I gathered up the aventurine, and when I counted them at home, I had seventy-nine stones.

I would always come up short with McNeal. How did I not see this pattern?

After the jade rendezvous, and after he was sequestered at the lookout, he wrote a lament about his distressed state.

May 14, 1993
Carbondale Lookout

Dear Mary,

Well I felt like shit in leaving but felt psychically cornered and knew that there was nothing I could do just then to help you; I also knew that my fragile psyche was not up for more torment. I'm not happy at all Mary and I'm sorry to have brought you more pain as it makes me feel even worse. I'm in the midst of mid-Life Big Time as the saying goes, and I won't belabour the issue as I have done so enough already; but I'm really fed up with things on so many levels. I'm holed up trying to do this work, it's about all I can do just now....I seem to be approaching some kind of crisis. No, not a nervous breakdown as such, but a vast and searching reappraisal of just what the hell I am doing on planet earth....

You are free to visit anytime and I would pick you up in Pincher as you like—I would like. But I suspect you may not be down and that is OK too. Perhaps I deserve a celibate season without a loving goddess to lie naked with. What will be will be.

I'm messed up just now, I admit it, although I have been straight with you and feel no guilt. But I understand your pain as I have been there myself on a number of occasions. It is really the worst....You're a good person Mary and you mean a lot to me—I really enjoy talking to you and sharing intimacies. If I don't see you this summer I shall miss you deeply, believe me, but I just can't commit to this all-out Couple thing just now and you mustn't take it as any failing in yourself. If anything it is my own failing as it appears to be part of a larger pattern in my life. I don't know.

Write and tell me how you feel and I'll do the same. I've long passed the point where I want to sublimate things and "persona" my way through life. It's too damn short.

With love,
McNeal

I had never been involved with a man who at once feared and pursued committed relationships with such intensity. I fired back a blunt reply, which, due to his "fragile psyche," instigated a torrent of vitriolic correspondence between us, so despicable that I contemplated burning those letters, something I was loath to do, given my propensity to archive correspondence. There was one in particular, a modern-day hex, in which he vowed I would be afflicted, for the rest of my life, with a reverse Midas touch. Everything you touch will turn, not to gold, McNeal chastised, but to destruction. I showed it to Athena for her appraisal. She read quietly, and then in earnest said, "Oh Mary, burn this." I took her advice and torched all the malicious letters.

On my birthday, later in May, Athena invited me to her home, to catch up, she said. I climbed the familiar stairs and was met by a chorus of "Surprise!" Six women friends, including Dinah, celebrated me with lilacs, always in bloom at this time of year in Calgary, plenty of wine, and cake. We sat in a circle in Athena's living room, the women's friendship a healing balm.

Throughout this time, I never speculated that McNeal's erratic behaviour might have been symptoms of depression. I consistently interpreted his emotional extremes as a character flaw, as proof he was a manipulative rogue.

Regardless of the correct diagnosis, the jade relapse motivated me to devise an exit plan, a way out of Calgary and the constant reminders of fire lookouts. From so many places in the city, the Rocky Mountains were visible on the western horizon; in the southwest of the city, on a clear day, I could spot the outline of Moose Mountain. To rebuild my life and build a reservoir of feminine strength, I needed new surroundings. I'd read about nicotine-addicted smokers who moved to new houses, cities, and even countries to successfully quit. Surely my metamorphosis would be less difficult?

It was a curious phenomenon, but after making a commitment to change my life, there was a lag, a window of regression, as though the vibration of my intentions needed time to synchronize with the rhythm of the universe. My timing was dreadful. In 1993, the unemployment rate rose into double digits, as high as it had been during the recession of the early eighties. Unemployment levels would never, in the following twenty-five years, be this high again.

Because I had quit the job supporting clients with disabilities, I stepped backwards into retail mayhem and accepted a full-time job as assistant manager at Community Natural Foods. I told myself it was a temporary situation, but the decision felt like defeat. I had come full circle, the place I had been when I first met Daniel seven years earlier.

If it was a cosmic joke, I was not laughing.

My duties, aside from purchasing stock, centred on hiring and supervising the sales associates who worked on the retail floor. And the floor at Community Natural was much larger than it had been when I worked there in the eighties. The natural foods business had exploded in the early nineties, and to accommodate escalating growth, the owner had purchased a six-thousand-square-foot building and converted it to retail space. We were the Whole Foods of Calgary.

I worked for almost a year at Community Natural, before carrying out my exit plan. The following summer, I rented a small U-Haul trailer and with the help of a few good friends moved to Edmonton. I had enrolled in graduate courses in counselling psychology at the University of Alberta; officially, I was an unclassified student, but I calculated that if I performed well, and then applied to the formal program, the department would open the gates and let me in. Incremental persuasion.

When I unpacked my collection of motley belongings in a ground-level apartment suite off Whyte Avenue, I surveyed the bare white rooms, and loneliness overpowered me. I had no support network in the city, and at university I was fifteen years older than most students in my classes. But, I told myself, by severing connections with Calgary, I could focus on new relationships and intellectual challenges.

No sooner had my self-imposed exile begun in Edmonton than I received a letter from Daniel in exile on Moose Mountain.

August 10, 1994
Moose Mountain

It's violet here, hazy—and I feel like I'm sitting on an egg of earth. My mind is kind of stunned when I think that you've actually moved to Edmonton! Not that it's the end of the earth or anything but I get sad a bit because it's just that much farther. Well, 3 hours is all. North of Calgary…

I can get quite sad about all this relationship strain. "Strain"—well it makes me sad and that's something of a strain (I think?). Of course I'm playing *The Piano* soundtrack—which is not exactly uplifting (a brooding melancholy more aptly put).

We sure do have a past together, yes—have done lots of stuff. I know that I seem to be a master @ avoidance—but I can get so sad when I feel how frustrating life is. This morning, I felt pretty good—even though sad—as though I had energy to actually make pots and do things without getting bogged down. Then I went to bed again! Brian came up in the afternoon and we fixed a propane leak, then I went to bed again! Somehow I have to overcome this block of energy and motivation. My personal challenge. (I did spray paint my radio cabinets today—very nice, another small step of "niceness" for the [lookout] cabin).

I really do miss you, I mean over the last couple of years. This lookout life sure has screwed some things up for me, moving back and forth. But then if I had a career that was rooted in one town that would be weird too. Some folks do. Or none. I'm glad I have something. Anytime I did those career counselling things, the lookout looked okay, sort of. Very self-centred I guess. But I don't like being alone so much, so I guess I do want a relationship. Well, I'd like some meaning to life, of some sort….One has to be a few bricks short of a load to really believe in some of the off the shelf worldviews these days….

Anyway—it's good you are going to University. This is what you want and are therefore doing. Good…I'm still thinking pots and darkroom work (a bit). Hooking up that gas kiln could be the rightest thing to do. I'm pondering. Mostly I want to pay off the car ASAP and credit cards too.

I keep thinking "maybe Prozac," exercise/fitness center. Ah, the fall, what a winter awaits? I get frustrated thinking of not having a 4X4 to scoot around in, of the debt I most likely still have, of sickness, of death. Mr. Bleak. Mister Bleak Buddhist. Bleak, bleak, bleak.

It's foggy now. I'm a turtle-paced person.

There come some hikers and in an attempt to preserve freshness of prose I'm going to mail this to you without saying much else! Perhaps this will be your first mail [in Edmonton]?

Take care,
I love you, Daniel.
Good luck finding work. Let me know if I can help w/ $ in a tight spot.

Mr. Bleak's mention of Prozac and death made me wonder if Daniel was depressed. He must have been dreading another cloudy Okanagan winter, alone, on Silver Star Mountain. The reference to *The Piano* was an important clue to his ruminating mood, which I deciphered when we spoke long after the lookout season.

During the spring of that year, before going back to Moose Mountain, Daniel had gone to see the Jane Campion film *The Piano* at the Towne Theatre in Vernon. The film told an emotionally charged, nineteenth-century story from the perspective of the female protagonist, Ada McGrath, a mute pianist, whose husband cut off her finger after learning she was attracted to, and had been intimate with, another man, Baines. This man had tattooed his face in the Maori tradition and, unlike Ada's husband, appreciated her passion for playing the piano.

As Daniel looked out across the bobble of heads inside the theatre, he caught his breath. That was John in the audience, his brown ponytail tied back neatly. Mesmerized by Campion's visual images and the melancholy score—in fact, he went back and viewed it again—mysteriously, beyond his control, the first viewing he watched with John.

When the house lights came up, John had disappeared, leaving Daniel dumbstruck by the synchronicity.

The next day, Daniel dropped by Sunseed, a natural foods café on the main street of Vernon, across the street from the theatre. No sooner was he inside the door than he spotted John drinking coffee alone.

"I saw you at *The Piano* last night," Daniel said, hovering next to the table.

"Yeaaah—I was there," John replied in his familiar drawl.

"What did you think of the film?" Daniel thought it inconceivable an artist could not be affected by the beauty of the work.

"I didn't like it," said John. "Didn't like it at all."

"Really!" Daniel exclaimed. He hesitated; this was the perfect moment for John to offer an apology or allude to his Big Jealous Violent Mistake. I'll go first and kick-start the conversation, thought Daniel. "Well, sorry about everything that happened," he said. He was referring to his own impulsivity at the time, blasting the news about John's attack on Dinah far and wide. Now, two years later, he doubted his actions in publicly shaming John.

"Sure, okay," said John, accepting Daniel's apology.

Daniel fidgeted, waiting for John to reciprocate, to apologize for the violence against Dinah.

Stalemate.

John sipped the coffee, his eyes concealed by sunglasses.

"I wanted to know what he was really feeling," said Daniel when he told me about the chance meeting. "I couldn't see his eyes, I couldn't know for sure, but I felt he was not about to apologize for anything."

Interpreting John's silence as intransigence, Daniel walked away. Their paths never intersected again.

I was moved by that story of synchronicity, and listened with the hope there would be a good ending. In my imagination, John would confess: "I sure screwed up that summer. I'm so sorry about what I did. I hope we can still be friends."

Sometimes the world, in its mystery, offers us a chance to make things right but, curiously we might choose to plod the same miserable path and ignore grace, preferring to endure the smoky prison of our own small mind.

Around the same time I received the *Piano* letter from Daniel, Tomas wrote from Mockingbird Lookout with an assessment of the past.

> I have respect for your sensibility and intelligence to be able to bypass the paint strokes with McN and D and all the other sources interwoven with our little isolated social web, the nucleus being the once upon a time ago "supper club," as Jim described it. A "supper club," which with one series of psychic explosions after another disintegrated into many bits and pieces....
>
> The other day in the evening I had a huge owl visit me. It flew about a meter or two from my head as if wanting to land on me; I had to lift my arm in defense against its sharp claws

and beak. We looked each other in the eyes. Three times it came very close trying to land on me so it seemed. The symbolism of this of course is death, a death perhaps physically or psychically. Never seen anything like it. Perhaps this will be my last season on Mockingbird Hill.

Tomas was right; in our separate realities, we all persisted in trying to understand how the Lookout Supper Club had suddenly disintegrated.

In the fall, he wrote again after coming down from Mockingbird Lookout.

November 8, 1994
Calgary

The mountains look pink this morning; visibility 40 km, in haze, chinook winds with lenticular clouds, warm temperatures, residual warmth from the south Pacific blowing across the mountains. All this with a coffee and cigarette to start the day…

I came down from the lookout and there is a bit of difficulty in the transition; each year the diffusion into the city is a problem. Each season increasingly difficult…

Indirectly I heard from McN the other day, via Keith, my Marlboro Man, the initial attack crew leader at the Ghost [ranger station]. He drove McN to the airport after he left the lookout. He told Keith to pass on a message to me, rather a short one-liner:

"Catch you in the rebound of life."

Brilliant! Ha? Sounds just like good old McNeal with his refined tapestry of words. There is humour to it all; in my imagination he will always be remembered as a most unique case study—he definitely taught me a lot. And son of a gun, the ending of our relationship now seems like something out of a black comedy….Whatever, I miss the man and I remain with good feelings toward him.

Christ Almighty Mary; I am sorry to hear the pressures with this bankruptcy stuff. This is the last pressure a person needs in academia land, especially at this time of year….You know this is what I like about the lookout, for at least five months of the year my brain functions without the pressure of god damn money—what a privilege in that regard....

You sound like you have no shortage of trials and tribulations in your Edmonton saga.

Take care up there Mary, what more can be said?

With best wishes and love,
Tomas

This was the last letter I received from Tomas. I let our correspondence lapse, in part as a strategy to reinvent myself and as a method of protection from laconic updates about McNeal.

After the fall equinox, darkness and cold enveloped Edmonton. The Rocky Mountains, three hours west, were a world away.

I attended my classes, got a part-time job at the university library, and volunteered at Planned Parenthood on the pregnancy crisis telephone line. To survive on a meagre budget, I abandoned organic foods, but fortunately, my type A blood was suited to a low-protein, vegetarian diet, which, technically, I adhered to on a regime of Campbell's soup and grilled cheese.

Despite the fact that I had earned excellent grades in three graduate counselling psychology courses, the following spring my application to the full-time master's program was rejected. Then my job at the library was terminated. Confounding the situation, Ralph Klein, the newly elected Conservative premier, slashed and gutted public spending, in particular health and education budgets, pushing me and thousands of Albertans into debt and unemployment. The weak argument Klein promulgated about the need for austerity to pay down government deficits made no sense given Alberta's billions in subsidies to oil and gas corporations.

While I endured unemployment, loneliness, and grilled mozzarella in Edmonton, Daniel went back to work on the fire lookout—and kept sending letters.

May 1995
Moose Mountain

Hiyuh, Huyuh, Ho! Tons of snow here this year. May 26th they
got me up, 6 feet of snow on the helipad. No sign of the cougar
yet! Tho' I worry. As per usual, I've been taking it easy-ish. I
feel like I'm on a melting ice-floe....Got some clay and a wheel
here....

As I tidy up here I come across all sorts of reminders of
my "past life." Pictures, letters, memories. More than the snow.
Of course I remember you hiking up in the snow. Everyone else
seems utterly freaked out about hiking up period, let alone in the
weathers you did! Of course you know that amuses me. Fetching
snow-hid beer!

I'm scared about my future, just am. Feel a sense of urgency,
"times runninoutishness." I know you don't like to hear that but
I want to do something more.

In July he wrote again, telling me that in addition to the rainy weather
and his own bleak mood, Moose Mountain had attracted a depressed male
hiker.

A hiker who's been hanging around a lot started telling me of
his suicide plans last weekend (go off his antidepressant medication, get drunk, jump off cliff nearby, after he finishes his mem-
oirs—about 10 days more work he figured). What could I say?
I could hardly find any emotional response in myself....What
would <u>instant</u> death be like I wonder.

The hiker was Warren. He was clinically depressed, and he had befriended
Daniel, who, based on his letters, was contemplating Prozac for himself.

Warren was different from other hikers; he bushwhacked up the
mountain from various directions, rarely bothering with the popular, well-
worn hiking trail from the east. He was intrepid, trekking in from the
south and southwest, as though the wilderness of Moose Mountain were
an extension of his backyard. Sometimes he climbed up the south side of
the Moose Dome, starting out from the Bragg Creek ice caves above Canyon Creek. On other occasions he meandered farther west along Canyon
Creek, until he found a little-used trail crossing Moose Mountain Creek,
and approached the lookout from the southwest.

After the arduous ascent, Warren would bound onto the catwalk and wait for Daniel to open the door and invite him inside. Daniel said Warren confided in him—how he struggled with depression, how his doctors had trouble getting the medication right, and how the pharmaceutcals caused weight gain. When Daniel asked him about the cut marks on his arms, Warren insisted they were the outcome of adventurous shortcuts through the brush. Prickly wild rose bushes. He told Daniel everything about his life: he was unemployed, never dated, and often thought about committing suicide. After unburdening himself, Warren would hike off and leave Daniel in solitude.

One evening in August, Warren popped into Daniel's viewfinder, breathless from the climb, striding with purpose toward the lookout door. The last hiker of the day. Once inside, Warren pulled a bottle of peach schnapps from his pack.

"This is the night," he declared. "I'm going to end my life."

Warren shoved the bottle toward Daniel.

"Go ahead, have a shot."

Wanting to be supportive, Daniel obliged, pouring a modest shot of peach schnapps into his vanilla soy latte.

"Tonight, really? How are you planning on doing it?"

"Alcohol and pills."

"Well, thanks for sharing the schnapps," said Daniel. "Sure it's okay if I imbibe? You might need it all, you know."

"No, go ahead. I have a bottle of pills, so have as much of the schnapps as you like, man. I saved up my medication for the last few weeks, and I think this is enough to do the job." Warren flashed the prescription bottle. "I'm gonna sit here for a while though."

"Sure, stay as long as you want."

Daniel ran scenarios through his mind. Should he call the ranger over the radio and ask them to send a helicopter for a suicidal hiker? Warren would probably dart and refuse to board the chopper. He imagined a manhunt from the air for Warren, an experienced hiker intimate with the ridges and contours of the mountain. Besides, if they caught Warren, apprehending him like a criminal, where would the pilot drop him? At the district ranger station? At a hospital in Calgary? Maybe he should try to wrestle the pills from Warren? But Daniel didn't want to convince anyone to do anything. So, he sat with Warren and listened to the details of the suicide plan. In preparation, Warren said he had visited his mother the night before and together they watched the Pink Floyd movie *The Wall* in Dolby stereo sound.

In the cult-status rock opera, the depressed anti-hero, Pink, walls himself off from the rest of the world. As Pink places the last brick in the wall, Roger Waters sings the quiet track "Goodbye Cruel World."

For Warren, Moose Mountain was the last brick. The mountain had certainly tested Daniel over the years: on Moose he had let go of Faith, me, Zip, and John.

The evening was auspicious. It was undercast; huge, billowy clouds floated below the lookout in all directions like a sea of white foam. The cloud and fog crept along the edges of the ridges, obscuring the valleys, suspending the lookout in time and space, sealing it off from the world below. In the west, above the clouds, the setting sun glowed reddish yellow, and in the east, a round full moon rose.

Warren relaxed, legs dangling off the side of the bed, now and then taking shots of the liqueur, content to share his final hours with the lookout man. Daniel refused the offers of more schnapps, revolted by the soy shooter. After a while Warren said, "I better get moving. I wanna get down to the ice caves before I take the pills."

"Well, it sounds like you've made up your mind."

"Yup."

"It's been nice knowing you, Warren."

Daniel empathized with the depressed man's predicament; but if Warren wanted to put in the last brick, Daniel would not fight him. As a young Mr. Bleak, he matched Warren's stoicism. There was nothing in our culture that had equipped him for intervening in a depressed man's plans.

When Warren hiked off, Daniel stood on the catwalk and tracked him through the binoculars as the man scrambled downhill, a lonely figure disappearing against the wash of grey rock and fog. Half an hour later, Warren came back into view on the high ridge above Canyon Creek, and Daniel blew the conch, waiting for the sound to travel through space. In a few seconds, Warren stopped and waved back, a speck of suffering engulfed by white clouds.

The full red moon rose higher and higher in the sky. Later that evening, Daniel sat on the bed, holding his sarod, and played a raga, in a minor key, to honour Warren.

"Far be it from me to stop him," said Daniel when he told me the story. "Warren had tried everything: medication, exercise, talk therapy."

About a week later, a couple of guys from the Fish and Wildlife department stopped by the lookout, and Daniel told them about Warren.

"Do you know if anyone found an abandoned vehicle down at the trailhead to the ice caves?" he asked.

"No, definitely not." The men said they were sure no one had reported anything unusual in the area. "Not a lot you could have done," they agreed.

How strange, Daniel mused; Warren had struck him as decisive that night.

Later that month, Daniel glimpsed a lone figure approaching from out of the grey rock formations right below the lookout. Ambushed again.

"Hey, how are you!" Daniel exclaimed. "What happened?"

Warren came inside, eager to tell his story. "Well, I swallowed all those pills, but I couldn't keep them down. They didn't mix with the schnapps. By the time I got to the ice caves I was vomiting like crazy."

"Oh geez, and you kept hiking?"

"Well, yeah. I had no reason to stay. I had to get outa there, right? I was so goddamn sick, but I dragged myself back to the car in the dark."

"Warren." Daniel smiled. "It's good to see you, buddy. The door here is always open."

Maybe he was unsure how to help a guy with suicidal thoughts, but friendship was a good beginning.

I have seen the Smoky One, whose mantra is dhoom, the inauspicious crone goddess, an outcast, wandering and travelling nowhere, ugly, without protection or companion, the raven of misfortune at her side, bestowing the grace of disappointment and failure to all on her path.

She abides in dry, burned forests, where smoke curls from the ashes of dead, blackened trees, their charred trunks like jagged headstones, pointing upwards into a grey, empty sky. She appears after the fire and flames are spent, at peace in the desolate, bleak remains, at ease in the parched valley of death.

Dare you look into her aged eyes? Her smoky gaze obscures and obliterates all hope, all passion, guiding you to utter Emptiness, total Freedom, and the Void of pure Being. She is not Mary, Athena, or Magdalene, Diana, Alicia, or Sophia; she is the dissolution of all forms.

One winter night, the Smoky One begged at the table of the Supper Club, wearing filthy rags, eating and drinking nothing, her smoky presence dissolving the unions, desires, and carefree hopes of our youth, casting us from the table of friendship and plenty.

As we dispersed among the skeletons of blackened trees, would we sense the stirring of new growth underfoot, awakened by heat and nourished by ash?

The blessing of loss and disappointment is that it forces us to look inward, shaking us into the mystery that all forms will pass away, and the conviction that we came here for a reason. In running between fire lookouts, up and down mountains, and back and forth between cities, I had avoided looking inward. The world presented me with a binary dilemma that was unsolvable, because the real issue was not a relationship with Daniel versus one with McNeal; it was the inner development of my own strength, creativity, and power. When I say power, I mean the power to assert myself, as a woman in the world, without apology, and to express my own individual purpose.

Both men may have struggled with depression at times, exacerbated by a job of isolation and aloneness, but as a supportive woman I was always at the ready to console them, buttress *their* adventure, their talents. The propensity to be helpful and supportive was etched so deeply into my psyche, by social convention, family, and history, I was unable to spot it.

Daniel had manifested his creative inventiveness, building and firing a rare sixteenth-century Japanese pottery kiln. McNeal had proved his intellectual prowess, researching and producing a dissertation grounded in second-century Egyptian religious sects. Where had I been in all this male initiative? What had evolved and taken outer shape in my life?

I had dabbled in counselling, community dance, holistic health, and living in a yurt—built by a man.

Not only had I failed to consistently nurture my own talents, I had sabotaged my own plans, applying to graduate school to train for a profession and then abandoning opportunity when personal crisis loomed. My life decisions had been guided by relationship influences, the agreement and approval of others, which in itself was not a terrible thing, but neither was it the ideal way to identify and fulfil my own purpose.

Daniel, in his fluid, spontaneous, and affable way, would likely have adapted to my desires, but my motivations were lodged in a blind spot, hidden by my own unconscious. Instead of negotiating with him for what I wanted, exploring mutuality and brainstorming solutions to our different goals, I fell in love with someone else, a man who represented the unrealized aspects of myself.

This understanding about self-expression and romantic triangles was incremental and permeated my awareness over a period of years.

Right now, the first step was admitting my move to Edmonton had been a geographic fix, a self-imposed hoax. After a year and a half, I packed up my queen-sized futon, pine table, television, clothes, and books and travelled back down Highway 2 to Calgary, knowing it was impossible to retrieve my old life.

Soon, I would be immersed in graduate studies at the University of Calgary, and I would complete a master's degree in communication studies, an interdisciplinary approach to knowledge, and there I would learn the basics of qualitative research practices, which later would serve me to work for academic teams in health and gender research.

For years, I would miss the long hike up Moose Mountain, the exhilaration of climbing to the summit, finding the door open, and knowing I had been sighted through the binoculars, that the lookout man anticipated my presence.

Not long ago, I dreamt about everyone from the fire lookout days, and in the dream we were intersecting points of light, tiny stars connected by rays of energy, separate flecks within a whole radiant universe.

Photos

Mary and Daniel outside the fire lookout on Mockingbird Hill, 1988. Photo credit Pat Goettler.

Mary and Daniel on the catwalk at Moose Mountain Lookout, 1994. Photo credit Daniel Stark

Daniel on the scree trail about 50 metres below Moose Mountain Lookout, 1995.
Photo by unknown female hiker.

Christos and Alice outside their farm house, Bearspaw Road, near Calgary, 1986.
Photo credit Daniel Stark.

Daniel on a low fire hazard day inside Moose Mountain Lookout, 1998. Photo credit Susan Heling.

Dinah outside the farm house, Bearspaw Road, near Calgary, 1986. Photo credit Daniel Stark.

Daniel working as a relief fire observer, Junction Lookout, 2000. Photo by unknown hiker.

Jack Carter (1936-1989), Permanent Lookoutman, visiting Sugarloaf Lookout for inventory inspections, 1980. Photo credit Daniel Stark.

Moose Mountain Lookout, southwest of Bragg Creek, Alberta, shot from helicopter, 1992. Photo credit Daniel Stark.

Mary and Daniel boffing in the meadow on Mockingbird Hill, 1988. Photo credit Pat Goettler.

Mary enjoying a brew in the kitchen at Mockingbird Lookout, 1987. Photo credit Daniel Stark.

Notes

1. Jack Kerouac, *Lonesome Traveler* (New York: Grove Press, 1988), 127-128.

2. Alberta Agriculture and Forestry. 2017. *Alberta Wildfire. Lookout Observer*. Position qualifications. Website updated August 18, 2016. http://wildfire.alberta.ca/recruitment/lookout-observer.aspx

3. Kerouac, *Lonesome Traveler*, 129.

4. Kerouac, *Lonesome Traveler*, 128.

5. Kerouac, *Lonesome Traveler*, 127.

6. Jack Kerouac, *On the Road* (New York: Penguin Putnam Inc., 1959), 5-6

7. Thomas Cleary, translator, *I Ching the Book of Change* (Boston, Massachusetts: Shambhala Publications, Inc., 1992), 54.

8. Anne McGuire, translator, *The Thunder: Perfect Mind,* 2010. Available at http://www.stoa.org/diotima/anthology/thunder.shtml

9. Martha Graham, *Blood Memory* (New York: Doubleday, 1991), 134.

Acknowledgements

Many thanks to Daniel for your constant generosity in sharing lookout stories and pondering my infinite questions about people and events. Thank you, Dinah, for your willingness to recount and relive the events on Cline Lookout and your assistance in reviewing sections of the manuscript. Appreciations to Christos and Alice for contributing your memories from our lookout days and discussing those events after so many years. Many thanks to my sister, Dr. Patty, for her support, feedback, and ideas about language.

I would like to express gratitude to my writing mentors, Denise Chong and Karen Connelly. I feel honoured to have crossed paths with you both. Denise, you inspired my direction in the earliest stages. Karen, your forthright honesty and insight were invaluable. Thank you to Rebecca Hendry for your thoughtful editorial report, and to Vici Johnstone for taking a chance with an unknown writer.

I am grateful to the Access Copyright Foundation for supporting early research for this project.

Narrative non-fiction presents the writer with choices unique to the genre; for instance, individual characters have varying degrees of openness about the details of their life becoming more widely known. As such, John, Tomas, McNeal, and Catherine are pseudonyms, assigned to provide privacy.